FIGHTING HEART D
THE HISTORY OF THE
BRITISH HEART FOUNDA
1961–1988

WENDY WILLIAMS

HRH the Duke of Edinburgh
Patron, the British Heart Foundation

FIGHTING HEART DISEASE

THE HISTORY OF THE
BRITISH HEART FOUNDATION
1961–1988

DAVID N. MATTHEWS

FOREWORD BY
THE RIGHT HONOURABLE
VISCOUNT TONYPANDY
PC, DCL
PRESIDENT OF THE
BRITISH HEART FOUNDATION

THE BRITISH HEART FOUNDATION
IN ASSOCIATION WITH
BLACKWELL SCIENTIFIC PUBLICATIONS
OXFORD LONDON EDINBURGH BOSTON
MELBOURNE PARIS BERLIN VIENNA

© 1990 by
Blackwell Scientific Publications
Editorial Offices:
Osney Mead, Oxford OX2 0EL
25 John Street, London WC1N 2BL
23 Ainslie Place, Edinburgh EH3 6AJ
3 Cambridge Center, Suite 208
   Cambridge, Massachusetts 02142, USA
54 University Street, Carlton
   Victoria 3053, Australia

Other Editorial Offices:
Arnette SA
2, rue Casimir-Delavigne
75006 Paris
France

Blackwell Wissenschaft
Meinekestrasse 4
D-1000 Berlin 15
West Germany

Blackwell MZV
Feldgasse 13
A-1238 Wien
Austria

All rights reserved. No part of this publication
may be reproduced, stored in a retrieval
system, or transmitted, in any form or by any
means, electronic, mechanical, photocopying,
recording or otherwise without the prior
permission of the copyright owner

First published 1990

Set by Excel Typesetters, Hong Kong
Printed in Great Britain at
the Alden Press, Oxford, and bound
at the Green Street Bindery, Oxford

DISTRIBUTORS

Marston Book Services Ltd
PO Box 87
Oxford OX2 0DT
(*Orders*: Tel. 0865 791155
           Fax: 0865 791927
           Telex: 837515)

USA
Mosby-Year Book, Inc.
200 North LaSalle Street
Chicago, Illinois 60601
(*Orders*: Tel: (312) 726-9733)

Canada
Mosby-Year Book, Inc.
5240 Finch Avenue East
Scarborough, Ontario
(*Orders*: Tel. (416) 298-1588)

Australia
Blackwell Scientific Publications
(Australia) Pty Ltd
54 University Street
Carlton, Victoria 3053
(*Orders*: Tel: (03) 347-0300)

British Library
Cataloguing in Publication Data

Matthews, David N.
  Fighting heart disease.
  1. Great Britain. Man. Cardiovascular
  system. Diseases. Research organisations.
  British Heart Foundation
  I. Title
  616.100941

ISBN 0-632-02874-2
ISBN 0-632-02876-9 pbk

CONTENTS

LIST OF ILLUSTRATIONS   vii

FOREWORD *by Viscount Tonypandy*   xi

PREFACE   xii

ACKNOWLEDGEMENTS   xv

1   THE BEGINNING   1
The British Cardiac Society – the Chest and Heart Association – Dr William Evans – Dr Harley Williams – Founding Committee Members – Founding Committee Meetings

2   THE EARLY YEARS: 1961–1966   18
The Appeal – The Appeal Policy Committee – Involvement of Industry – Relations with the Chest and Heart Association – Council Structure – Memorandum and Articles of Association – Premises – Appeal Committee – Science Committee – Consultant Advisers – Research Policy – Research Grants – Administration – Public Appeal – Reorganization – Annual General Meetings – The Origin of Future Success

3   THE MIDDLE YEARS: 1966–1976   40
Covenants: Industry – Fund-raising Events – Administration – Reorganization of Committee Structure – Professorial Chairs – Regional Network – Annual General Meetings and Public Meetings – *Heart* Journal and *Bulletin* – Personnel – The End of an Era

4   THE YEARS OF EXPANSION: 1976–1988   68
Brigadier Thursby Pelham – Research Policy – Education Policy – Media Coverage – Head Office – The Finance and General Purposes Committee – The Council – Annual General Meetings and Public Meetings – Appeals Department – Advertising – The Press Office – The *Bulletin* – Joan Scott Public Relations Consultancy – Special and National Events – The Donations Department – The Legacy Department – The Regions

5   THE MEDICAL DEPARTMENT   111
Science Committee – Project Grants – Medical Department Committee Structure – Personnel – Professor Shillingford – Scientific Advisory Committee –

v

The Research Funds Committee — Chairs and Research Groups Committee — The British Heart Foundation Prize and Gold Medal — Endowed Chairs Established by the Foundation — The British Heart Foundation Personal Chairs — Research Groups — Fellowships Committee — The Education Committee — Appendix A: Titles of Symposia — Appendix B: Titles of Workshops — Appendix C: Fact File Subjects — Appendix D: Publications List — The Cardiac Care Committee —

6 THE REGIONS   192
Development — Reorganization — Regional Geographical Patterns — Regional Histories — Fraud and Deception

7 THE WAY AHEAD: 1987   242
Policy — Anniversary Review — Annual Report 1987 — Reorganization — Medical Policy Decisions — Achievements — Objectives

INDEX   258

LIST OF ILLUSTRATIONS

Frontispiece: HRH The Duke of Edinburgh, Patron, the British Heart Foundation

1. The four Founding Members appointed by the British Cardiac Society: (a) Dr Maurice Campbell; (b) Dr Paul Wood; (c) Dr Evan Bedford; (d) Dr William Evans.   7
2. Dr Harley Williams, Secretary of the British Heart Foundation and of the Chest and Heart Association.   13
3. Field Marshal the Earl Alexander of Tunis, the first President of the British Heart Foundation.   15
4. Lord Evans, Physician to Her Majesty Queen Elizabeth II.   19
5. Seating plan showing those present at the dinner party, held at Lord Evans's house on 17 July 1961, to launch an Appeal Committee.   20
6. (a) Sir Charles Dodds, first Chairman of the Science Committee; (b) Sir John McMichael, Chairman of Council and of the Research Funds Committee.   27
7. Brigadier Ereld Cardiff, Director of Appeals 1964–66, and Director General 1966–76.   35
8. Her Majesty Queen Elizabeth, the Queen Mother, and Margaret, Countess of Tunis, at the gala performance at the London Palladium.   42
9. Poster announcing Ascot Race Day for the British Heart Foundation in 1973, which raised over £66,000.   43
10. Garden party at Walmer Castle. Left to right: Mrs du Boulay, Geoffrey Davison, Sir Robert Menzies and Mrs Perez (Chairman of the Deal and District Committee).   45
11. Charity match between the Arsenal Football Club and 29 children treated for heart disease, arranged by Jimmy Saville.   46
12. Julie Jarrold, Winner of the national 'Nurse of 1970' competition, sponsored by the Green Shield Stamp Company.   47

List of Illustrations

13	Presidents of the Foundation following Earl Alexander: (a) Lord Cobbold, 1969–76; (b) Viscount De L'Isle, 1976–84; (c) Viscount Tonypandy.	51
14	Brigadier Christopher Thursby Pelham, Director General 1976–86.	52
15	The regional pattern in 1967.	61
16	Income and expense/income ratios for the decade 1977–86.	68
17	The income from voluntary sources, and the advertising and publicity expenditure for the decade 1977–86.	69
18	Annual expenditure on research for the decade 1977–86, with illustration of percentage of disposable income.	72
19	Colonel James Malcolm, Director of Appeals during the years of expansion.	79
20	The conference room at headquarters, used for administrative and medical meetings. Furnished and equipped by Ciba-Geigy Pharmaceuticals.	83
21	Seating plan showing those attending 25th anniversary dinner at the Cavalry and Guards Club 17 July 1986.	87
22	The successful poster produced in the early days entitled 'The Crossed-out Man'.	92
23	Comparison of legacy and *in memoriam* income with the advertising expenditure over the period 1977–87.	93
24	His Royal Highness the Duke of Edinburgh, Patron of the Foundation, enjoying a joke with Eric Morecambe, who did so much to help raise money for the Foundation.	101
25	Medical Directors of the Foundation: (a) Professor John (Jack) Shillingford; (b) Professor Desmond Julian.	123
26	Analysis of expenditure on research grants 1972–88.	128
27	Analysis of distribution of funds on research grants 1979–85.	129
28	Analysis of expenditure 1982–86.	132
29	Total income, and expenditure on research, chairs and education 1963–88.	133
30	British Heart Foundation display stand at the 6th World Congress of Cardiology in London in 1970.	165
31	Resuscitation poster produced in 1969 and illustrated in the *Bulletin* of the summer of 1971.	172

List of Illustrations

32 His Royal Highness Prince Philip, Duke of Edinburgh, Patron of the Foundation, seen with Professor Sir John McMichael, Chairman of Council (left), and Lord Cobbold, President of the Foundation (right), attending the première of the film, *One in Every Two of Us*, at the Shell Centre on 11 November 1971.   174
33 The value of awards by the Cardiac Care Committee from the BHF budget, and 'local' or 'conditional' awards between 1977 and 1988.   187
34 'Dos and Don'ts' for fund-raisers as recommended by Colonel Malcolm, Director of Appeals.   197
35 Map of the regions published in the *Bulletin* in 1971.   198
36 Map of the eleven large regions of the Foundation in 1988.   200
37 Chart showing the regional income 1963–88.   203
38 Scottish Queen of Hearts 1980. Loraine Kelly receiving her prize of two return tickets to Rio de Janeiro from Mr Gordon Mason (right). General Manager of British Caledonian Airways in Scotland, and Mr George Young, President of the Scottish Appeal and Chairman of the judges.   207

FOREWORD
BY THE RIGHT HONOURABLE
VISCOUNT TONYPANDY PC, DCL

I AM HONOURED to be asked to provide this foreword to the History of the British Heart Foundation. Dr David Matthews is to be congratulated on his painstaking research covering the Foundation's history from its earliest origins when it was just an idea in the minds of a few far-sighted individuals. He traces its progress through the early years of its existence and its subsequent development until it is now the largest source of charitable funding for heart research in the United Kingdom. He includes a wealth of detail about those involved in this remarkable achievement over a period of 25 years.

I am proud to have been the Foundation's President.

Tonypandy

PREFACE

WITHIN A FEW MONTHS of taking up my appointment as Medical Spokesman in 1983 I had need, on several occasions, to seek some detail from the past history of the Foundation, either to answer an enquiry or to assist in the promotion of public awareness.

It soon became clear to me that, although factual information on matters of policy and finance were available through committee minutes, the number of people who knew the history of the Foundation from personal experience was small, and unavoidably shrinking with the passage of time. Information about the early days was very hard to get.

It seemed, therefore, that it would be worth while to try to fill this gap, and the idea was welcomed by Sir Harry Moore, Brigadier Thursby Pelham and Professor Shillingford, all of whom I consulted.

Having set myself the task I obtained as many of the old records as were available, and read and annotated them. After familiarizing myself with all these documents had to offer, I made tape-recorded interviews with as many of the men and women as I could find who had been associated with the Foundation over a long period of time, and I am greatly indebted to the 27 who responded so generously. Many others, whom I could not reach directly in this way, assisted by correspondence and by patiently answering many telephone calls.

This book is the combined distillate of committee records and all these personal recollections. The information it contains is necessarily limited by the availability of the pioneers for consultation and by the degree of success of my researches. Details are sometimes lacking, but the facts, as stated, are all substantiated; avoidable omissions represent failures in my research, and will not, I hope, cause disappointment or annoyance.

Drawing the line between being too parochial and too impersonal is a personal decision. There will be some who are firmly convinced I have erred one way or the other. Whilst accepting the risk of the accusation of parochialism, I believe that, in recording the history of an organization as comparatively youthful as the BHF, it is right to give personal acknowledgement to as many as possible of the few who by their endeavours, however, humble, built the structure on which so much has been set. This, it seems to me, is the essence of a history of a charity. Basically it is all about people with a vision, and the determination to make a dream a reality.

Turning to the structure of the book as I have set it out, I appreciate that there is a wide variety of choice, and that there will be those who are certain that setting it out differently would have been better. As H.G. Wells put it: 'There is no passion on earth, neither love nor hate, as great as the passion to alter someone else's draft.' After considering all the material I had researched, however, the history of the Foundation seemed to me to fit naturally into the four periods I have chosen. 'The Beginning' and 'The Early Years' record the conception and the birth pangs, whilst 'The Middle Years' and 'The Years of Expansion' fall as mantles round the dominant figures of the two Directors General. Unavoidably this method of presentation leads to some degree of repetition since continuity of effort and continuing expansion of the same or similar themes is in reality an overlap from one era to the next. But I hope that the amount of repetition is small enough to be acceptable, and large enough to ensure continuity for the reader.

'The Medical Department' and 'The Regions' appeared to me to need separate chapters in order to give an overall picture. The Medical Department, representing the objective of the whole endeavour, is the big spender, and it owes its continuing expansion to the success of the fund-raisers, who have assumed ever-increasing importance through the regional framework. I regret that the detail in the chapter concerning the regions is of uneven quality and quantity; this reflects considerable variation in the response to attempts to get information about regional histories and personalities from some of those I hoped might have the answers. I suspect that some skeletons were kept firmly locked in cupboards.

The closer a historian gets to the present day the easier it is for a knowledgeable reader to criticize a 'history' for failing to record the most recent changes in personnel resulting from retirements, resignations or new appointments. Similarly, in an active, lively organization such as the Foundation, there are always new moves afoot which have not yet become established policy or practice. In order, therefore, to avoid the criticism that the book is out of date it is necessary to set a cut-off point, and leave subsequent changes and developments to a future historian. It seemed to me that 1988 was as near to the present day as it was possible to go without risking errors and inaccuracies.

'The Way Ahead' is not a fantasy or pipe-dream, on neither of which would I be qualified to ponder, since I am not a cardiologist, but summarizes the most recent steps taken to lead the Foundation to continuing and increasing successes in the years to come.

Finally I wish to record my indebtedness to everyone who has helped me, and to those who have encouraged me to undertake this task, and have sustained me in its execution. I hope it will give pleasure to those who read it and be a rewarding source of information to those who want to know about the Foundation. Its shortcomings are mine — and mine alone.

DAVID N. MATTHEWS
1990

ACKNOWLEDGEMENTS

I GRATEFULLY ACKNOWLEDGE my indebtedness to the 27 members of staff, past and present, who gave me hour-long tape-recorded talks about the Foundation, and to the very many others who wrote to me of their experiences and answered numerous telephone calls. In particular I wish to record my thanks to Frances Neal and Ron Trebell for the time and thought they have given me in recalling people and events from bygone days, and to Brigadier Thursby Pelham for the trouble he has taken in preparing all the charts and diagrams which are included.

Of the many others who have helped me I wish to mention Mrs Sue McNally and her staff for their patience in looking out documents for me, Mrs Kalli Alcock for transcribing the tape-recorded interviews and summaries of committee minutes, and Mrs Tisha Browne, my secretary, for all the time she has spent tracing, and verifying the accuracy of recording of, innumerable items of special interest. The preparation of photographs presented a difficult problem since most of the originals had been lost; the Misses Jane Landon and Elaine Snell, in the press office, took much trouble in getting acceptable reproductions from copies of the *Bulletin*, some of which were more than 20 years old.

My thanks, too, to Sir Harry Moore, Brigadier Thursby Pelham, Professor Desmond Julian and Sir Richard Lloyd for reading the printout and making valuable comments, together with suggestions which I have incorporated in the final text.

I also wish to record my thanks to my neighbour, Mrs Eva Collier, for loaning me the computer and word processor and teaching me how to use it, and to my wife for her forbearance over the inordinate length of time I have been closeted in my study instead of being around and about.

Finally I wish to record my thanks to everyone concerned with the production of this book; to Wellcome P.L.C. for a very generous grant with which to supplement the outlay of the Finance and General Purposes Committee, which made publication possible; to my Publication Advisers, Mr Peter Collier and Mr Tom Colverson for much-needed advice and technical help very willingly given; and to Mr Julian Grover, of Blackwell Scientific Publications, for his knowledge and skill which have resulted in the production of such an attractive volume.

DAVID N. MATTHEWS
1990

ONE

THE BEGINNING

A STUDY OF THE RECORDS makes it plain that many people and several organizations combined to create the British Heart Foundation: it had multiple beginnings. All were prompted, however, by the common desire to provide funds to finance research into heart disease because of the heavy toll it takes of life and health.

In the late 1950s when the endeavour began the amount of money available in Britain for cardiovascular research was woefully small in comparison with resources in other countries. An appeal document prepared for the Foundation some years later states that in 1958 America raised over $20,000,000, Canada in its first appeal raised nearly $1,000,000, and Australia had raised £2,000,000 by an appeal on just one Sunday morning.

Speaking of these times at the launch of an appeal for the British Heart Foundation in 1963 Professor McMichael (later Sir John), Vice-Chairman of the Science Committee at the time, said:

> The amount of money available for research on the heart and circulation from official sources is very limited indeed. The Medical Research Council budget only totals about two-thirds of one per cent of the whole cost of running the National Health Service ... probably the amount they spend on heart and vascular disease does not exceed say fifty thousand pounds a year ... medical schools of the Universities have been given no additional support in the current quinquennium ... it is for these reasons that we must appeal direct to the public for their generous assistance.

The two organizations which played major roles in the creation of the Foundation were the British Cardiac Society and the Chest and Heart Association: the Royal Colleges were also importantly supportive and the Medical Research Council gave freely of their wide experience.

THE BRITISH CARDIAC SOCIETY

The British Cardiac Society (BCS) is a professional specialist body to which 'election to membership is by peer review'. Its membership includes leading clinical and academic cardiologists and those with like interests in other disciplines, for example, radiology and pathology. The main object of the Society is 'the advancement of knowledge of Diseases of the Heart and Circulation for the benefit of the public'. It rightly has an authoritative voice in all matters dealing with its speciality, having been in existence over 50 years (1937), and itself growing from the Cardiac Club, which dates back to 1922.

THE CHEST AND HEART ASSOCIATION

The Chest and Heart Association (CHA) is a charity which developed from the National Association for the Prevention of Tuberculosis (NAPT). This had existed for over 60 years before changing its name to the Chest and Heart Association in 1959. It changed again to its present format in 1975 by adding 'Stroke' to its title (CH&SA).

The decision to change the name and widen its objectives in 1959 was due to the success which had been achieved in the treatment of tuberculosis; it was made, however, only after protracted discussion over several years. But as soon as it became the Chest and Heart Association it was an obvious source of potential conflict of interest with the British Cardiac Society. This was enhanced by the fact that it already had well-advanced plans for launching an appeal for £1,000,000 to finance heart research.

This expansion of interest coincided with the British Cardiac Society's decision to explore the possibility of creating a fund-raising body to promote research into diseases of the heart and circulation.

The records contain a copy of a letter to members of the British Cardiac Society from the President, Dr Maurice Campbell, dated 31 October 1958, reminding them that at the last meeting of the Society he had spoken briefly about two possibilities: either that the Society should take steps to form an association for raising money for research or that it should seek some form of cooperation with NAPT. His letter continues:

I reported that the Council had appointed myself and Drs Paul Wood and Morgan Jones to meet representatives of NAPT to discuss the possibility, without power to commit the Society. This meeting took place in a friendly atmosphere and a special meeting of Council was held on October 30th 1958 to discuss the report of these negotiations and to decide future policy.

The Council decided that no further negotiations should take place with

The Beginning

NAPT at present, and that they should not accept the suggestion of NAPT to put forward names of members of the Society for election by NAPT to their Council. The Council also decided to appoint a committee to determine what steps should be taken to form a new association for raising money for cardiovascular research and possibly for other purposes. The Council thought that two decisions of such importance to the Society as a whole should be communicated to members at once, and that there might be further information to give them at the next meeting of the Society.

This is followed by a second letter to members from the President, Dr Maurice Campbell, dated 24 June 1959. It runs:

You will remember that the Council appointed a Committee consisting of Drs Evan Bedford, Rae Gilchrist and Paul Wood to consider what steps should be taken to form an organization to raise funds for cardiological research and for other purposes.

The Committee have considered the question and after informal discussions with the President of the Royal College of Physicians and the Secretary of the Medical Research Council have made some preliminary suggestions. They recommend that such an organization should be established and that it should be independent of the British Cardiac Society (BCS). It might be called the National Heart Foundation (NHF) or Council (NHC). It is suggested that the Governing Body or Council of the NHF should consist of medical and lay members and that the number of lay members should not exceed the number of medical members. The medical members would be appointed by the British Cardiac Society, the Royal Colleges of Physicians of London and Edinburgh, the British Postgraduate Medical Federation and perhaps other bodies. The main purposes of the NHF would be:
1 To raise funds for cardiological research.
2 To assist existing cardiological centres in their research projects by grants by appointing fellows and in other ways; and
3 to act as a national representative body in certain directions.

A special meeting of the Council of the BCS is being held in the near future to discuss these recommendations. If the Council approves these and asks the same or an enlarged Committee to proceed on these lines they and the British Cardiac Society will have no further direct control over the activities of the NHF except in so far as they appoint some members of the Governing Body or Council of the NHF.

I believe some such plan will be approved by the Council and that it will be carrying out the wishes of most members of the BCS. If I am wrong in this assumption I wish to give members the opportunity of letting me know or of making any other suggestions and I will see that any such letters are brought before the Council at its next meeting.

It seems that the Council meeting of the BCS referred to decided to promote the creation of a British Heart Foundation (not a National

Heart Foundation) which would ultimately become a separate entity and that in the mean time they would foster it through a Founding Committee with a nucleus of four of their own Council members.

DR WILLIAM EVANS

Complementary to these records Dr William Evans, Consultant Physician to the London Hospital at the time, has written in a personal communication as follows:

> In 1948 I was invited to be Guest-Lecturer at the Centenary Meeting of the Royal Melbourne Hospital ... I took a great interest in the research work carried out there with the aid of the monies donated by a National Appeal Fund. This fund had been initiated to support research work in heart disease. An appeal was supported by Industry and Commerce and launched to the public on a Sunday morning when a sum of £2 million was raised in a single day. It was this which caused me to suggest that a similar effort should be made in this country to collect monies to support research work in heart disease.
>
> Thus at a meeting of the Council of the British Cardiac Society in the spring of 1959 under the item 'any other business' I proposed that a National Heart Foundation should be formed. A short discussion took place and the Secretary, Dr Patrick Mouncey, was requested to place it on the agenda of the next meeting. At the next meeting of the BCS a Founding Committee was formed comprising Dr Maurice Campbell, Dr Evan Bedford, Dr Paul Wood and myself. At this stage it became necessary to win the support of the Chest and Heart Association, with Dr Harley Williams, a tough negotiator, as its Secretary. Consequently it was arranged that Paul Wood and myself should meet Harley Williams.

Dr William Evans also sent me his original aide-mémoire, which outlines the points he wished to make and the discussions which ensued. Judging from this document Dr Evans was an equally tough negotiator and it reads as though Dr Harley Williams was grilled comprehensively with the happy upshot that, for the most part, the two organizations pulled well together.

Dr Evans concludes his letter: 'On September 8th 1959 the Founding Committee of the Cardiac Society and the other co-opted members met at the Royal College of Physicians in Trafalgar Square.'

Doubtless Dr Evans was in the forefront of discussions, formal and informal, amongst cardiologists at that time as the result of his experiences in Australia, and he would have known from the President's letter of the talks with the NAPT in 1958. It is in keeping

The Beginning

with his enthusiasm that he should have been the member of Council to encourage the Cardiac Society to make haste in sponsoring the endeavour following the decision not to pursue the matter further with the NAPT.

DR HARLEY WILLIAMS

A discussion document prepared by Dr Harley Williams for the Council of the Chest and Heart Association dated May 1959 entitled 'Proposed Cardiac Appeal' outlines the objectives as:

(a) To endow 20 research Fellowships at different medical schools in the UK or the Commonwealth, each Fellowship to continue for 5–7 years, and awarded to a young research doctor together with expenses and necessary equipment. It would decide later what main lines of research would be pursued by these Fellows.
(b) The establishment of a university chair in cardiology at some British or Commonwealth medical school. At present there is no such chair in any British university.
(c) Monetary grants to individuals and cardiac departments for clinical research and necessary equipment.
(d) Scholarships for doctors from the Commonwealth to study cardiac work in the UK.
(e) A National Cardiac After-Care Fund to provide social help for the victims of cardiac disease.
(f) Setting up a model unit for rehabilitation of cardiac patients and social research in cardiology therewith.

The document also goes into some detail about the organization of the appeal, the methods to be employed and their cost: it also puts forward the names of prominent personages who might be approached with invitations to form the appeal committee. With their plans so far advanced it is little wonder that Dr Evans saw the need to approach the Chest and Heart Association again without delay.

It is also important to remember that the Association was a well-established going concern with premises from which to work and an experienced staff. Besides Dr Harley Williams as Secretary-General, there was a Deputy (Mr A.J. Mantripp) and a secretariat, an accounts department, secretarial staff to service the Council and its finance and science committees, and a doctor as scientific adviser. At this time the British Heart Foundation was only a dream.

Chapter 1

From Dr Evans's notes it seems that when he and Dr Paul Wood met Dr Harley Williams, the latter agreed (presumably subject to his Council's concurrence) to drop their proposed appeal and that, instead, an appeal should be launched 'solely from the British Heart Foundation as an independent body'. This was a remarkable concession and in exchange for it there was agreement that members of the CHA should join the Founding Committee of the BHF. It says much for the negotiating skills of Dr Evans and Dr Wood, and equally for the breadth of vision of Dr Harley Williams, that so much agreement was reached in so short a time.

FOUNDING COMMITTEE MEMBERS (Figure 1)

Since the four members selected by the Council of the British Cardiac Society to form the nucleus of the Founding Committee played such an important part in the creation of the Foundation, and afterwards, in nursing it through many ups and downs in its early years as an independent body, it is fitting to include a small cameo of each.

Dr Evan Bedford was the President of the BCS at the time and it was to some extent because of this that he became involved. He was a very busy and highly successful consultant cardiologist at the Middlesex Hospital with a large practice. He appeared somewhat rigid and orthodox in his views and outlook to some of his colleagues and was not basically orientated to research. None the less he worked very hard for the Foundation, having undertaken to foster it.

Dr William Evans, the son of a farmer, was a lovable dynamic Welshman who was, at first, a bank clerk and local preacher. When he decided to turn to medicine he earned enough money to see himself through medical school at the London Hospital where he became a consultant physician. With his chief, Sir John Parkinson, he ran the cardiac department and was also elected to the staff of the National Heart Hospital. He was always interested in research and helped many young men as assistants in the department to develop successful careers, and some to pursue academic research; Professor Shillingford was one of them. Like most practising physicians at the time, however, Dr Evans had received no formal training in research skills. His efforts were unavoidably limited to usage of the results of his clinical experience: to these he added a native Welsh shrewdness and intuition. Much of the development of the modern electrocardio-

Figure 1 *The four Founding Members appointed by the British Cardiac Society: (a) Dr Maurice Campbell; (b) Dr Paul Wood; (c) Dr Evan Bedford; (d) Dr William Evans.*

graph is due to his efforts. He enthused his juniors, who had great affection for him. He was a 'character'. Fastidious in dress with black coat, striped trousers and spats, professionally meticulous and dedicated to punctuality, he was a well-known figure on the national and international scene of the time.

The Foundation was fortunate to have such an illustrious and enthusiastic pioneer in its formative years, and to continue to receive his support throughout his professional life and into his retirement so long as his health lasted. He responded generously to repeated requests to address medical and social fund-raising events. His engaging personality and great clinical experience combined to make him a very popular and successful speaker; his natural ability was helped by the possession of native Welsh fervour and a genuine liking for public speaking.

It is consistent with the charismatic nature of his personality that his trainees and disciples have set down a record of a hundred of his best-known aphorisms. They are pithy, pertinent and sometimes impertinent, with the clear intent to debunk pomposity and humbug.

Reflecting philosophically he observed: 'There is no loss so finite as lost opportunity; the search for it is futile,' and again, 'One's past is either the dust-bin of lost opportunities, or the granary of accumulated wisdom,' and 'Immortality depends largely on other people's memories.'

Speaking of the innocent systolic murmur he remarked: 'It is an advantage to a cardiologist to be a little deaf,' and 'To diagnose a systolic murmur in the mitral area as "mitral incompetence" is incompetent but not mitral.'

Amongst his many remarks directed to his undergraduate students he said: 'Should a garrulous patient frustrate your examination of him, take his mouth temperature,' and 'It's better to do nothing than something when nothing needs to be done,' adding sometimes: 'Through the years I have been amazed at the healing properties of coloured water, especially the red kind.'

Finally, amongst his references to research is the observation that: 'Man is being preferred to the rat for investigation for two reasons: he is a more docile animal and has better veins.'

On receiving a letter from Professor Shillingford in 1984 telling him that the Foundation's annual income had exceeded £6,000,000 he wrote back saying: 'To have been in the van of a movement which collects from a generous public a sum of money exceeding six million pounds in a single year in support of a crusade which aims to deal with ailing hearts, creates a belief that the Nation's heart continues to beat unerringly true.'

Dr Paul Wood was an Australian. He was amongst the first

scientifically orientated research workers in cardiology. He was essentially a basic physiologist and rapidly gained a great international reputation; he was a pioneer of the application of cardiac catheterization and other physiological principles to the practice of cardiology. He was an excellent teacher and became the Director of the Cardiological Institute at the National Heart Hospital where he remained until his sudden and untimely death from a heart attack in 1962. Ironically he failed to diagnose the pain in his shoulder and sought orthopaedic advice for it. Moves were afoot at the time to put his name forward for a Nobel Peace Prize, such was his reputation. His textbook of cardiology was the standard work for many years.

Dr Maurice Campbell was a physician at Guy's Hospital with a special interest in paediatric cardiology. He was very conscientious and did everything he undertook very well. These qualities were of great service to the Foundation, for which he was the ideal leader and Chairman in the early days. He was fair in his dealings with those of differing opinions although he had a reputation for not suffering fools gladly. He was the hard-working, punctilious editor of the *British Heart Journal* for very many years and won for it a great reputation for accuracy of content and for presentation. He was a quiet modest man who never drove a car and lived most of his professional life in the same house. Some have said that his unassuming nature led to lack of the public recognition which he merited.

FOUNDING COMMITTEE MEETINGS

The first meeting of the Founding Committee was held at the Royal College of Physicians on 8 September 1959. It was attended by the four representatives of the British Cardiac Society and there were some apologies for absence from others who had been invited. Dr Maurice Campbell was elected Chairman and Dr Paul Wood Secretary.

The meeting first addressed itself to its membership and its decisions read as follows:

(a) Eight representatives from the British Cardiac Society: Professor Melville Arnott, Dr D. Evan Bedford, Dr Maurice Campbell, Dr William Evans, Dr Rae Gilchrist, Dr A. Morgan Jones, Professor E.J. Wayne and Dr Paul Wood.

It was understood that these eight members would resign as soon as the

British Heart Foundation was officially inaugurated, when they would be replaced by six members nominated to serve on the Governing body of the Foundation.
(b) Two representatives from the Royal College of Physicians of London, Sir Robert Platt and Lord Evans.
(c) One representative from the Royal College of Surgeons of England, Mr T. Holmes Sellors.
(d) One representative from the Royal College of Physicians of Edinburgh, Professor Ian Hill.
(e) One representative from the Royal Faculty of Physicians and Surgeons of Glasgow, Dr J.H. Wright.
(f) One representative from the British Postgraduate Medical Federation, Dr Graham Hayward.

It was agreed that a small number of lay members should also be invited to join the Founding Committee. A subcommittee consisting of Lord Evans and Dr Evan Bedford was formed to look into this matter and advise. This subcommittee was also asked to consider lay members who might serve on the Governing Body of the Foundation. It was agreed that Mr Michael Perrin (later Sir Michael) of the Wellcome Foundation should be invited to join the Founding Committee forthwith.

It was tacitly assumed that members of the Founding Committee, other than representatives of the British Cardiac Society, would be expected to serve on the Council of the Governing Body of the Foundation as soon as it was formed.

It was agreed that if negotiations with the Chest and Heart Association were concluded successfully an appropriate number of representatives from the CHA would be four. It was acknowledged, however, that the CHA hoped to have six representatives.

The objects of the BHF were considered and approved provisionally as follows:
1 To raise funds for several purposes, which, in order of priority, were:
(a) Research relating to diseases of the heart and circulation.
(b) Postgraduate education in cardiology.
(c) Patients' welfare and education of the lay public in cardiological matters. (Just what function, if any, the BHF might have in relation to the practice of cardiology was not settled.)
2 To promote such research and postgraduate education by creating Fellowships, making grants, and providing equipment and other fa-

The Beginning

cilities in established cardiological centres and, if thought desirable, elsewhere.

3   To improve patients' welfare and the education of the lay public in cardiological matters through the agency of the CHA, should negotiations with that body reach a satisfactory conclusion.

4   To act as a national representative body in cardiological matters in relation to other bodies concerned with raising and distributing money (such as the International Society of Cardiology Foundation) and also, where appropriate, in relation to other organizations that might, from time to time, have interests similar to those of the BHF (such as the Ministry of Health and the World Health Organization).

5   To take any other action that might seem appropriate to advance cardiology.

The committee then met two representatives of the CHA (Drs Harley Williams and Lloyd Rusby) and the record of their discussions reads as follows:

1   The general principles of the proposed appeal, and any subsequent appeals, and the distribution of all monies received would be decided by the BHF, which would be totally independent of both the BCS and the CHA, although its formation gave it an obligation to serve the interests of both bodies in certain specified ways.

2   The appeal, and any subsequent appeal, would be conducted in the name of the BHF and all money received would be paid to the BHF.

3   The CHA would offer its secretarial staff, office and other facilities to expedite the appeal, and perhaps in helping the future administration of the BHF. Expenses incurred by the CHA in conducting the appeal would, of course, be the first charge on any money collected.

4   The CHA realised that the primary object of the BHF was to raise money for research relating to diseases of the heart and circulation, and that its secondary object was to help postgraduate education in cardiology; on the other hand, the BHF recognised that it would have an obligation to the CHA to give it a proportion of money received for the welfare and rehabilitation of patients with heart disease, and for educating the lay public in cardiological matters, the proportion to be decided by the BHF. It was agreed that these last three objectives should be the primary concern of the CHA, and that matters relating to cardiovascular research and postgraduate education in cardiology should be dealt with by the BHF.

5   Both Dr Harley Williams and Dr Lloyd Rusby felt that the CHA should be represented by six members on the Founding Committee and later on the Council of the BHF. The present Founding Committee, on the other hand, thought that CHA representation should be limited to four.

6   It was stressed repeatedly that negotiations between the BHF and the

CHA should be conducted with the idea of permanent cooperation between the two bodies, and not as a temporary expedient for conducting the appeal. 7 It was understood that the CHA had already decided to make an appeal for £1,000,000 for cardiological purposes, and the CHA now understood that the BHF was going to make a similar appeal. [Clearly it was hoped that some suitable arrangement could be reached to avoid two appeals of this kind by independent organizations simultaneously.]

It was agreed that Dr William Evans and Dr Paul Wood should serve on a subcommittee to continue negotiations with the CHA, and the Chairman and Secretary agreed to act as a subcommittee to initiate the necessary legal steps to establish the British Heart Foundation.

The records also contain a document prepared by Dr Maurice Campbell with the same date as the meeting of the Founding Committee (8 September 1959) for transmission to the Council of the CHA and headed 'Summary of proposals approved provisionally by the Founding Committee and representatives of the Chest and Heart Association'. It is in essence the same as the record of the discussions here set out except in relation to CHA representation. It states: 'Four to six members chosen by CHA (from Drs Shirley Smith, Bruce Perry, C. Parsons, A. Leatham, Lloyd Rusby and Harley Williams) should be invited to join the medical members of the Founding Committee and some, or all, of them should be appointed later to the Council.'

The second meeting of the Founding Committee was held on 29 October 1959. After discussion of the report of the subcommittee negotiating with the CHA four of its representatives joined the meeting by invitation. A modification of the previous statement of intent was agreed and reads as follows: 'Research and postgraduate education, jointly and severally, would receive paramount consideration over welfare and health education. At the same time the Founding Committee agreed that a reasonable proportion of monies collected should be allocated for patient welfare and health education, to safeguard these CHA interests.'

It was also agreed that the Secretary-General of the CHA should become the Secretary of the BHF. The Secretary was instructed to open a bank account for the Founding Committee to cover immediate needs; this was opened with Glyn Mills Bank and the first credit received was for £100 from the BCS.

The third meeting of the Founding Committee was held on 26

The Beginning

November 1959 at 51 Wimpole Street by permission of the National Heart Hospital. It was reported that the CHA had accepted the recommendation that it should have four members on the Committee and named them (Drs Shirley Smith, Lloyd Rusby and Clifford Parsons, and Professor Bruce Perry). Dr Paul Wood then proposed that Dr Harley Williams should become Secretary of the Founding Committee (Figure 2) as from the close of the present meeting. This was agreed and Dr Wood was appointed Treasurer.

It was announced that Mr C.F. Cooper, a solicitor and partner in the firm of Slaughter & May, had promised, as a personal commitment, to draft a legal instrument embodying the Constitution of the Foundation. This he did, going to much trouble satisfying the Board

Figure 2 *Dr Harley Williams. Secretary of the British Heart Foundation and of the Chest and Heart Association.*

of Trade in answer to a number of questions raised before their approval was granted.

This meeting also addressed itself to the question of lay membership of the Governing Body of the Foundation and its committees; after discussion the matter was referred to a subcommittee consisting of the Chairman and Secretary, Lord Evans and Dr Evan Bedford.

The fourth meeting of the Founding Committee was held at the British Medical Association (BMA) House on 18 January 1960 when the composition of the Council was the principal item for discussion. It was agreed to add one representative of the College of General Practitioners and four doctors elected by the Council 'on the grounds of their personal qualifications and usefulness to the Foundation and thereafter up to 19 laymen also elected by the Council'.

The Council was to have power to elect from its own members a small Executive Committee to act between Council meetings for research, appeal and other purposes with power granted by the Council to co-opt. The possible need, subject to legal advice, to create a larger body called, perhaps, an Advisory Committee or a Consultative Committee was considered; it was suggested that this might have a total of 100 members including 40 Council members.

The name of Viscount Alexander of Tunis was proposed as the first President of the Foundation and the names of five distinguished laymen were put forward for Council membership: Mr C.F. Cooper (legal adviser), Mr Harry Moore (Chairman, Board of Governors, London Hospital), Mr Charles Forte (Trust Houses Forte), Mr Norman Collins (Associated Television) and Lord Cowdray.

Dr Harley Williams suggested that a 5,000-word statement of intent and objectives, couched in lay terms, was needed for publicity in advance of the appeal and Drs William Evans and Paul Wood were entrusted with this task. They drew on the text and content of the document already produced by the CHA in anticipation of their appeal and the resulting printed leaflet for the Foundation was entitled *The Heart Problem*. It is the first publication produced by the Foundation and a copy is still extant.

For clarification Dr Harley Williams spelled out to the Committee the decision that the BHF would be responsible for all policy matters regarding the appeal and the CHA for its management including the initial expenses incurred.

The fifth meeting of the Founding Committee took place at BMA

The Beginning 15

House on 2 May 1960 when the Chairman welcomed Earl Alexander of Tunis to his first meeting as President (Figure 3). Earl Alexander offered to approach His Royal Highness the Duke of Edinburgh to ask him if he would become the Patron of the Foundation and the favourable response by the Duke was received with pleasure at the next meeting of the Committee. This meeting was attended for the first time by three lay members, Mr Michael Perrin, Mr Charles Forte and Mr Harry Moore, and an apology for absence from Mr Norman Collins is recorded.

The Memorandum and Articles of Association prepared by the Honorary Solicitor, Mr C.F. Cooper, were presented and discussed at length prior to approval with modifications for submission to the Board of Trade with a request that the Foundation be now 'incorporated'. The lay membership of Council was defined in the Memorandum as: '6 to be elected by Council and 12 by the Annual General Meeting of Members'. The principal item of discussion concerned the Foundation's commitment to accept the Secretary of the CHA as its Secretary in perpetuity. This was unacceptable to

Figure 3 *Field Marshal the Earl Alexander of Tunis, the first President of the British Heart Foundation.*

many members of the Committee and the matter was left for resolution by Mr Cooper of Slaughter & May and Messrs Hastie, solicitors for the CHA. This was successfully accomplished and an agreement was ready for signature as soon as the BHF was legally constituted. It reads as follows:

This Agreement is made between the British Heart Foundation (hereinafter called the Foundation) and the Chest and Heart Association (hereinafter called the Association)
WHEREAS:
(1) The Foundation was incorporated on the Twenty Eighth day of July one Thousand Nine Hundred and Sixty One as a Limited Company by Guarantee and not having a share capital.
(2) It was provided by Clause 3 (1) of the Memorandum of Association of the Foundation that the Foundation was established (*inter alia*) to raise funds by public appeal or otherwise for the following purposes:
>   (a) The primary purpose being to undertake and promote medical and scientific research relating to diseases of the heart and circulation and subjects related thereto and to promote postgraduate medical training in cardiology.
>   (b) The secondary objective being to promote through the Association, so long as the Association retains the status of a charity, the welfare and rehabilitation of patients who have suffered from heart disease, and health education in subjects relating to the heart and circulation.

(3) It has been agreed between the parties hereto that the Association shall undertake the said secondary objective of the Foundation on the terms and conditions hereinafter contained.
NOW IT IS HEREBY AGREED as follows:
1 The Association shall, so long as it retains its status as a charity, undertake the exclusive promotion for the Foundation of (a) the welfare and rehabilitation of patients who have suffered heart disease and (b) health education in subjects relating to the heart and circulation.
2 The Secretary-General for the time being of the Association shall be the Secretary of the Foundation, and the Association shall undertake all the necessary administrative and secretarial work of the Foundation from the offices of the Association PROVIDED that any future Secretary-General shall be appointed by the Association in agreement with the Foundation.
3 (a) The Foundation shall reimburse the Association for the expenses incurred by the Association in connection with any public appeal for funds undertaken by the Association in agreement with the Foundation.
  (b) The Foundation shall pay to the Association a reasonable proportion of the funds it shall have available for distribution to enable the Association to undertake the work described in Clause 1 hereof.
4 THIS Agreement shall remain in force until such a time as shall be agreed between the parties.

The Beginning

At this fifth meeting of the Founding Committee an Appeal Policy Committee was also set up consisting of Dr Maurice Campbell (Chairman), Dr William Evans, Mr Charles Forte, Mr Harry Moore, Mr Michael Perrin and Dr Harley Williams (Secretary).

The sixth and final meeting of the Founding Committee was held on 6 February 1961; the next meeting would be the first meeting of the Council of the British Heart Foundation.

A report of the Appeal Policy Committee was received in which the target was set at £5,000,000 and it was agreed to appeal privately to industry before launching a public appeal. Lord Evans refused an invitation to become Chairman of the Appeal Committee but agreed to become Vice-Chairman, jointly, with Dr William Evans.

An Executive Committee was also appointed consisting of the members of the Appeal Policy Committee (Dr Evans, Mr Forte, Mr Moore and Mr Perrin) with the addition of Dr Evan Bedford and the chairman of each committee as it was set up, with additional representation from the newly formed Science Committee since the justification for creating the Foundation was central to its recommendations. The Science Committee, also set up at this meeting of the Founding Committee, was asked to meet as soon as possible to consider plans for receiving applications for research grants, assessing them and, if satisfactory, financing them. It would need to consider policy matters as well as organizational requirements.

The Science Committee was composed of the following members: Professor Melville Arnott, Dr Evan Bedford, Dr Rae Gilchrist, Professor Ian Hill, Dr Morgan Jones, Professor Bruce Perry, Mr Holmes Sellors, Dr A.J. Thomas and Professor E.J. Wayne with Dr Paul Wood as convener. The Committee had powers to co-opt.

Finally it was agreed that one-third of the members of all committees should be elected annually to serve for three years, with one-third of the original committee retiring after one year with eligibility for reelection.

The Founding Committee had accomplished an enormous amount of work in a very short space of time and the scene was now set for the birth of the Foundation.

TWO

THE EARLY YEARS: 1961–1966

THE FOUNDATION became a reality on 28 July 1961 when the Board of Trade, having approved its Memorandum and Articles of Association, issued its Certificate of Incorporation as a Company.

THE APPEAL

The most urgent task was to organize an appeal for funds with which to finance research, the promotion of which was the Foundation's principal objective. The Appeal Policy Committee set up at the fifth meeting of the Founding Committee on 2 May 1960 had been very active, meeting on six occasions before it was dissolved on 31 January 1961. This was because the last meeting of the Founding Committee which had set it up was due to take place the following week on 8 February.

It was reported that the CHA had allocated £10,000 to meet the expenses of the appeal for £5,000,000 up to 31 March 1961; thereafter it was hoped that the appeal would be self-supporting.

It was agreed that plans should be made during the winter of 1960 to approach industry and commerce in 1961, and that this should be followed by a public appeal; the advantage of having a sum already collected before appealing to the public was well recognized. It was also appreciated that the Appeal Committee would need information about medical policy and administrative procedures in relation to the assessment of applications for research grants. This was the reason why the Science Committee had already been constituted before the Founding Committee was disbanded.

THE APPEAL POLICY COMMITTEE

The Appeal Policy Committee gave consideration to the possibility of setting up regional appeal committees, and to this end wrote to cardiologists in provincial centres, but the only encouraging reply

The Early Years

Figure 4 *Lord Evans, Physician to Her Majesty Queen Elizabeth II.*

came from Dr W.G.A. Swan in Newcastle; unfortunately therefore this early, and far-sighted, vision of a regional framework for appeals was frustrated by apathy.

The Appeal Policy Committee also gave much thought and time to the composition of the Appeal Committee and its officers. Following the refusal of Lord Evans (Figure 4), Physician to Her Majesty the Queen, to become the Chairman, it was agreed, at the suggestion of Mr Moore and Mr Perrin, to invite Mr H.G. (Leslie) Lazell, Chairman of the Beecham Group of Companies, to become Chairman. He agreed to do so with Lord Evans and Dr William Evans as his Vice-Chairmen.

INVOLVEMENT OF INDUSTRY

Lord Evans then informed the Committee that he would be prepared to approach a number of the leading industrialists and businessmen who were personally known to him to try to enlist their interest in, and financial support of, the Foundation. This offer was gratefully accepted and resulted in a dinner party in Lord Evans's home on 17

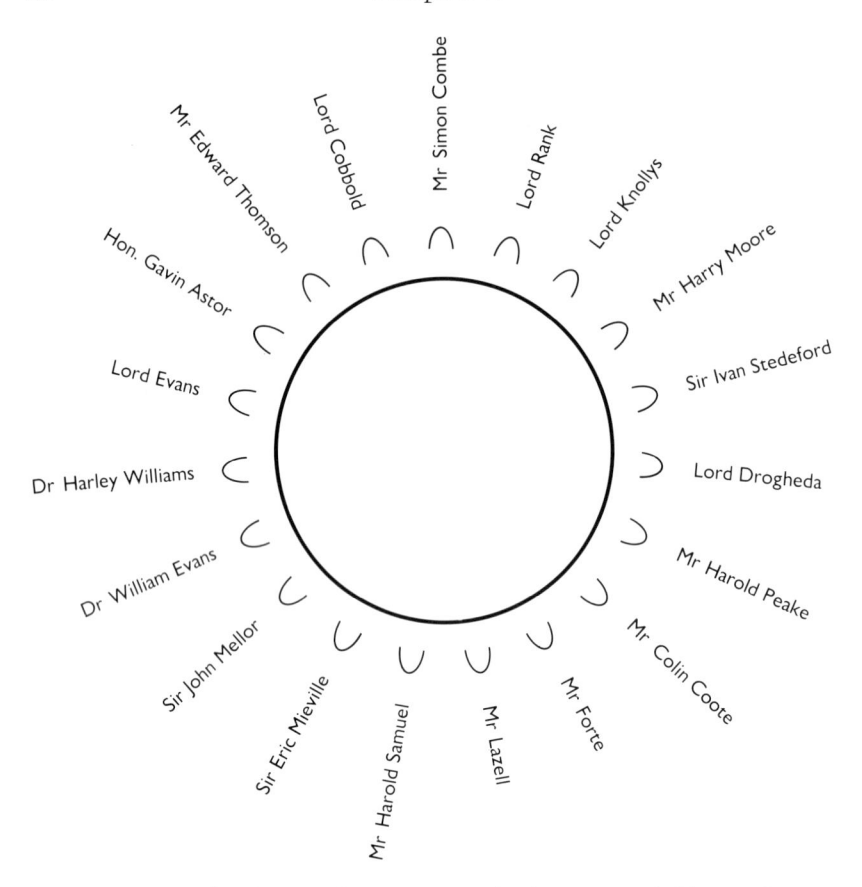

Figure 5 *Seating plan showing those present at the dinner party, held at Lord Evans's house on 17 July 1961, to launch an Appeal Committee.*

July 1961 (Figure 5). This occasion was a very important milestone in the development of the Foundation since it engaged the attention of the country's captains of industry, and resulted in promises of personal support of the appeal, either by advancing the cause of the Foundation, or as members of the Appeal Committee, or both, in addition to financial support by donations or covenants. Ultimately the officers of the Appeal Committee were recruited as a result of this dinner party, but several of those present needed clarification of the relationship of the Chest and Heart Association to the Foundation and of the method of electing Council members before they would agree to participate. Amongst these was Mr Leslie Lazell, the prospective Chairman of the Appeal Committee.

RELATIONS WITH THE CHEST AND HEART ASSOCIATION

This matter was very serious since unless the difficulties were resolved the viability of the Appeal Committee without participation by leading public figures would have been jeopardized. The Executive Committee met on 4 September 1961 to tackle the problem. The nature of the objections which had been raised was ably put to the Committee by Mr Harry Moore, who had been at the meeting at Lord Evans's house in July. His wise counsel also did much towards securing agreement between members of the Executive Committee as to the best way to meet Mr Lazell's objections, in preparation for a meeting between him and representatives of the BHF and CHA, which was arranged for the following week. Mr George Pope, Deputy Manager of *The Times* newspaper, who was a member of the CHA Council, also took a prominent and constructive part in these deliberations.

The problems were resolved by agreement that there should be a single appeal conducted by the BHF and that all monies raised would be at the disposal of the Foundation for heart research; the CHA would undertake not to make any appeal during this time, and subsequently to make such an appeal only if it did not conflict with a continuing appeal by the BHF. At the same time the Foundation accepted that public education and welfare for heart patients formed 'an essential part of heart research'. The Foundation would regard the CHA as its agent in respect of education and welfare of cardiac patients and would pay the CHA to carry out these functions. The amount of money given for these purposes was to be entirely controlled by the Foundation.

COUNCIL STRUCTURE

It was agreed, at Mr Lazell's insistence, that the British Cardiac Society and the Chest and Heart Association could *nominate* members to the Council of the BHF but not *appoint* them; the BHF Council would be the only body responsible for the constitution of its Council. He also refused to accept that the Secretary-General of the CHA would automatically be the Secretary of the BHF in perpetuity. The agreement that Dr Harley Williams was to be the Foundation's

Secretary was to be for three years in the first instance and renewable. Furthermore the whole agreement between the BHF and the CHA already negotiated was to be terminable after three years on one year's notice. It was also agreed that, whilst the CHA secretariat would continue to be employed on BHF business at present, a time was envisaged when a separate staff would be needed. He also insisted that although the CHA staff would continue to work from their own offices in the BMA at Tavistock House North the BHF must have a separate address in a different room if it were in the same building. The solicitors of the two organizations were instructed to draft the necessary documents.

MEMORANDUM AND ARTICLES OF ASSOCIATION

In due course the Board of Trade accepted the amendments to the Memorandum and Articles of Association and they were approved at an extraordinary meeting of the BHF held in the Rygate Room, Tavistock House North, on 12 December 1962.

The objectives of the BHF remained unaltered (see p. 10) but the wording was changed to exclude all direct reference to the Chest and Heart Association. The ability to cooperate with them was, however, safeguarded by Clause 4 of the objectives, which reads as follows: 'To establish, subsidise, promote, amalgamate, co-operate or federate with, affiliate or become affiliated to, act as trustee or agent for or manage or lend money or assistance to any association, society, company or other body, whether or not incorporated, whose objects are wholly of a charitable nature etc.' At the same time the agreement between the BHF and the CHA was redrafted to include the amendments and was subsequently ratified.

PREMISES

In compliance with the requirement that the BHF should have its own premises the Council, at its first meeting on 17 October 1961, authorized the Secretary, Dr Harley Williams, to accept the two rooms offered by the BMA on the third floor of Tavistock House North at a rental of £500 per annum, the money being put up by the CHA on the Foundation's behalf.

APPEAL COMMITTEE

Lord Evans, who had been present at all the discussions which these difficulties precipitated, undertook to convene a second meeting of the public figures who had attended the dinner given by him in July, with some additions, in order to inform them of the satisfactory outcome of the negotiations and to encourage the creation of an Appeal Committee. This meeting took place at Lord Evans's house on 5 February 1962 and resulted in the formation of a powerful Appeal Committee with the Hon. Gavin Astor as President, Mr Leslie Lazell as Chairman and Lord Cobbold as Treasurer. The Hon. Gavin Astor was the Proprietor of *The Times* newspaper, Mr Lazell the Chairman of the Beecham Group of Companies and Lord Cobbold the Governor of the Bank of England. Lord Evans proposed that all those present should become members of the Appeal Committee and all agreed to do so.

It is impossible to overstate the importance of Lord Evans's support of the Foundation. Besides being a public figure in consequence of his royal appointment he was widely known, well liked and held in universally high regard by all sections of the medical profession. His popularity was merited, not only because of his clinical acumen, but also because of his personality. He was larger than life, which he enjoyed to the full. He laughed a lot and made others laugh with him. He shared with his wife, Helen, a passion for horses and horse racing, and was never happier than when having a day at the races. He enjoyed a 'flutter', but it is said that his wife was the more knowledgeable punter. He was in a position to influence many important people to support the Foundation and he was tireless in this endeavour. His interest in, and publicly expressed enthusiasm for, the Foundation and its objectives guaranteed its respectability in the eyes of a profession which tends to view new medical institutions with a healthy scepticism until of proven worth. Their approval was essential for the Foundation's survival and Horace Evans was uniquely placed to influence this. The Foundation lost a strong, tall and elegant pillar of support with his untimely death at an early age.

The first meeting of the Appeal Committee was held on 1 May 1962 at the London Press Exchange. A draft leaflet for use in connection with the appeal, which had been prepared by the London Press Exchange, was considered and approved with some amendments. The Chairman undertook to have it printed in suitable form for distribution.

The first promises of support for the Foundation were announced and were as follows:

Harold Samuel Esq., £100,000 over 7-year covenant.
Unilever Ltd, £7,500 over 7-year covenant.
Shell Trading & Transport, £7,500 over 7-year covenant.
Watney Mann Ltd, £5,000 over 7-year covenant.
Beecham Group Ltd, £5,000 over 7-year covenant.
Glaxo Laboratories Ltd, £5000 over 7-year covenant.
Mr Charles Forte, £2,500 personal covenant over 7 years.

It was also announced that members of the Committee would undertake to approach companies on a list which had been circulated, each dealing with the industry in which he was a leading figure. Such was the diversity of expertise of members of the Committee that this resolution secured coverage of life assurance, the pharmaceutical industry, oil companies, ICI and Courtauld's, banks, insurance companies, newspapers and the brewing industry.

The records contain a copy of a letter used by members to elicit financial support written by Mr Rudolf de Trafford, a partner in the merchant bankers Philip Hill, who had joined Lord Evans and Dr William Evans as an additional Vice-Chairman of the Appeal Committee.

It was also decided to engage a firm of appeal consultants (John F. Rich & Co.) at a fee of £1,200 to make a survey and prepare a detailed campaign plan over a four-month period.

So successful were the initial efforts of the Appeal Committee that the Annual Report for 1962, submitted to the Annual General Meeting, was able to announce that after only one year's work nearly £1,000,000 had been promised and more than £80,000 received. The archives contain documents showing that donations, most as covenants, amounted to £1,168,002 in March 1963 and had reached £2,548,528 by March 1965.

SCIENCE COMMITTEE

While the Appeal Policy Committee had been engaged on the difficult task of setting up the Appeal Committee, the Science Committee had been busy fulfilling its supporting role, which was to provide the Appeal Committee with as much information as possible about the nature of the research to be undertaken and the way in which grant applications would be judged and awards made.

The first meeting of the Science Committee took place on 6 March 1961. It was a committee of the newly formed Council although, in the event, the Council did not hold its first meeting until October 1961; in the mean time the Science Committee reported to the Executive Committee.

Dr Paul Wood was appointed Vice-Chairman and took the chair at the first three meetings of the Science Committee whilst a Chairman from outside the Council of the Foundation was sought, although the members of the Committee did in fact try their utmost to persuade Mr Michael Perrin (later Sir Michael), a lay member of the council, to become Chairman. But he declined as he felt that his acceptance might be questioned on ethical grounds because he was already Chairman of the Wellcome Foundation. The acceptance of the chairmanship by Sir Charles Dodds, President of the Royal College of Physicians and an eminent biochemist, was announced at the meeting of the Executive Committee on 18 July 1962. Within a few days Dr Paul Wood died suddenly and unexpectedly from a heart attack. He was a great loss to the Foundation and generous tributes were paid to him by the chairmen of all committees of the Foundation. He had worked tirelessly for it since the first meeting of the Founding Committee and his warm personality, his wise counsel and his ability to go to the root of a problem quicker than most people, combined with his ability to listen to others, had smoothed many rough paths.

CONSULTANT ADVISERS

It was soon realized by the Science Committee that expertise would be needed in many subspecialities. This was obtained by inviting experts to act as Consultant Advisers, attending meetings when their special knowledge was needed, without the onus of regular attendance. This scheme worked well and many distinguished men served the Committee including Professor Donald Reid (epidemiology and statistics), Dr Clifford Parsons (paediatrics), Dr Robert Steiner (radiology) and Professor Wayne (pharmacology). Later, at the suggestion of Mr Lazell, industrial scientists were added to the Advisory

Panel. In this way the assistance of Sir Ronald Holroyd, Dr E.G. Woodroofe (later Sir Edward) and Dr G.J. Popjak, who all held senior positions in industry, became available. They were later joined by others of equal eminence.

RESEARCH POLICY

Discussion as to the general policy of the Committee in regard to research and to postgraduate education took much time. It was agreed that the Foundation should consider support of both collective and individual research, that it should grant individual research Fellowships for study in Britain and abroad and that it should strive to improve the knowledge and practice of cardiology. Serious consideration was given to the possibility of putting money into bricks and mortar and the possibility of founding and funding an Institute of Cardiological Research was not finally abandoned for a number of years. It is interesting to note, moreover, that, despite considerable reservation being expressed about the desirability and feasibility of this course by many members of the Committee from the start, the idea has been put forward again several times over the years, and always with the same result.

RESEARCH GRANTS

The Committee was asked by the Appeal Committee to list research projects which would attract and interest the public. Their list included cardiac metabolism and electrophysiology, cardiomyopathies, all aspects of coronary disease, including life-style factors, atheroma and blood lipids, thrombosis and artificial and natural thrombolysis. To these they added hypertension, congenital heart disease, cardiac surgery, cardiac failure, emergency cardiac resuscitation and long-term community studies into cardiac disease. The list would not need much modification or expansion if compiled today nearly 30 years later.

The Committee did not meet again for over a year (between July 1961 and August 1962) since the appeal had not, until then, progressed sufficiently to make desirable a public announcement about the availability of money for research. However, at a meeting on 13 November 1962, with Sir Charles Dodds in the chair and Dr McMichael (later Sir John) as Vice-Chairman (Figure 6) in succession

Figure 6 *(a) Sir Charles Dodds, first Chairman of the Science Committee; (b) Sir John McMichael, Chairman of Council and of the Research Funds Committee.*

to the late Dr Paul Wood, the advisability of holding a press conference was discussed. It was generally agreed that this should coincide with the launch of a public appeal on behalf of the Foundation.

It was decided that grants should not be made before this since, to date, only members of the Science Committee were in a position to know of the possible availability of money. But Mr Lazell, the Chairman of the Appeal Committee, was understandably keen that some research should be funded as soon as possible after the launch of the public appeal in June 1962, provided of course there were applications worthy of support. Consequently the Science Committee spent time assessing the applications already received in readiness for this, and the Council, at its meeting on 18 July 1962, authorized the Science Committee to spend up to £40,000 in the year 1962–63. In the event £19,513 was awarded out of a gross income of £170,017. It was at this time that the Council decided that two members of the Finance Committee, Mr Harry Moore and Mr Charles Forte, should be asked to serve on the Science Committee as the availability of money for research became a reality.

ADMINISTRATION

During this early formative period the Council was continually called on to make decisions on policy matters and to initiate executive action on a wide variety of matters, both directly, and indirectly through its committees.

Registration

An early problem concerned registration of the Foundation as a charity, which seems to have been overlooked; the Charity Commissioners issued registration on 20 March 1963 and related this back to the date of the Foundation's incorporation, 28 July 1961. But the Inland Revenue were not so accommodating and it was only after persistent representations by Mr Cooper, the Foundation's solicitor, and Lord Cobbold, the Treasurer, that they relented and allowed payment in full of claims on covenants amounting to £38,400.

Membership

Another problem concerned membership of the Foundation. The Appeal Committee saw this as a valuable source of income and a membership application form was ultimately agreed. The Council was wary, however, of surrendering *carteblanche* voting powers to all comers and limited membership, at first, to Council members; all were asked to join so that they could vote at the Extraordinary General Meeting in 1962 to alter the Memorandum and Articles of Association. But the Appeal Committee ultimately had its way and three classes of membership were agreed: life at £105, and ordinary at £5 a year, both with voting rights, and associate, without voting rights, at £2 a year. At the fifth meeting of Council in October 1963 it was reported that there were 179 life members, 700 ordinary members and 1,321 associates.

Welfare

Implementation of the Foundation's undertaking to pay the CHA as its agents for welfare and rehabilitation of cardiac patients also engaged the Council's attention. A grant of £20,000 per annum was made for the years 1962–63 and 1963–64; this was increased in February 1964 to £22,500 per annum for the next three years and raised again to £25,000 per annum for 1967–68 and 1968–69 when the arrangement terminated.

Personnel

During these years there were many changes in personnel and many newcomers who assisted the Council and its committees. Lord Cobbold, Treasurer of the Foundation, became Chairman of the Finance and General Purposes Committee, and Mr Rudolf de Trafford became Chairman of the Investment Subcommittee before succeeding Lord Cobbold as Treasurer. The Publicity Subcommittee of the Appeal Committee was under the Chairmanship of Mr A.B. McKay of the *Daily Mirror* group. Dr Maurice Campbell resigned as Chairman of Council in October 1965 and was succeeded by the Vice-Chairman, Dr Evan Bedford, who was succeeded as Vice-Chairman by Sir Charles Dodds. In 1963 Mr Charles Forte and Mr Harold Samuel accepted the Council's invitation to become the Foundation's first Vice-Presidents. They were followed early in 1964 by Lord Marks. The honour was conferred on him following his munificent gift of £200,000, which formed the basic financial backing of the first BHF-endowed Professorial Chair of Cardiology, the Simon Marks Chair at the Cardio-Thoracic Institute. Unhappily he died shortly afterwards, and the Council was very pleased when his widow, Miriam Lady Marks, agreed to become Vice-President in his stead.

A notable newcomer was Dr John Shillingford (later Professor), who joined the Council in 1963 on the nomination of the British Cardiac Society, of which he was Secretary at the time; this marked the beginning of 24 years of service to the BHF.

PUBLIC APPEAL

This was launched, after much hard preparatory work by Dr Harley Williams and the Secretariat of the CHA headed by Mr A.J. Mantripp and Mrs M. Davis, at a press conference held at the headquarters of the Royal Society at Burlington House on 11 June 1963. In an introductory speech the President, Field Marshal Alexander, the Rt. Hon. the Earl of Tunis, Kg, explained that he had suffered a heart attack five years previously and went on: 'It is in gratitude for the skill of the medicos that I head this Foundation, and also for others who may be stricken as I was.'

After explaining the urgent need for money with which to finance research he concluded:

The heart is a muscle which can long outlast most other parts of our bodies – it is a wonderful little muscle which is quite happy to go on pumping day and night for a hundred years. It really is too absurd that it should be allowed to fail us prematurely. We must find out the reasons why it fails us – and we will find out the reason if we have the means. This is what the British Heart Foundation has set out to do.

Lord Alexander was followed by Lord Evans, Vice-Chairman of the Appeal Committee, who enlarged upon the nature and scope of the research needed to investigate heart disease in both children and adults. He concluded: 'What we of the Foundation have to do is to provide them [research workers] with the opportunities, adequate equipment, economic security at least as good as that in other branches of medicine, and with other facilities, and with a channel by means of which their individual contributions may be coordinated into a single programme of attack.'

Professor Sir John McMichael, formerly Professor of Medicine. University of London Postgraduate Medical School and currently Director of Postgraduate Medical Education, University of London, then addressed the meeting in his capacity as Vice-Chairman of the Foundation's Science Committee. He said: 'The reason for launching this appeal is that heart and vascular disease is the cause of over 50% of all the deaths in this country.' He went on to explain how the Science Committee would try to ensure that the money entrusted to the Foundation by the public was used to the best advantage, adding: 'I also want to say that the Science Committee will not itself direct research. It will rather try to find the able and original minded young investigators and give them the support they need.' He summarized the philosophy which underlay the creation of the Foundation when he said:

Some people have said that we could leave all this costly work to the Americans, who have so much more to spend on it than we have. My answer is that you cannot buy genius with money and that genius is just as likely to be available on these islands as in any other country. A country which fails to develop its research would be committing national suicide because our cultural leadership depends on it.

Sir John McMichael was followed by Mr H.G. Lazell, Chairman of the Beecham Group of Companies, and Chairman of the Appeal Committee, who said that in the first seven years the BHF 'will need

£500,000 a year to finance research on an adequate scale. Our aim is to raise a fund of at least three and a half million pounds to provide continuity of research over this period.' He also pointed out that the prevalence of heart disease meant that 'there is a potential victim in every family' and continued: 'I also support the Foundation as a businessman because heart disease has become a great menace to industry and commerce. It threatens the careers of some of our most able employees.' He ended his remarks by saying: 'I believe that industry and commerce should support the Foundation, not just as a charity, but as a form of insurance for their staff and their businesses.'

The press conference was concluded by a short speech from Lord Woolton, who was also a member of the Appeal Committee. He was very well known to the public as a highly successful Minister of Food in the harsh days of wartime rationing. In characteristically robust style he declared: 'I beg you to applaud the courage and far-sightedness of the Committee which asks for this large sum – you have heard the experts. They tell us it can be done. I know they will tell you money cannot buy it, but it can give encouragement to the men who can accomplish it.'

Following the press conference sustained efforts were made to secure maximum publicity through the press and media backed by articles in magazines and by direct mailing. Twelve thousand companies were approached by personally signed letters and life membership was sought from five thousand individuals. Half a million householders received invitations of membership or associate membership.

As time went by, regional fund-raising organizations were created with regional organizers in charge. Some of the first were in Northern Ireland (W/Cdr C.G. Masters), Scotland (Major R. Andrew McIntosh), the North based on Newcastle (Mr R.G. Hill) and London (Mrs Doreen Nicholson and Mr W.E. Cutts). A wide variety of fund-raising activities was organized both in the regions and at headquarters from the earliest days.

The press conference was followed three days later by announcements in the medical press that money was available for cardiac research and inviting the submission of applications for grants. These were processed by the Science Committee and when necessary by the Advisory Panel.

The public appeal was directed by General Vivian Street, who was appointed Appeal Director by the Council in February 1964. He was a distinguished soldier destined for the highest offices in the army command when he had to retire following a heart attack. Unhappily his health was not good enough to support such strenuous work in a field so closely allied to his own disability, and, on the orders of his doctor, he resigned after 18 months. He was succeeded by Brigadier Ereld Cardiff, who was to play a long and important part in the Foundation's affairs. He was an officer in the Scots Guards with a distinguished war record, being for some time Assistant Adjutant Quartermaster-General (A/Q) to the 7th Armoured Division with responsibility for the provision of all supplies including fighting equipment. He was then posted to the Joint Services College in America, after which he served with Far East Land Forces (1955–58), before becoming, for five years (1958–63), the Personal Assistant to General Norstadt, the NATO commander at the headquarters of SHAPE (Supreme Headquarters Allied Powers in Europe) in Paris. His retirement from the army in November 1963 was a stroke of good fortune for the Foundation since he was a very experienced administrator and well known in high places. He was a genial man, a very good mixer and an enthusiast, all of which qualities made him an ideal choice as Appeal Director. He was assisted by Captain Noel Lyster-Binns as Deputy Director of Appeals and Dr Harley Williams, the General Secretary, both of whom worked closely with him. These three served the Appeal Committee very ably and did much towards the success of the appeal. The fostering of development of the regions was the special responsibility of Captain Lyster-Binns.

In spite of everyone's efforts, however, progress was disappointingly slow at first. Only about £350,000 were added in the first year and it says much for the dedication of all concerned that they persisted with unabated enthusiasm despite early disappointment.

REORGANIZATION

At the meeting of Council on 7 May 1963 the Chairman reported that the Executive Committee had expressed concern regarding the future organization of the BHF and it was agreed that a committee should be set up to consider the matter and make a report. This important committee consisted of the chairmen of the four existing committees (Dr Maurice Campbell, Lord Cobbold, Sir Charles Dodds and Mr

The Early Years

Lazell) together with Dr Evan Bedford, Lord Evans, Mr Harry Moore and Mr Michael Perrin.

The Finance and General Purposes Committee

It was agreed by the Council meeting on 29 October 1964 that the present Executive Committee should be wound up and that a Finance and General Purposes Committee (F&GP) should be set up to 'act as an executive channel for the conduct of the affairs of the BHF'.

It was stipulated that it should be composed of Council members and that it should be responsible to the Council. It met monthly at first and has subsequently met every two months up to the present time. It was also agreed that the Council would meet only twice a year and would work through the F&GP, instead of through all the committees as heretofore. The Science Committee and the Appeal Committee would therefore become responsible directly to the F&GP. A new Investment Committee, also responsible to the F&GP, was set up under the chairmanship of the Teasurer with a membership of four; not all of these had to be Council members. Mr Rudolf de Trafford became the first Chairman of the F&GP and Mr Lazell the first Deputy Chairman. The members were the Chairman and Vice-Chairman of Council, the Chairman of the Science Committee or his Deputy, Mr A.B. McKay, the Director of Appeals and the Secretary. This streamlining was successful and the structure has remained essentially the same to the present day apart from modifications of committee membership and the addition of new committees responsible to the F&GP as necessary.

The Chest and Heart Association

It was not long before the F&GP turned its attention to the relationship of the BHF with the Chest and Heart Association. Through its chairman it commissioned the well-known accountancy firm of Peet, Marwick & Mitchell to 'examine and report on the existing administration and organization of the British Heart Foundation and to make recommendations as to any changes which seem necessary'. The report, which is very detailed, was completed on 1 September 1965 and its date of publication was 7 December 1965.

The report was debated at length by the Council on 23 March

1966. It recommended the termination of the existing agreement with the CHA, which was due for renewal in December 1966. Mr de Trafford reported that since one year's notice of this intent was mandatory such notice had already been given to the CHA. Many changes followed.

It was agreed that as from 1 April 1966 the BHF would take over all financial matters and book-keeping and that at a mutually convenient date in the autumn of 1966 all administrative and secretarial work would be transferred to 57 Gloucester Place, where the Appeal Department already had offices. This address became the registered office of the Foundation. The office at Tavistock House North in the premises of the British Medical Association was kept on for the work of the Science Committee and became known as the Medical Department of the BHF until, after a short spell in 69 Gloucester Place, the Foundation was able to acquire accommodation in 59 Gloucester Place in 1970. With some internal rearrangement, including knocking a hole in a wall between the two buildings, the Medical Department became physically joined up with the Foundation's headquarters next door!

It was also agreed at the council meeting on 23 March 1966 that Dr Harley Williams's appointment as Secretary of the BHF should terminate on 30 September 1966, but that he should continue with the work of the Science Committee and as editor of the journal *Heart* with the title of Administrative Medical Director. This journal was a four-page broadsheet which had been produced quarterly since the start of the Foundation and was mainly to encourage and congratulate fund-raisers on their efforts; it was a successful propaganda vehicle.

It was also agreed at the same Council meeting that the BHF would seek a successor in 1968 to Dr Harley Williams, who was happy to stay on to help the transition for a few months. His successor was Dr Margaret Haigh.

The Director General and Secretary

The same Council meeting also resolved that Brigadier Cardiff (Figure 7), the Director of Appeals, should be appointed Director General of the Foundation to take effect on the day of Dr Harley Williams's resignation as Secretary (30 September 1966). This he did and also became the Acting Secretary until the appointment of Mr Denis

The Early Years

Figure 7 *Brigadier Ereld Cardiff. Director of Appeals 1964–66, and Director General 1966–76.*

Blake. At the same time Captain Lyster-Binns resigned as Deputy Director of Appeals and Mr Geoffrey Davison, who had been working for the British Epilepsy Association, became Deputy Director General with special responsibility for the development of regional fund-raising organizations.

Welfare

The only remaining outstanding matter of reorganization was the work of welfare and rehabilitation, for which the CHA had been acting as the agent of the BHF. This was resolved by a new agreement in which the Foundation undertook to reimburse the CHA at the increased rate of £25,000 a year with termination fixed at 31 March 1969. Medical members of Council, headed by Drs Maurice Campbell and Lloyd Rusby, strongly urged continuing cooperation between the two charities and a subcommittee was set up to try to ensure this; it is a measure of the success of these discussions that the two organizations have continued to work harmoniously alongside each other over the years. It is also a lasting tribute to the qualities of the Treasurer of the CHA, Lord Kirkwood, and the Treasurer of the BHF, Mr de Trafford, that such radical changes were made so smoothly. At a meeting of Council on 29 June 1966, at which the new agreement between the two bodies for the ensuing three years was ratified, the Chairman had recorded in the minutes that 'warm congratulations were due to the Treasurers for their efforts'.

ANNUAL GENERAL MEETINGS

The first of these was held on 12 December 1962 at the Foundation's headquarters in Tavistock House immediately following the Extraordinary General Meeting at which changes in the Memorandum and Articles of Association were agreed. The Annual Report of Council was presented by the Chairman, Dr Maurice Campbell. It gave an account of the Foundation's objectives and a summary of the committee structure set up to pursue them. The progress made during the first year of the Foundation's existence was outlined with special reference to the auspicious start made by the Appeal Committee in securing promises amounting to nearly £1,000,000. Generous tribute was also paid to the untiring work of the late Paul Wood. The Chairman also outlined the Council structure, after which elections were held to fill vacancies from a previously circulated list of nominations. The Treasurer, Lord Cobbold, then presented the accounts, which were duly adopted. The meeting concluded with the election of Messrs Lord, Foster & Co as auditors and a vote of thanks.

The second and third Annual General Meetings in 1963 and 1964 were also held at Tavistock House and had the same general format.

In 1963 the Chairman reported that the Science Committee had recommended 34 awards totalling £180,000 and in 1964 the meeting received a message from the Patron, His Royal Highness the Duke of

Edinburgh, which read: 'The British Heart Foundation should make it possible to plan and execute a thoroughly comprehensive programme of research. I send my best wishes to the Foundation on its inauguration and I hope it will receive all the support it needs.'

At the fourth Annual General Meeting held on 14 July 1965, the format was changed in that it was immediately followed by a public meeting open to anyone interested. The increasing number of people wishing to attend also necessitated a change of venue, and both meetings were held in the lecture theatre of the Royal College of Physicians in Regent's Park. Two hundred people attended. At the public meeting a message was read from the President, Lord Alexander. He wrote:

It is now two years since the Foundation launched its public appeal, and I congratulate the Foundation on the results it has achieved, and on the number of research projects in operation. I am extremely sorry not to be able to be present this afternoon and only an important engagement in my capacity as Lord Lieutenant of the County of London would have prevented my attendance.

Mr McKay, the Chairman of the Publicity Subcommittee of the Appeal Committee, arranged for a display of photographs presented by the International Publishing Corporation illustrating the work of the Foundation. Six short papers were also delivered. Mr Lazell, Chairman of the Appeal Committee, reported that nearly £2,000,000 had been raised but that much more was needed to ensure the provision of £500,000 a year for research. He urged the creation of a nation-wide network of fund-gathering volunteers and stressed the value of *in memoriam* gifts stating that 'if only 10% of friends and relatives who mourn would make an *in memoriam* donation to the Heart Foundation in place of the more normal floral tribute we would raise all the money we require'. At about this time income from *in memoriam* gifts was starting to rise substantially.

Dr Maurice Campbell, Chairman of the Council, emphasized that the Foundation was already contributing to the saving of some lives by the distribution of apparatus to correct irregularities of rhythm and was researching the problems of atheroma. Sir Charles Dodds, Chairman of the Science Committee, announced new awards totalling £50,000 over three years and said that previous awards totalled £377,000; 120 research workers were now in receipt of grants from the Foundation. He went on to outline the Committee's interest in possible funding in the field of molecular biology, which was then only in its infancy. Sir John McMichael, Vice-Chairman of the Science Committee, followed by reporting the support given to research into paediatric cardiology, heart surgery for diseased valves, hypertension and coronary occlusion. Dr Walter Somerville spoke about the value of recently introduced intensive care units, in which the BHF had played a part, and the techniques of cardiac resuscitation and defibrillation, both of which had been supported. The meeting was concluded by Dr Berwick Wright, the doctor in charge of the medical department of the Institute of Directors, who was in receipt of a grant from the Foundation to study the life-style of business executives and its relation to heart disease. He reported the start of an analysis of risk factors identical to those generally listed today, and exhorted businessmen and the firms for which they work to 'look after yourself at least as well as you look after your car'.

The meeting seems to have been such a success that the 200 who attended increased to 500 the following year, 1966. The lecture theatre was too small and the meeting was transferred to the large Edward Lumley Hall at the Royal College of Surgeons in Lincoln's Inn Fields, where it was held for a number of succeeding years and in much the same form. This was large enough to allow ingenious innovations such as curtaining off part as a hospital ward with beds containing volunteer patients who happily told their success stories of treatment resulting from research! Less dramatic innovations included the demonstration of new apparatus used in the diagnosis and treatment of patients and for research. The Annual Reports during these years were published in full in the *Heart Journal*.

THE ORIGIN OF FUTURE SUCCESS

Reference has already been made to the diversity of matters which the Council and its committees had to consider and on which they had to make decisions. It would not be right, therefore, to conclude this chapter on the early years without recording the vision of these early pioneers whose deliberations led to the development of so many of the important activities of the organization today.

The possibility of setting up university professorial chairs was discussed by the Council as early as February 1964 and agreed in principle. Negotiations were commenced with the University of London and the Cardio-Thoracic Institute which resulted in the presentation of the first cheque from the Foundation to the Principal of the University by Miriam, Lady Marks, on 24 May 1964 for the establishment of the Simon Marks Chair of Cardiology in memory of her husband, Lord Marks, who had died three months earlier. In October 1965 Dr Swan, cardiologist in Newcastle, and a member of Council, raised the possibility of establishing an Academic Chair at Newcastle University, which eventually came about.

At the same meeting in February 1964 the Council also agreed in principle to the recommendation of the Science Committee that the Foundation should set up a number of seven-year research Fellowships costing approximately £20,000 each.

At the next Council meeting in May 1964 the development of the Cardiac Care Committee was foreshadowed by granting seven out of eight applications, each for £1,000, to purchase equipment for cardiac resuscitation and defibrillation in cardiac units in general hospitals, to attract publicity to the Foundation and its appeal. It was agreed that resuscitation was a valid aspect of research to support, and the availability of money for such equipment had been announced at a meeting of the British Cardiac Society. The equipment supplied included cardioverters (defibrillators) and electrocardiograph machines.

Finally it is to be recorded that Sir John McMichael, in presenting the report of the Science Committee to Council in October 1965, said that he had discussed with Dr Surgenor of the American Heart Association proposals for an exchange of research Fellows to which the AHA would contribute $10,000 for each Fellow (originally proposed $15,000) and the BHF $5,000 for each. The award of the first two British–American Exchange Fellowships from this country under this agreement was announced at the Council meeting a year later. The recipients were Dr Michael Lee of Oxford and Dr B.M. Rifkind of Glasgow.

THREE

THE MIDDLE YEARS: 1966–1976

With the ending of the original agreement with the Chest and Heart Association (CHA) in 1966 the Foundation (BHF) became an independent organization and with the transference of its administration to 57 Gloucester Place, where the Appeal Department already had offices, it became physically separated. A 15-year lease on the whole of this building was subsequently signed in 1968 and two years later a similar lease was purchased on the adjoining terraced building at 59 Gloucester Place.

The Foundation enjoyed happy years in its new home and those who were members of its staff at the time look back nostalgically to the family atmosphere which prevailed. It was still a small charity and comparatively unknown despite the auspicious start which its distinguished medical and lay pioneers had made.

The urgent need was to intensify and enlarge the appeal in order to obtain more money for research, and the Foundation was singularly fortunate in having Brigadier Cardiff as its Director General at this time. He inspired everyone who worked at headquarters to give of their best and to turn their hands to whatever the moment or occasion required. He also had a very wide circle of influential friends in the business and social worlds, on whom he exerted his natural charm, engaging personality and unfailing good humour for the good of the Foundation's cause. Everyone who knew him has spoken in glowing terms of his qualities and of the debt the Foundation will always owe him. Dr Morris Butler, at one time Medical Administrator to the Foundation, said: 'He had a wonderful image to the public; one could trust him completely, and obviously the public did. He was charming to everyone.'

COVENANTS: INDUSTRY

The initial funding of the appeal was mainly through covenants from industry, obtained by solicitation by business leaders serving on the

The Middle Years

Appeal Committee, and there was some well-founded anxiety by the Council as to whether these would be renewed when the seven-year expiry date approached; most had been made at the beginning in 1961. Sir Harry Moore, a well-known banker, who has been associated with the Foundation since the days of the Founding Committee, described the attitude of the donors of covenants as: 'Our function is to help you get started but we reckon this gives you time to interest the general public because they are really the people who have got to support this.' He went on: 'A number of them did in fact renew their covenants, not always for quite as much ... they were very generous ... but we were quite firmly told that industry saw its role really as getting it started but not to be the main source of income in the long run. And I think it has worked out quite well that way.'

FUND-RAISING EVENTS

Brigadier Cardiff set about engaging the interest of the public. The fashion of the time was to organize big, well-publicized, fund-raising events which brought in a lot of money and increased awareness of the existence and aims of the charity. The Foundation enjoyed a generous slice of this glamorous cake with 'first-nights', gala performances, fashion shows, prestigious auctions, sponsored race meetings, flag days, balls and dances to list but a few.

To attempt a full account of these events would be inappropriate and certain to fail, but they played such an important part in the Foundation's development and so characterized an era that a record of some of the most outstanding occasions is proper.

A Gala Variety Performance was held at the London Palladium Theatre in the presence of Her Majesty Queen Elizabeth, the Queen Mother, on 1 May 1972 as part of the public appeal for £250,000 to endow a Professorial Chair of Cardiology at Oxford University to the memory of the Foundation's first President, Field Marshal the Earl Alexander of Tunis, who had died in 1969. It was a glittering occasion with his widow, Margaret, Countess of Tunis, supporting it as Chairman of the Ticket Selling Committee (Figure 8). The cast was made up of the leading entertainers of the day including Arthur Askey, Morecambe and Wise, the Beverley Sisters, Harry Secombe and Kenneth McKeller with Vera Lynn, the Forces Sweetheart, lending

Figure 8 *Her Majesty Queen Elizabeth, the Queen Mother, and Margaret, Countess of Tunis, at the gala performance at the London Palladium.*

the name of her famous wartime song, 'We'll Meet Again', as the title of the performance. Besides raising over £40,000 for the appeal the evening gave the Foundation much good publicity.

The world of theatre has always been very generous to charities and the Foundation has benefited many times. Amongst the special occasions was a preview of the play *Lloyd George Knew my Father* at the Savoy Theatre in 1972 in the presence of Princess Marina; this event was obtained by the Petersfield Committee from Mr William Douglas Hume but organized by the staff at headquarters. Through Mr Lew Grade, who was a member of the Council at the time, the Foundation enjoyed the proceeds of the European première of the musical *Mame* and the first-night of the Golden Boy Show at Grosvenor House Hotel by Sammy Davis Junior, both in 1975. In the same year Mr Alan Tillotson, also a member of the Council, obtained a share of the proceeds of a very popular concert given by Elton John at Wembley Stadium for the Foundation. Of a number of radio appeals those by Eric Morecambe, David Kossof and Peter Sellers were outstandingly successful.

There were many balls and dances held in different parts of the

Figure 9 *Poster announcing Ascot Race Day for the British Heart Foundation in 1973, which raised over £66,000.*

country, amongst which one of the earliest and most successful was in Glasgow in 1967 when £1,500 were raised, and another, equally successful, was organized by the Derby Committee, at Chatsworth House by permission of the Duke of Devonshire, in 1971 and attended by the Duchess of Gloucester.

Two very successful race days were held at Ascot in 1973 (Figure 9) and 1977 in support of the Foundation. On both occasions they were under the auspices of Lord Porchester, Racing Manager to Her Majesty the Queen. On the first occasion Sir Charles Forte (later Lord Forte) gave a lunch party for 250 guests and Lord Porchester acted as auctioneer at a generously supported auction sale during the luncheon. In 1973 races were sponsored by Beecham's, the Green Shield Company, Dry Fly Sherry and the Chiltonbury Stud and in 1977 by Taylor Woodrow, Phillips Electrical, William Hill, Argos and the Ewar Stud. A profit of over £66,000 was made at the meeting in 1973 and almost as much in 1977. The event in 1973 was a new venture for the BHF and the first held by a charity. It was organized from headquarters by Rosalind Ross assisted by Ginny Hills and was such a success that Miss Ross was in demand for organizing similar race meetings for other charities for several years, returning to the Foundation to run the second meeting in 1977.

Two successful occasions were held at London's Festival Hall. In 1969 Marks and Spencer, who were very generous to the Foundation right from the beginning, put on a fashion show which attracted much interest; the master of ceremonies was Bob Monkhouse, the well-known artist, and he was assisted by Coco, the clown. The following year the Foundation promoted a gala evening concert in honour of the Sixth World Congress of Cardiology, which was being held in London at the time, with Sir John Barbirolli conducting the Hallé Orchestra. Fashion shows were also popular fund-raising events and many were held throughout the country; among the earliest was one at the Fairfield Hall in Croydon in 1969 which raised nearly £1,000.

Outdoor events were of course popular and of great variety; only a few can be mentioned although countless others, organized by the hard work and enthusiasm of unsung friends, were equally worthy.

Flag days were much in vogue and Brigadier Cardiff was keen to get the Foundation involved. They were first held in the London area in 1966, and repeated in 1967 and 1969. They were repeated from

Figure 10 *Garden party at Walmer Castle. Left to right: Mrs du Boulay, Geoffrey Davison, Sir Robert Menzies and Mrs Perez (Chairman of the Deal and District Committee).*

time to time during the seventies and were also successfully run in many regions. In London they were organized by Frances Neal, assistant to Geoffrey Davison, in the early days. All the small band of headquarters staff were press-ganged to help and one gets the impression from the recollections of those who took part that despite the hard work they were enjoyed by everyone. One of the problems was to get a sufficient number of volunteers to rattle collecting tins and this was largely resolved by radio appeals each year for helpers by Jack de Manio, the presenter of a very popular morning programme. The staff had to set up depots at railway stations and other likely collecting points and arrange the collection of tins and their transport to local banks, which cooperated by counting the proceeds. Flag days were never great money-spinners in London and brought in each year only around £6,000 after much expenditure of time and effort, but they were invaluable for increasing public awareness of the Foundation and thus indirectly greatly increased its income.

An early event which is looked back to with nostalgic pleasure was a garden party held in 1967 by Sir Robert Menzies, Prime Minister of Australia, at Walmer Castle in his capacity as Warden of the Cinque Ports (Figure 10). This was the brainchild of Group Captain G. Du Boulay, who was regional organizer for Kent at the time.

In 1967 Alderman Jansen, the Mayor of Hounslow, nominated the BHF as his charity for his year of office, and collected over £10,000. Of this £2,500 was raised from a sponsored walk and this gave Mollie Chandler, the organizer for Sussex, the idea of adapting this concept to a sponsored swim. She organized the first in Britain in 1969 and raised over £1,000 at a swim in Worthing. By the end of the year the BHF had benefited by around £11,000 from other similar events.

Football also helped to raise money both by participation by well-known teams and through football pools. On one occasion there was a charity match, played on the Arsenal ground at Highbury, between the Arsenal team and 29 children successfully treated for cardiac conditions at the Hospital for Sick Children, Great Ormond Street (Figure 11), and on another the Birmingham team turned out to support the local appeal. As early as 1965 the Foundation obtained a concession of one and a half pence on every shilling paid to the foot-

Figure 11 *Charity Match between the Arsenal Football Club and 29 children treated for heart disease, arranged by Jimmy Saville.*

The Middle Years

ball pools promoters and the income from this grew dramatically. In a week in October 1965 the income was six shillings; in the comparable week a year later it was £96. By 1967 the average weekly total had risen to £125.

Students also played their part by raising money through street collections and rag weeks. The students of Southampton University were amongst the first, donating part of the proceeds of their rag week as early as 1966. In 1972 the students of Aberystwyth raised £9,000, the largest sum then raised by a single event.

The National Sponsored Slim, which was very successful for many years, made its appearance in these middle years. It was originally the idea of Dorothy Curtis, who has been the regional organizer for the Hampshire area since 1968. She ran a Regional Slim, which was taken up at headquarters by Geoffrey Davison, Assistant to the Director General; he organized it nationally in 1975 when it raised £16,000. Since then, under the sponsorship of Cadbury Marvel, who underwrite all the expenses and provide the prizes, it has raised many times this amount in recent years.

In 1969 a fund-raising scheme called the Mend-a-Heart Campaign was introduced in schools. Children were given cardboard cutouts of a heart with perforations in it and a set of Heart Foundation stamps of differing monetary value which they stuck on to cover the holes as

Figure 12 *Julie Jarrold, winner of the national 'Nurse of 1970' competition, sponsored by the Green Shield Stamp Company.*

they collected money for performing services. They received pin-on badges of varying distinction according to the number of completed cards they returned. The scheme, which was devised by Geoffrey Davison, was popular and financially successful. It was revived with equal success many years later.

In 1970 the Green Shield Stamp Company allowed the Foundation to place tins, into which stamps could be put by recipients, at some 87,000 retail outlets such as garages and shops. The monetary value of these donated stamps was then used to purchase equipment for coronary care units. Again the venture was successful, and it was backed by a competition, promoted by the BHF, to choose the 'Nurse of 1970' to spearhead the Green Shield Campaign. The competition was nation-wide and the final round was judged at a party given by the Green Shield Company at the Royal Lancaster Hotel in London. The winner was Julie Jarrold, a student nurse at King's College Hospital (Figure 12).

ADMINISTRATION

The governing body of the Foundation, as hitherto, was the Council, which met twice a year, and the executive management was in the hands of the Finance and General Purposes Committee, which continued to meet every two months. This committee was small enough to be accommodated at the Foundation's headquarters in Gloucester Place but the Council was too large. For a time it continued to meet at Tavistock House, the home of the British Medical Association, but subsequently it enjoyed the hospitality of the London Press Exchange through the good offices of Mr Rudolf de Trafford, Chairman of the F&GP. In 1970 it transferred to the Royal Society of Medicine for a short time before becoming regularly hosted by Marks and Spencer, in their boardroom, at the invitation of Mr B.W. Goodman, the managing director, who was a member of the Foundation Council.

REORGANIZATION OF COMMITTEE STRUCTURE

Over the years there were many changes in personnel and in committee structure. At the Annual General Meeting in 1966 the Constitution was amended to increase the number of laymen who could be co-opted on to the Council from 6 to 14 in order to secure the help of more industrialists.

In 1966 Mr. C.F. Cooper, the partner in Slaughter & May, the Foundation's solicitors, who had done such an outstandingly able job in the long and delicate negotiations with the Chest and Heart Association, left the Council on the expiry of his term of office. His vacancy was filled by Mr Lew Grade, who had a big hand in securing the interest and help of artists and producers in the world of stage and screen.

Early in 1967 Mr Lazell resigned as Chairman of the Appeal Committee and was succeeded by Mr Alex McKay but continued as a member of Council until 1969. Speaking of him Sir Harry Moore said: 'He was a very able man. He transformed the place and did a marvellous job for us.' Also in 1967 Sir Ronald Bodley Scott succeeded Sir Charles Dodds as Chairman of the Science Committee and Professor Melville Arnott (later Sir Melville) of Birmingham University became Vice-Chairman in succession to Sir John McMichael; Sir Charles Dodds remained a member of Council. In 1968 Dr Evan Bedford resigned as Chairman of Council and was succeeded by Sir John McMichael with Dr John Shillingford (later Professor) as his Vice-Chairman. Two years later (1970) Dr Evan Bedford and Dr Maurice Campbell, both members of the original Founding Committee, resigned from Council. At the same time Dr F.H.K. Green, who had been Scientific Adviser to the Foundation since its inception, resigned due to ill health. He was also at the time Scientific Adviser to the CHA as well as Scientific Secretary to the Wellcome Foundation.

Dr Harley Williams, Secretary of the Foundation from the days of the Founding Committee until 1966, ended his association with the Foundation as Administrative Medical Director on 31 March 1969, being succeeded as Medical Administrator by Dr Margaret Haigh, who was, in turn, succeeded by Dr Morris Butler in 1973. This year also saw Sir John McMichael succeeded as Chairman of Council by Sir Thomas Holmes Sellors, the President of the Royal College of Surgeons of England; he in turn was succeeded in 1976 by Sir Ronald Bodley Scott with Professor Shillingford as Vice-Chairman in succession to Dr Graham Hayward.

Sir Ronald served the Foundation continuously from 1967 until his tragic death in a road accident in 1982. He was, in turn, Chairman of the Science Committee, the Research Funds Committee and the Council, to all of which appointments he brought wise counsel and fair judgement, which contributed significantly to the reputation the Foundation gained for integrity and unbiased comment on contentious issues of the day.

In a quiet unassuming way, which was characteristic of him, he controlled the fervour of competing interests, and achieved harmonious progress during a period in which the influence and material resources of the Foundation were increasing rapidly. He was adept at smoothing paths behind the scenes to everyone's satisfaction. It is a rare gift and one which he used unsparingly to the benefit of the Foundation.

The year 1970 was very important for the administration of the Foundation. At the meeting of Council in February the Science Committee was replaced by the Research Funds Committee with Sir Ronald Bodley Scott as Chairman and Professor Shillingford as Vice-Chairman. The Postgraduate Education Funds Committee and the Cardiac Care Committee were also established at the same meeting and a Scientific Advisory Council was set up but this was disbanded in 1973 since it was found that its work was adequately covered by the other committees.

The function of the Cardiac Care Committee was to provide life-saving equipment to front-line situations, which included hospitals, ambulances and rescue services. This was understandably popular with local fund-raisers, and good 'seed corn' to spread awareness of the Foundation and to foster goodwill.

At its first meeting the following month the Research Funds Committee recommended 23 awards totalling £105,000, and in 1971 Dr Haigh reported to Council that the Cardiac Care Committee had also met and recommended the acceptance of four requests totalling £5,382; it met again three months later and recommended the expenditure of approximately the same amount of money, and in 1972, with Dr Walter Somerville as Chairman, it made four awards totalling £11,500.

At the Council meeting in June 1970 the Finance and General Purposes Committee was reconstituted to meet current needs and was composed of the Chairman and Vice-Chairman of Council, the Treasurer, the Director General, the Chairman or Vice-Chairman of the Research Funds Committee, the President or Chairman of the

Figure 13 *Presidents of the Foundation following Earl Alexander: (a) Lord Cobbold, 1969–76; (b) Viscount De L'Isle, 1976–84; (c) Viscount Tonypandy.*

Appeal Committee with the co-option of one member of the Council and one member of the Scientific Advisory Committee. The Committee had power to appoint its own Chairman and Sir Rudolph de Trafford was re-elected. He remained Chairman until his retirement in 1974 when he was succeeded by Sir Harry Moore.

In 1974 Mr Bryan Basset, Managing Director of Philip Hill Investment Trust, succeeded Sir Rudolph de Trafford as Treasurer of the Foundation and Mr Alex McKay retired from Council on

Figure 14 *Brigadier Christopher Thursby Pelham, Director General 1976–86.*

completion of ten years' service. In the same year the Foundation lost a loyal friend through the death of Mr B.W. Goodman of Marks and Spencer.

The previous year the Appeal Committee, which had not been active for some while, was re-formed with Mr Allen Tillotson, the industrialist, as Chairman and Mr Basset a member.

On 1 January 1976 Viscount De L'Isle, VC (Figure 13) succeeded Lord Cobbold as President of the Foundation and Lord Cobbold was elected Vice-President. At the same time Sir Cyril Clarke, lately President of the Royal College of Physicians of London, joined the Council and succeeded Sir Ronald Bodley Scott as Chairman of the Research Funds Committee, with Professor R.J. Linden of Birmingham University succeeding Professor Shillingford as Vice-Chairman.

In the autumn of the same year Brigadier Thursby Pelham succeeded Brigadier Cardiff as Director General (Figure 14).

PROFESSORIAL CHAIRS

At the Council meeting in June 1969 the policy regarding the award of research grants was debated at length. Initially as many grants as possible were made to worthy projects in order to publicize the existence of the Foundation, even though this meant giving only small sums because of limited resources. Another limiting factor at that time was that the appeal was restricted to a once-and-for-all collection of £3,500,000.

As time went by the amount of money available increased and the concept changed to an ongoing appeal without limitation of size or time. In consequence a change of policy was agreed whereby larger sums would be given, even if this meant at first a smaller number of awards, in order to support projects of major importance more generously. This change was strongly supported by Mr Goodman, managing director of Marks and Spencer, who was a lay member of the Science Committee at the time.

By 1971, however, the number of acceptable applications for grants was falling. This was partly because of discouragement in academic circles caused by poor career prospects for research, and partly because of better prospects in the clinical field. The response of the Foundation was to promote the establishment of academic professorial units as centres of excellence to which those with an interest in research would be attracted. It was a far-sighted decision and it is difficult to imagine the position of heart research in Britain today if it had not been made.

The Simon Marks Chair of Cardiology was already established at the Institute of Cardiology in London but the financial support was inadequate for its needs, and in 1971 the Research Funds Committee recommended the provision of £100,000 in addition to the £6,000 per annum as previously agreed. This was accepted by the Council.

Chapter 3

In the mean time the death of Earl Alexander, the Foundation's President, in 1969 had led to discussions with the University of Oxford about the creation of a professorial chair in his memory. A special appeal was launched with Mr Harold Macmillan (later Viscount Stockton) as President and Viscount De L'Isle as Chairman, for £250,000 with which to endow it. The money was raised and the chair was inaugurated on 30 September 1973 at a ceremony attended by Queen Elizabeth, the Queen Mother.

Denis Blake, the Foundation's Secretary, recalls that this included the presentation of a bronze bust of the Field Marshal in the presence of its sculptor, Oscar Nemon, whose increasing agitation became apparent during Harold Macmillan's acceptance speech as he leant his outstretched arm in characteristically relaxed pose against the flimsy plinth on which it stood. For he was one of the few present who knew that because the bronze was not yet complete a fragile plaster of Paris replica was doing duty on the day. Happily no disaster occurred and the drama was the subject of much merriment, shared by the Queen Mother, at the luncheon which followed.

Also at this time, through the good offices of the philanthropist Mr Isadore Walton, the Foundation became involved in the creation of a Chair of Cardiology, and another of Cardiac Surgery, in the City of Glasgow. In 1966 Mr Walton had set up a Personal Chair of Cardiology for Professor T.D.V. Lawrie through a covenanted gift. In 1973 the University was handed a cheque for £70,000, of which half was donated by the BHF and half by Mr Walton, to endow in perpetuity the Walton Chair of Cardiology. A year later the Foundation donated £70,000 and Mr Walton £100,000 by covenant to establish the Chair of Cardiac Surgery.

Professorial Chairs of Cardiology followed at Birmingham (1971), Leeds (1973) and Newcastle (1974), and a Chair of Paediatric Cardiology was endowed at the Hospital for Sick Children in 1975 in the sum of £250,000, of which £150,000 was provided by the Foundation and £100,000 by the Vandervell Foundation. With the endowment of the Duke of Edinburgh Chair in Edinburgh, agreed in 1976, and the Sir John McMichael Chair at the Royal Postgraduate Hospital in London in 1977, the Foundation had created nine centres of excellence by the end of the middle years, and established itself as the leading support of academic cardiology in the country. It capitalized on this excellent start in the succeeding decade.

In 1976 the Foundation also started awarding personal chairs, as opposed to endowed chairs. A personal chair is for the working lifetime of a particular research worker and is not automatically renewable by advertisement. The concept has several advantages: it is less expensive than an endowed chair; it keeps an outstanding research worker in the field of cardiology at senior level; and the Foundation does not lose control of the appointment of successors, as in endowed chairs, since there is no succession unless the Foundation has someone it wants to promote. The first personal chair in which the Foundation was involved was the Joseph Levy Foundation Chair of Paediatric Cardiac Morphology at the Brompton Hospital awarded to Professor Robert Anderson. It was funded by the Levy Foundation in the sum of £150,000, of which the BHF made a loan of £50,000 repayable over ten years.

REGIONAL NETWORK

Although this important part of the Foundation's fund-raising effort will be dealt with in depth in a separate chapter (p. 192) it needs also to be recorded in this account of the middle years, since it was during this period that beginnings were made in what has become such a large and successful enterprise.

Brigadier Cardiff appreciated the crucial role of a regional fund-raising network as soon as he became Director of Appeal in 1964, and set about its creation with vigour. One of the first attempts was in Scotland, where the Chest and Heart Association already had an office, run by Miss N.B. Hume. He enlisted her help and after some initial difficulties a powerful Scottish Appeal Committee was established under the Presidency of Sir Alexander King with Dr Rae Gilchrist, a member of the original Founding Committee, as Chairman. Later Mr Isadore Walton became President after the death of Sir Alexander in 1973. In the mean time a Region for the West of Scotland was established in Glasgow and another for the rest of Scotland in Edinburgh. Other early endeavours were to set up a Northern Region based on Newcastle, a Region in Northern Ireland based on Belfast, and a North West Region in Liverpool; a little later an active committee was formed in Birmingham.

When Brigadier Cardiff became Director General in 1966 Geoffrey Davison was appointed as his deputy, charged with the special task of developing the regions, and to him must go much of the credit for the early successes. He was assisted at head office by Mrs Doreen Nicholson and Mr Patrick Anderson. At first they were mainly concerned with setting up an organization for London, but later Mrs Nicholson enlarged her sphere of activity to include help with the founding of several other regions, whilst Mr Anderson continued to help London until Marjorie Barron took over. He also supervised the building up of an organization covering a large part of the Thames Valley, besides running the sale and distribution of Christmas cards, which was his main duty at head office.

By 1966 the Director General could announce the establishment of 13 committees in South East England extending from Bromley to Canterbury and Chichester, and in 1969 the establishment of 17 regions, followed a year later by 100 active committees.

Despite these successes, however, there was considerable fluidity at local committee level, since they usually depended for their success, and even their survival, on the enthusiastic drive of a single individual or of only a handful. Lack of sustained interest for any reason could lead to collapse of a committee, and even regional organizations were vulnerable to similar mischance. None the less the network was sufficiently well established by 1971 for the *Heart Bulletin* to publish a map in its April issue outlining 17 regions with the names of the Regional Organizers and their addresses. There are several exhortations at about this time in the *Bulletin* to encourage regional fund-raising activities, to offset fears of a reduction in income from covenants which were due to come up for renewal. It is pleasing also to read messages of thanks and congratulation for successes at this critical time for the Foundation, in spite of economic depression which made it a lean time for collecting money.

ANNUAL GENERAL MEETINGS AND PUBLIC MEETINGS

Annual General Meetings continued to be held around midsummer at the Edward Lumley Hall at the Royal College of Surgeons in Lincoln's Inn Fields.

The Annual Report was usually presented by the Chairman of Council, but in 1967 it was presented by the Foundation's President, Lord Alexander; unhappily it was the last time he presided before his death in 1969. The accounts were presented by the Treasurer.

The public meeting which followed and was open to anyone interested, including the press, aimed to publicize the work of the Foundation and to increase public awareness of its existence. A theme was chosen and speakers invited to give short talks in lay terms on a particular aspect of heart disease. In 1966 the theme was 'Research' with talks by Dr Michael Oliver (Physician, Royal Infirmary, Edinburgh) on diet and heart disease, Dr Berwick Wright (Director, Medical Centre, Institute of Directors) on business stresses and heart disease, and Professor Ernst Chain (Professor of Biochemistry, Imperial College of Science and Technology) on recent achievements of biochemical research into heart disease. In 1967, with 'Research in Heart Disease' again the theme, the speakers were Professor W.J. Butterfield (Professor of Medicine at Guy's Hospital), Sir Thomas Holmes Sellors (Thoracic Surgeon, Middlesex Hospital) and Professor Shillingford (Physician, Hammersmith Hospital). In 1968 the speakers were Professor K.W. Donald (Edinburgh), Dr R.E. Bonham Carter (Hospital for Sick Children) and Dr Somerville (Middlesex Hospital).

In 1969 the speakers were Professor G.K. Morris (Medical Research Council), Dr Celia Oakley (Hammersmith) and Dr Aubrey Leatham (St George's). In 1970 the pattern was changed by showing the recently produced and highly successful film entitled *One in Every Two of Us*.

In 1971 the theme was 'Advances in Cardiovascular Drugs and Equipment' with talks by Professor C.T. Dollery (Hammersmith), Dr Edgar Sowton (Guy's), Dr A.M. Breckenridge (Liverpool) and Dr Somerville (Middlesex), and an exhibition of modern equipment. In 1972 the theme was 'The Cardiac Patient' and talks were by Mr Woodruffe on the ambulance service, Sister Susan Harrison on nursing in the coronary care unit, and Miss Anne Molloy on community care. There was also a display of instruments used for cardiac investigations and cardiac operations arranged by the suppliers, Simonsen & Weil, with staff to explain their use; this attracted much interest.

In 1973 an extract was shown from a BBC television programme in the series entitled *Tomorrow's World* dealing with heart disease and its treatment, and questions were answered by Dr Somerville (Middlesex), Dr Malcolm Carruthers (St Mary's) and Dr Peter Taggart (Middlesex). In 1974 the public meeting was addressed by Mr James Davidson on his experiences before and after an operation for double heart valve replacement. Questions were answered by Drs Somerville and Shillingford and by Mr W.G. Williams (Cardiac Surgeon, Coventry). In 1975 the theme was 'The Treatment of Heart Disease in Infancy' and was presented by the team from the Brompton Hospital consisting of Dr Elliot Shinebourne, Dr Robert Anderson and Mr Christopher Lincoln. They brought a number of children treated in their unit to accompany their presentation. In 1976 the public meeting was addressed by Professor Peter Sleight from Oxford on high blood pressure and Dr Ann Coxon from Hammersmith on stroke.

Speaking of these talks Dr Morris Butler, the Medical Administrator, said: 'It was always difficult; it's rather like trying to understand Voltaire if you don't speak French. Trying to mix talks to laymen by doctors with the technical side is always awkward. But after all the public were the people who gave us the money and they rightly wanted to know where it was going.'

Of course public meetings of this kind inevitably attract their fair share of eccentrics and cranks who enjoy being centre stage with questions. The Foundation was no exception and included a number who were bent on getting free consultations. Sarah Hillard, who was Geoffrey Davison's assistant, recalls being detailed to sit next to an eccentric old man who had a religious mania and quoted the Bible at length, and without relation to context, whenever the mood took him. Her task was to ply him with sweets to try to prevent his outbursts. 'Sometimes it worked and sometimes it didn't,' she recalls. But he was none the less welcome since he always pulled handfuls of pound notes out of his pockets for the Foundation at the end of every meeting!

HEART JOURNAL AND *BULLETIN*

The decision to publish a journal was taken as soon as the Foundation was established. The President announced the intention in the Annual Report of 1962–63 saying that in order 'to keep our members and friends in touch with the Foundation, our journal *Heart* will be issued regularly. It is meant for the average reader who likes to be kept informed of modern progress.'

The first issue appeared in June 1963 and it was published quarterly in the same form for exactly ten years. Its editor was Dr

Harley Williams until his retirement in 1969, when it was taken over by his successor, Dr Margaret Haigh, who edited it until she left at the end of 1972. Dr Morris Butler, her successor as Medical Administrator, then assumed responsibility for it, although the format was changed in 1973.

It was a praiseworthy achievement to produce such an informative and professional journal so regularly, and reflects much credit on the editors, particularly Dr Harley Williams, who had so much else to do in establishing the Foundation. The conception was probably his because he was already editing a similar journal for the Chest and Heart Association, of which he was also the Secretary.

Each number edited by Dr Harley Williams included a chatty, lightly written editorial on an aspect of heart disease of public interest, and was followed by short specialist articles on a wide-ranging variety of research projects, together with simply worded explanations of current clinical practice.

In the Annual Report for 1963–64 the Chairman stated that: 'the *Heart* journal has been established as a quarterly journal to report the activities of the Foundation, especially its research programmes', and he went on: 'it will be kept lively and informative and will attract fresh interest into the Foundation. It has been well received by the Foundation's members and a wider readership.' The report is signed by Alexander of Tunis, President, Maurice Campbell, Chairman, Rudolph de Trafford, Treasurer, and Harley Williams, Secretary.

The subjects of medical articles in the early editions included congenital heart disease, coronary thrombosis, cardiac cathetherization, intensive care units, blue babies, radiology of the heart, air travel and heart disease, ultrasound, resuscitation, surgery for coronary disease, angina and computers in medicine.

Starting in 1969 there also appeared a series of five articles which subsequently became the first five numbers in the highly successful Heart Research Series Pamphlets.

Each year the Annual Report was published in full in the autumn number and periodically lists of research grant awards.

Although the main thrust of the journal was medical instruction, later numbers reported, increasingly, successes in fund-raising, mentioning especially generous corporate covenants and efforts to set up regional organizations.

There are also numerous exhortations to canvass new members, and an annual plea to assist by purchasing the Foundation's Christmas cards. In 1970 this was augmented by offering for sale packets of notelets, and birthday, get-well and best-wishes cards, together with ties, ball-point pens, wallets, address books, diaries, calendars, wrapping paper and what are described as 'stocking fillers'; this seems to have been the beginnings of the now well-established Christmas Catalogue.

From time to time the names of all Council and Committee members were published and changes in personnel recorded. There are also photographs and short pen portraits of leading figures in the Foundation. As early as 1967 there is a list of the addresses of regional appeal offices (Figure 15).

The issue for Christmas 1967, when Dr Haigh took over, showed a change in the front cover with the title, the *Journal of the British Heart Foundation*, and a heart symbol on it; at the same time the editorial was replaced by a 'quiz' on the heart and its problems with the answers on the back page. These numbers also published readers' comments on the published articles. The number for Christmas 1972, which is the first edited by Dr Morris Butler, carried, for the first time, the BHF logo.

In spite of all the information carried by the journal *Heart* it was felt that there was a need for a publication specially designed to foster the rapidly expanding regional fund-raising activities. In consequence the *Heart Bulletin* was started, once again with the indomitable Harley Williams as editor. This too was published quarterly, and continued in this form until recent times. Volume 1, issue 1, appeared in July 1967, and recorded events as widely spread as Hounslow, Newcastle, Walmer, Eastbourne, Inverness, Merseyside, Glasgow and Lambeth.

Subsequent numbers recorded fund-raising events of all kinds, large and small. A feature of every number was the profusion of photographs of organizers and participants, together with pictures of new committee members. As many events as possible were covered, and the whole strung together with interesting and light-hearted editorial comment. In the summer of 1968, pending the retirement of Dr Harley Williams, Geoffrey Davison took over as editor, and continued until the issue for spring 1977, which was edited jointly by him and his assistant Sarah Corbin. The editor of the next issue, summer 1977, was Sarah Hillard (née Corbin), who continued to do this work until 1982.

Exciting Regional Developments

DURING 1967, the Foundation was able to establish a number of new Regions and all the signs point to this pattern being continued in 1968. This work is greatly assisted by many of our supporters who generously give their free time to committee work and a host of fund raising and publicity activities.

The Foundation now has over 40 local committees hard at work. Their work has undoubtedly contributed in no small measure to the considerable progress being made.

Region No. 10 has now been re-organised and Surrey has been added to Region 7 and the Weald of Kent to Region 8.

HARTNELL FASHION SHOW

NORMAN HARTNELL, the Queen's dress maker, personally presented his Spring Collection in the Glasgow City Chambers on the 27th February in aid of the Foundation's Scottish Appeal. The show included a cocktail reception and wine and cheese tasting and was under the patronage of the Lord and Lady Provost of Glasgow.

Six of Scotland's top models displayed the collection before an audience of 800. There was considerable publicity and it is expected that funds will benefit by over £600.

Left to right: Mrs. M. Robinson, Mrs. E. M. Peel (Northern Region Organiser) and Mrs. B. Smith (Chairman of South Shields Committee). Mrs. Robinson was the first person in the world to be fitted with a Star Valve in her heart 4½ years ago. Both Mrs. Robinson and Mrs. Smith work energetically for the Foundation. To date, the Committee has raised £1,000.

Photo: The Shields Gazette.

KEY	REGIONS	ORGANISER
1	Scotland	Major R. Andrew-McIntosh
2 & 2a	Northern & Teeside	Mrs. E. Peel
3	Merseyside	Mrs. K. Keenan
4	Midland	Mr. G. W. Hands
5	East Midlands	Regional Development Officer Mrs. D. Nicholson
6	North London	Mr. P. Anderson
7	S. W. London and Metropolitan Surrey	Mrs. L. Higgs
8	S. E. London & N. Kent	Mrs. M. Barron
9	S. E. Kent	Group Capt. G. Du Boulay
11	Sussex	Miss M. Chandler
12	Hampshire	Rear Admiral R. Alexander
13	Wiltshire & Dorset	Lt. Col. D. Swift

NEWS ITEMS PLEASE

A number of committees still appear to be a little shy about providing information for the Bulletin. We want others to know what you are doing, so please let us have news and photographs of your various events. Please remember to give dates and names of people concerned.

Figure 15 *A page from the journal showing the regional pattern in 1967.*

The issue for September 1970 recorded a personal donation from Her Majesty the Queen, and the issue for September 1972 records the words of the President, Lord Cobbold, at the Annual General Meeting, at which he congratulated all concerned on a record income, mentioning especially 'the Foundation's regions and in particular the many local committees and groups who give so generously of their time.'

In 1973 the journal *Heart* and the *Bulletin* were, in a sense, amalgamated. A new series of the *Bulletin* was commenced with the spring issue carrying the subtitle *Heart Survival through Research*, and incorporating a four-page broadsheet entitled 'Medical News' edited by Morris Butler. Introducing this Brigadier Cardiff, the Director General, wrote:

> This is similar in size to previous *Heart Bulletins* but it also represents an amalgamation of this and the journal *Heart*; a special four-page Medical News Section, complete in itself, will make possible much wider coverage of the Foundation's research activities and should appeal to both the medical world and the lay public. I hope you will find it informative and rewarding.

In this new form the *Bulletin* provided the stimulus and reward of publicity for fund-raisers, and also a continuation of scientific and medical information. It also reported the widening activities of the Foundation by the creation of professorial chairs, by medical and public education, and by the provision of life-saving medical equipment to hospitals and emergency services in need. A series of articles, spanning several issues, written by Mr James Davison Ross, a journalist who had undergone an operation for double heart valve replacement, highlighted the activities and research projects under way at professorial units funded by the Foundation.

The *Bulletin* also chronicled the development of the regional network and reported the appointment of Regional Organizers, together with changes of personnel which occurred over the years. It was, and has continued to be, highly successful in keeping everyone in touch with activities nation-wide, and with the Foundation's financial position, policies and achievements. It both gives encouragement and acts as a catalyst.

PERSONNEL

It would not be right to conclude an account of the middle years without reference to the small band of dedicated staff at headquarters on whose shoulders the whole future of the Foundation rested.

The Middle Years

Equally, in a history of as big and powerful an organization as the Foundation has become, it would be out of place, and too parochial, to name everyone who helped to build it, even though everyone's contribution was important. In 1966 the Foundation was virtually unknown as a charity with a gross income of under £500,000; by the end of the middle years, in 1976, the gross income was over £1,500,000. Today's success is the legacy of the few who were in it at the start. Ron Trebell, who joined the Foundation in 1970 and is still an active member of headquarters staff, said: 'The emphasis was on fund-raising and everyone entered into it with a great sense of fun because it was all new. Enthusiastic amateurs; that's what I remember us as being.'

Tribute has already been paid to Brigadier Cardiff, who inspired both the enthusiasm and the sense of fun. He had the knack of keeping people happy and at the same time getting the best out of them for the benefit of the Foundation. He was principally responsible for the family atmosphere which prevailed throughout his time at Gloucester Place. He also had access to the people who could advance the Foundation's cause and finances. As Trebell put it: 'He turned many keys which opened cash flows.'

Sir Harry Moore echoed Trebell's recollection of the enjoyment and sense of fun which prevailed at head office in these early years when he said: 'there was always a lot of laughter and the importance of this is great. No one can enjoy their work without it, and a charity cannot hope to survive. Unless people are happy in their job, and show it, the venture is unlikely to succeed.'

Brigadier Cardiff's assistant, Geoffrey Davison, joined the Foundation in 1966 and stayed ten years. His tasks were to build a regional network and to advance the Foundation's publicity. He travelled extensively and served as an important link between headquarters and the Regional Organizers and their committees. He started with three regions and finished with 17. He was ably assisted by Sarah Hillard, who became his secretary in 1968 and was with the Foundation fourteen years. They were also helped by Bernie Lane, who came to the Foundation on a temporary basis in 1974 to organize a flag day and stayed eight years becoming, in turn, the Organizer of Special Fund-raising Events and later the Foundation's first Press Officer. In the former capacity she had charge of the organization of the annual National Slim Campaign and the London-to-Brighton bicycle ride, both of which have been outstandingly successful for many years.

On the office side Denis Blake was the Secretary and, at first, being a trained accountant, also the Foundation's Accountant. He joined the Foundation the same day as Geoffrey Davison in 1966 and stayed until 1981. His secretary was Frances Neal, who was known as the Administrator, and became, in effect, the General Office Manager; she too was with the Foundation from 1966 to 1981. She is a mine of information about the life and times of the Foundation in the middle years and has been unstinting in her help. Denis Blake described her as 'absolutely the right hand to me'. For many years she was assisted by Pauline Worsfold; and Denis Blake was assisted by Nathaniel Webster, as Assistant Accountant.

The Medical Department was very small in the early days and was run by Dr Harley Williams until his retirement in 1969. The Foundation is indebted to him for the hard work and wise counsel he gave for ten years from the first days of the Founding Committee, this in spite of his pre-existing, continuing and overriding responsibilities to the Chest and Heart Association as its Secretary throughout the whole of this period. He was followed by Dr Margaret Haigh, who saw the beginnings of expansion of the work of the Medical Department and took a leading role in its development. She was followed towards the end of 1972 by Dr Morris Butler, who was appointed Medical Administrator. His principal duties in the early days were to service the three medical committees, but he was also heavily involved in helping with the selection of grant-award winners, and later with the organization and running of symposia and lecture programmes.

Separation from the Chest and Heart Association in 1966 necessitated the assumption by the Foundation of all the responsibilities of office management, and it soon became apparent that automation of routine tasks was needed. This led first to the installation of the addressograph machine and the Gestetner printer, both of which served the Foundation well in their day. Indeed they soon became vital for the preparation of mailing and supporters lists, for record-keeping, and for the printing of a wide variety of items, ranging from appeal letters, brochures, sponsor forms and posters, to letterheads and the addressing of envelopes. As the regions developed the work increased rapidly and it was not long before the printing, post and stores departments were processing and shifting several tons of material produced in-house.

Trouble with the addressograph brought an engineer to the office to repair it. Not only did he do so but he joined the staff and remained with the Foundation until his death ten years later. He was Albert Jeff: he could turn his hand to anything and in the inimitable way so typical of a humble Londoner he smoothed many paths. He was also responsible for introducing Ron Trebell, his brother-in-law, to the Foundation, which has benefited from his hard work and experience for 18 years to date. Speaking of Jeff, Trebell says: 'He handed out the olive branches ... there are many things which happened in the Foundation which would not have happened without him, or if they did, they would not have happened so happily.'

THE END OF AN ERA

At the Council meeting of 25 June 1975 Brigadier Cardiff is recorded as having said: 'It must be considered that the days of Gala First Nights with very expensive tickets are over, and that regional fund-raising events are expected to produce a great proportion of income in the future.'

Policy document

Attached to these minutes is a document entitled 'A Suggested Policy for the BHF'. It reads as follows:

1 It is recommended that the Foundation should now work along the following general lines of policy:
(a) To concentrate its main efforts on maintaining the current level of effort of existing Chairs; and to recognise that these are likely to need additional funds to maintain their existing effort.
(b) A proportion of the funds must still be channelled to clinical projects.
(c) To supplement existing Chairs with funds for additional staff to meet their needs for further development. These needs will vary in different locations.
(d) Not to seek to establish, nor to commit itself to, any new Chairs for the next few years, other than those already agreed.
(e) To consider the creation of a number of new middle-grade career posts, which could be used as appropriate to carry out the objectives in (c) above.
(f) To reduce somewhat the annual allocation of one-off grants but to continue the existing policy of inviting applications under this heading, both from clinical sources and from existing academic areas – whether or not such units were established with the help of the Foundation.

2   It is also proposed that the Research Funds Committee should now be asked to put forward recommendations as to the number, type and grade of middle-grade career posts suggested in paragraph 1(e) above.

3   One further very important point is that the continuity of effort of the Foundation becomes even more essential in the present uncertainty and stringency. This can really only be achieved if a somewhat higher proportion of the annual income of the Foundation comes from its own invested resources.

In past years the accumulation of capital has been discouraged, on the grounds that reasonably full distribution of income each year provided the best discipline for raising more funds during the following year. In view of the growth of inflation, and of its effects, it is now recommended that the Foundation should for some years seek to put aside (say) £150,000 or perhaps a little more each year to its Capital fund. This, with the improvement one may hopefully expect in the Stock Market over the next two or three years, should ensure a reasonably solid base for the future of the Foundation.

The changes in the pattern of fund-raising were not only dictated by economic recession and inflation but also by a shift of public mood when support of charities by prestigious social occasions and personal munificence gave way to fund-raising through organized business management. Sponsorship became the vehicle of commercial advertising and charities were the beneficiaries. In turn charities had to sell themselves in competition with each other, and consequently public awareness of a charity's existence and objectives were vital to success. The public in Britain has always been generous in supporting good causes, even in hard times, provided the need is made plain, the approach to the problem well founded and the integrity of management beyond reproach.

It was inevitable that the family atmosphere would gradually fade as the size, wealth and influence of the Foundation increased; the changes were right and necessary to sustain continuing growth, but a nostalgic backward glance to the glamour of adolescence is also justifiable.

Brigadier Cardiff

The middle years are epitomized by Brigadier Cardiff, whose personality knitted the whole family together with such brilliant results. He retired in 1976 together with his deputy, Geoffrey Davison, and an equally successful new team arrived in the persons of

Brigadier Christopher Thursby Pelham as Director General, and Colonel James Malcolm as Director of Appeals; both were former Welsh Guards officers. In the same year Ereld Cardiff became Chairman of the Finance and General Purposes Committee in succession to Sir Harry Moore, who remained a member of Council.

Sir Harry Moore

This is an appropriate juncture to record an appreciation of the immense debt of gratitude which the Foundation owes to Sir Harry. He is easily the longest-serving councillor, having been one of the first lay members of the Founding Committee in 1959 and having served continuously to the present time. He and Sir Michael Perrin were the first laymen to be co-opted to the Science Committee and he has remained a member of the Research Funds Committee ever since, attending regularly the quarterly meetings at which research grants are made. In this committee and in Council and the F&GP, he has been a leader in important policy decisions. His wise counsel did much to assist the delicate negotiations with the CHA when the Appeal Committee was being set up, and in 1976 he played a major role in introducing a personal pension scheme for all full-time BHF staff. Sir Harry Moore's early association with the Foundation grew out of his membership of the Governing Body of the London Hospital (and subsequent Chairmanship) where Dr William Evans and Lord (Horace) Evans were both Consulting Physicians. Speaking of Lord Evans he said: 'He is a man I got to know very well and he is the man I admire most, more than anyone I have ever met.'

Sir Harry had much to do with Lord Evans's decision to invite prominent businessmen to the dinner in his house in 1961 to win their support for the newly formed Foundation and its Appeal Committee, and he was directly responsible for recruiting several of the men who have led the Foundation over the years; amongst these were General Vivien Street, Brigadier Ereld Cardiff and Sir Rudolf de Trafford.

FOUR
THE YEARS OF EXPANSION: 1976–1988

THE ANNUAL GROSS INCOME of the Foundation increased from £1,570,307 in 1976–77 to nearly £19,665,000 in 1987–88. Over the same period the value of its Investment Portfolio increased from £2,500,000 to over £40,000,000 and its disposable income increased

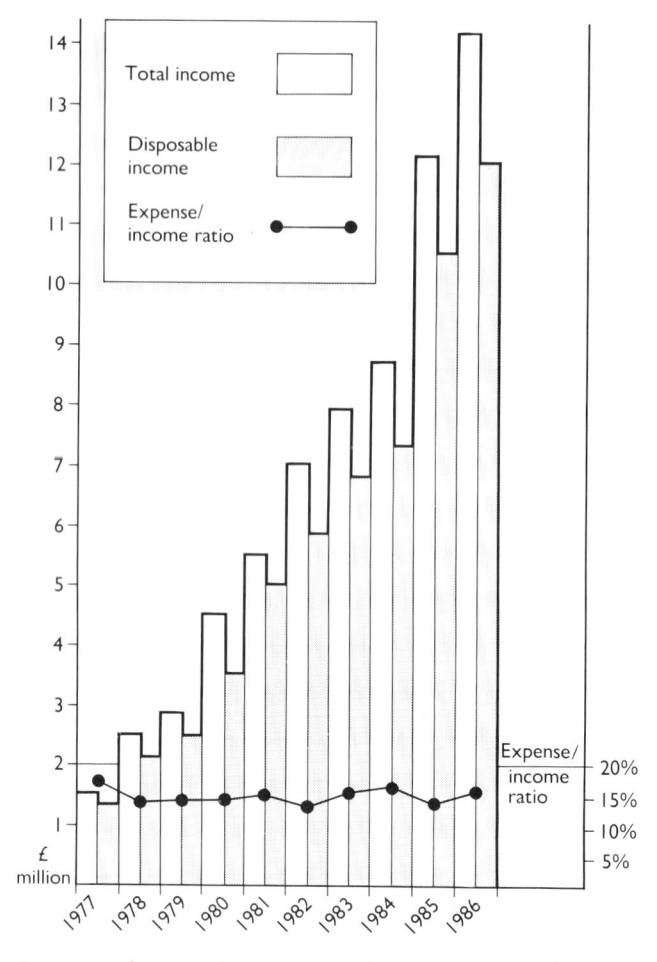

Figure 16 *Income and expense/income ratios for the decade 1977–86.*

The Years of Expansion

from £1,127,790 to £16,982,000. The General Fund Portfolio stands at £20,724,000 and the Chairs Fund Portfolio at £20,119,000.

Throughout this period of dramatic expansion the expense/income ratio was kept well below the 20% generally regarded as acceptable for medical charities. Administration averaged around 4% and fund-raising around 11%; in 1987–88 the figures were 2.7% and 11.0% respectively. Thus well over 80% of the money donated by the public was used to promote the Foundation's objectives (Figure 16).

These good results were achieved in spite of periods of severe

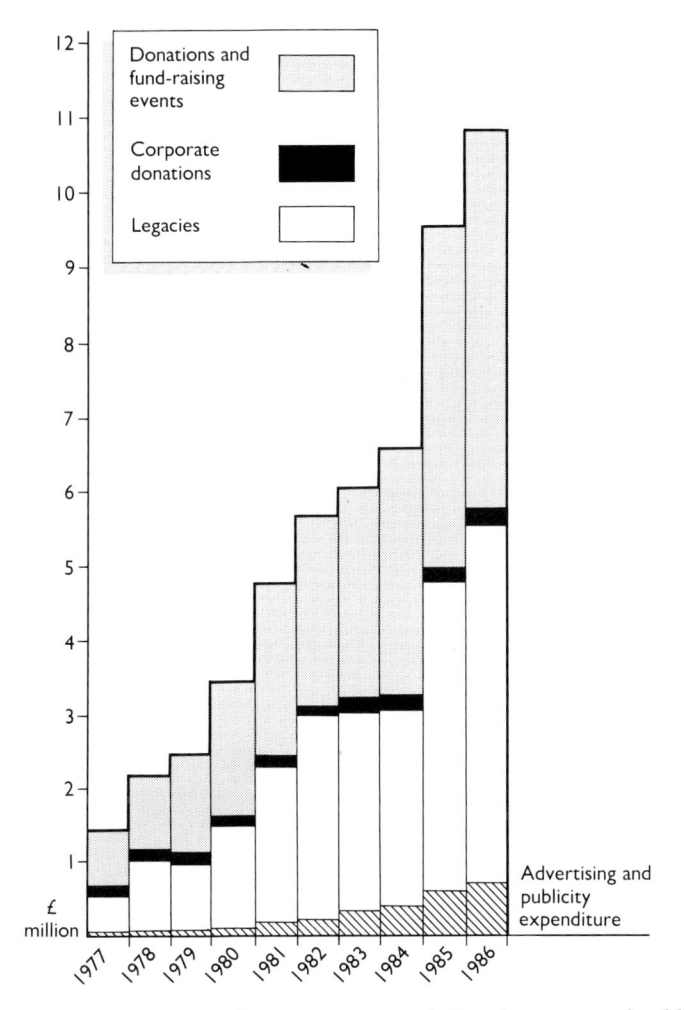

Figure 17 *The income from voluntary sources, and the advertising and publicity expenditure for the decade 1977–86.*

inflation, particularly in the late seventies, and a major recession, with a huge rise in unemployment, which followed, all of which provoked worrying fluctuations in Stock Exchange prices. Although increased national prosperity in the latter part of the decade coincided with an acceleration of the Foundation's financial expansion it is noteworthy that public generosity continued without interruption in bad times, and also that the level of regional donations was well maintained in the hardest hit areas. Not only does this represent a praiseworthy public response to the Foundation's needs but it also reflects credit on the skill and hard work of the staff at headquarters and in the regions (Figure 17).

BRIGADIER THURSBY PELHAM

Speaking of the early days of his appointment the Director General, Brigadier Thursby Pelham, said: 'I decided that, rather than make any changes in the fine structure built up by my predecessor, we should concentrate upon trying to expand the work in its existing form.' The objectives, which are reviewed annually by the Finance and General Purposes Committee, and passed to the Council for debate and ratification, remained substantially the same throughout the decade, namely to promote research into cardiovascular disease, to assist postgraduate medical education, and to provide life-saving cardiac equipment to front-line situations such as ambulances, rescue services and hospitals in need. Within these parameters, however, there was a variation of emphasis.

RESEARCH POLICY

At first there was a period when the number of applications for individual grants of sufficient merit for support was inadequate for the money available, and the Council decided to continue to expand its policy of financing professorships in universities as centres of excellence. This resulted in the creation of ten more chairs in these years of expansion, besides increasing the funding of the ten existing chairs by a further £100,000 each, to make them self-supporting, as agreed in the policy review of 1977–78.

Later, reduction of research budgets at universities and for the

Medical Research Council was reflected by an increase in the number of high-quality applications for research grants submitted to the Foundation, whilst the number of academics with the qualities and experience needed to lead centres of excellence as professors was reduced. There were many reasons for this: salary scales compared poorly with the rewards of clinical practice, soaring house prices in big cities, particularly London, were often prohibitive and the career structure in academic medicine was too precarious. The Foundation has concentrated much effort, and a very large part of its financial resources, on trying to make the professorial units as prestigious as possible. Besides increasing the endowment to universities it has provided a senior lecturer for each and increased the annual discretionary and equipment funds available to each professor. In 1985 the discretionary allowance was raised from £25,000 to £26,500 per annum and the equipment allowance from £10,000 to £12,500 per annum, both guaranteed for five years. In 1988 these amounts were again increased to £27,000 and £13,000 respectively. In 1987 it was calculated that each professorial chair costs the Foundation £70,000 per annum to maintain. The Foundation has set up 20 of the 22 chairs of cardiovascular medicine and surgery in Britain and has set aside, to date, more than £20,000,000 in the Chairs Maintenance Fund to meet this commitment (Figure 18).

Two other measures have been taken to assist chair holders. The first is an entitlement to one year's sabbatical leave every seven years, or six months every three and a half years, with travelling expenses and an arrangement for exchange professorships under some circumstances. The second is an entitlement to £2,500 per annum to host a professor, or other distinguished visitors from overseas, in their unit.

Salary scales are outside the remit of the Foundation, being governed by the universities, and indirectly the Government through the University Grants Committee, and there is no way in which astronomical house prices can be offset; London medical schools are particularly hard hit by housing costs, and salary limitations have led to loss of academic talent by emigration, nation-wide, in the past.

It has been possible, however, to take steps to improve career structure and the Foundation has helped to do this through Fellowships at three levels. Junior for one to two years, Intermediate for three years and Senior for five years. Recently security for non-clinical scientists, where the chances of promotion to a professorship with

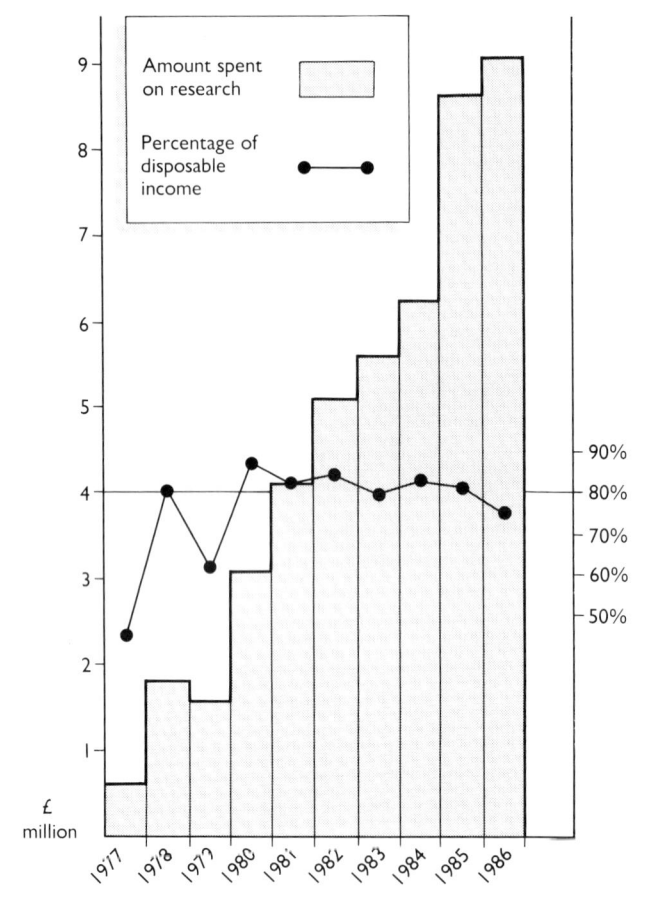

Figure 18 *Annual expenditure on research for the decade 1977–86, with illustration of percentage of disposable income.*

permanence of tenure are very limited, has been increased by the introduction of a roll-on scheme for Senior Fellows.

Further improvement in the career structure for potential academics at the beginning of their careers has been made by the allocation of more money to fund Ph.D. students, mostly in professorial centres, and by relaxation of the rules so that a professor can make an application for the funding of a Ph.D. studentship before the student can be named. Such is the shortage of top-quality applicants that the delay, caused by prohibition of application until a student is known to be interested, can result in the student taking an appointment elsewhere.

The Years of Expansion

EDUCATION POLICY

Postgraduate medical education has played an ever-increasing role in the work of the Foundation during the years of expansion and the subject will be dealt with in detail in the chapter concerned with the Medical Department (p. 111), but debate about the degree of involvement in public education by the Foundation has occupied much time in Council. There has been increasing pressure by the media to get the Foundation heavily committed, and this has been backed from time to time by some medical opinion. As far back as 1977 the Policy Review of Council contained the resolution, for the first time, that 'some provision should now be made for public education in addition to postgraduate education'. At the same time it endorsed continuing caution about giving advice on matters unproven scientifically. Three years later an article appeared in the *British Medical Journal* criticizing medical charities, notably cardiac and cancer, and naming the British Heart Foundation for not doing enough about public education and prevention. It also published a reply from Sir Ronald Bodley Scott, the Chairman of Council, reiterating that the Foundation was set up specifically to fund research. Shortly afterwards Sir Ronald represented the Foundation at a meeting at the Department of Health and Social Security called by the Parliamentary Under-Secretary to discuss public education and the prevention of heart disease where he repeated the Foundation's reluctance to pronounce on any but proven facts. Two cardiologists who taxed the Foundation on the same subject with special emphasis on exercise, and backed by the proprietor of a London gymnasium, were invited to submit their suggestions in writing as to the action the BHF should take. This they ultimately did, and their suggestions were put to 50 leading cardiologists for comment. The replies demonstrated conclusively the lack of unanimity of medical opinion and the Foundation resolved to continue its policy unchanged, whilst increasing the number of its Heart Research Series pamphlets (now renamed Heart Information Series). These are simple texts written for lay consumption on subjects of public concern such as high blood pressure, angina and stroke; they were immediately popular. In 1980 complete sets of the series were sent to 50 general practitioners in Essex as a pilot scheme and this was followed in 1981, because of their wide acceptability, by distribution, at a cost of £4,000, to 150 general practitioners chosen at random. The success of this venture led to a nation-wide distribution in 1983 costing £100,000. There are now 18 in the series and, to date, 10,000,000 copies have been given away free to the public and to the medical profession.

In 1981 Sir Ian Trethowan, Director General of the BBC, who was a Council member at the time, invited the Director General to meet him at Broadcasting House to discuss the role of the BHF with the media, as a result of which the Foundation took a larger part in medical programmes although with the same caution as before. There is no doubt that, although the Foundation's reluctance to become involved in a public debate that was spreading with prairie-fire speed and heat irritated some medical correspondents and some doctors, the policy paid handsome dividends. The Foundation acquired the status of honest broker, and its opinions, often sought, when given were noted with respect. The determination to steer a middle course between evangelism and nihilism on all unproven matters created for it a powerful voice when decisions were made. In November 1982, at the height of the debate, the Foundation convened a meeting of all the interested parties at its headquarters under the chairmanship of Dr Tom Meade, the Chairman of the Education Funds Committee. A consensus was reached which Dr Meade embodied in a policy document. After its circulation he called a second meeting in February 1984, when unanimous agreement was secured on the wording. This document now constitutes the official BHF guidelines on life-style, and forms the basis of Heart Information Series Pamphlet No. 14 entitled *Reducing the Risk of a Heart Attack*. This was a fine achievement by Dr Meade and the Foundation, since it reconciled widely differing views held by the leading protagonists.

Inevitably, however, because of its stature in the eyes of the public and the profession, the Foundation was drawn, increasingly, into the surge of public interest in heart disease. It responded in many ways. In 1979 it produced a film entitled *You've Got to Have a Heart*, which was, in essence, an explanation of some of the problems posed by heart disease and the Foundation's attempt to solve them by research. This was followed, in 1981, by a simple instruction film called *A Heart Attack: Learn What to Do*, after which it commissioned an English version of an attractive and amusing French cartoon film put together by Dr Roquebrun, a French cardiologist, on life-style. Recently (1988) a short video has been made recording the *Aims of the BHF* for use for fund-raising in the regions, and with an eye to possible legislation to permit advertising by charities on television.

In 1980 the Foundation agreed to finance the production and distribution of heart donor cards, and in 1985, in a national 'Heart Week' fund-raising campaign, with the slogan 'Research Saves Lives', a million leaflets were distributed, mostly through Sunday newspapers. Each contained three cards: a donor card, a cardiopulmonary resuscitation (CPR) instruction card and a returnable card requesting further information about the BHF. This was followed in the Foundation's Jubilee Year (1986) by the key-ring donor scheme in which 100,000 key-rings, incorporating a small donor card, were distributed to the public through headquarters, the regional offices and by the police, by ambulance services and by local radio stations following broadcasts. The scheme was hugely successful.

The Education Committee bore much of the brunt of the work resulting from the Foundation's increasing involvement with public education in these and other ways, and responded with enthusiasm and resource under the guidance of Cary Spink, its indefatigable Administrator. A fuller account of its history and activities will be found on p. 162.

As the voice of the Foundation was increasingly heard on matters of public education it became more closely associated with the Health Education Council (HEC), later reorganized as the Health Education Authority (HEA). In 1981 the Director General, the Medical Administrator and Professor Shillingford met Dr Keith Taylor, the Chief Medical officer of the HEC to discuss how the Foundation could cooperate in the field of Public Education to reduce the risks of heart attacks, and in 1985 the Foundation met Professor John Catford, who had been appointed Professor of Health Education for Wales and was working on the programme to be known as 'Heart Beat Wales'. There was clearly a potential conflict of interest in this with the BHF, which had already founded the Professorial Chair of Cardiology at the University of Wales Medical School in Cardiff, and had run a successful fund-raising organization in Wales based in Llandrindod Wells for 18 years, with Major John Probyn as Regional Organizer. Eventually a joint Welsh Heart Appeal was agreed and a satisfactory formula was worked out between the two organizations for the distribution of donations from the Principality, so avoiding harmful competition.

In 1986 the Foundation also assisted the newly formed Health

Education Authority by contributing £20,000 to the 'Save a Life' campaign which the Authority had recently undertaken. In addition the Foundation is currently involved in a joint project with the Authority to produce a pack for the use of school teachers, focusing on heart disease and the three ways in which children can help themselves: smoking, diet and exercise. Further support to the Authority is the financial help given to their production of a pamphlet to promote their 'Look after Your Heart' campaign. The Foundation has also produced its own pamphlet entitled *It'll Never Happen to Me*, which is subtitled a *Guide to a Healthy Heart*.

Most recently the Foundation has agreed to participate in a display for the public at the Science Museum showing the methods and results of cardiovascular research at a cost of £50,000 over three years.

MEDIA COVERAGE

In the early days the Foundation's contacts with radio and television, and with newspapers and periodicals, were generally restricted to publicizing its existence and objectives. Whenever opportunity offered it was welcomed and the response was usually from Geoffrey Davison or his deputy, Sarah Hillard. Later Brigadier Thursby Pelham filled this role with great success. He was lucid and enthusiastic; the media liked him and his style. Later he was assisted by Bernie Lane when she became Press Officer in 1981.

Increased media coverage of the Foundation's activities, however, has inevitably led to increased demands by the media, and particularly by medical correspondents, for authoritative opinions on medical issues thrown up by day-to-day comment, often at very short notice and usually at the hub of controversy. The Director General and Bernie Lane found these demands sometimes difficult to meet and something of a crisis developed towards the end of 1980 when regional organizers expressed annoyance that the Foundation had declined an invitation to participate in a BBC television programme entitled *Medical Express*.

In response the Council set up a medical panel whose members undertook to cover specific areas of enquiry. These included, for example, diet and epidemiology, public education and prevention, heart transplants, congenital heart disease, vivisection and general medical policy. This helped but it did not entirely solve the problem

The Years of Expansion

because of the unavoidable delay in getting in touch with the experts. So a questionnaire was compiled including a wide range of questions frequently asked, and others likely to be asked, which was sent to all members of the panel. Their answers were correlated and became a policy document to which anyone answering questions both at headquarters and in the regions could refer, to give an authoritative BHF reply.

Later, increasing involvement led to the appointment, in 1983, of a Medical Spokesman to take enquiries from the media and the public, and to answer on behalf of the Foundation with the assistance, when necessary, of the Medical Director.

It has never been envisaged, however, that the Foundation would provide a full-time answering service. This would necessitate an unjustifiable increase in medical staff. Gaps in the service are sometimes tiresome, but medical correspondents, and others who need information, soon get to know how to contact the Medical Spokesman or Medical Director quickly enough.

A further increase in cooperation with representatives of the media, pioneered by the Joan Scott Public Relations Consultancy, is the now well-established and successful custom of inviting them to informal lunches at headquarters. These started in 1985 and are held every few weeks; they are hosted by the Press Officer, the Medical Director, the Medical Spokesman and Joan Scott or one of her partners. This gives the guests an opportunity to ask about the work of the Foundation, and to seek copy for articles and stories to suit their particular needs, and the hosts an opportunity to report research projects and results of interest to the public.

The importance of public relations and media interest also led to the establishment in 1984 of regular weekly PR briefing meetings at headquarters chaired by the Director General and attended by the Medical Director and Spokesman, the Director of Appeals, the Press Officer and Joan Scott or deputy, together with the Organizer of National Events and the Education Committee Organizer. The purpose is both to recount the happenings of the previous week and to plan publicity strategy for the future, with critical assessment of how improvements can be made. These meetings, which were started at the suggestion of Professor Shillingford, have been very valuable in ensuring the close cooperation of all concerned with this very important part of the responsibilities of head office.

Chapter 4

HEAD OFFICE

The Foundation has been very fortunate in its candidates and wise in its selection of staff at all levels. In no department is this better illustrated than in its Chief Executives. The innovative skills of Brigadier Cardiff were ideally suited to fostering the small new charity in its early days. He laid the foundations and created the sound structure on which his successor could build as soon as the opportunity arose. Brigadier Thursby Pelham brought great administrative ability just when it was needed to guide the Foundation into the competitive business atmosphere of charity fund-raising. He also brought a robust optimism and a sense of humour in the face of difficulties, which was matched by undisguised intolerance of poor performance. He enjoyed speaking at a wide variety of fund-raising activities, great and small, and was well liked by the fund-raisers.

Headquarters staff

One very important and highly successful innovation made by the Brigadier immediately after his appointment in 1976 was to shed direct personal responsibility for the Appeals Department; it had become too big for this to continue to be feasible. The appointment of Colonel James Malcolm as Director of Appeals was an inspired choice and the two together have been largely responsible for the growth of the organization through the last decade (Figure 19). They were sustained by continuity of staffing at intermediate level; this was essential for day-to-day management and they were exceptionally well served. The nucleus was Denis Blake as Secretary and Accountant, Frances Neal as Office Manager and Pauline Worsfold as her secretary. James Malcolm had Sarah Hillard (née Corbin) and Bernie Lane as his assistants, whilst Ron Trebell (who joined the BHF in 1970), assisted by Stephen Johnston (1973), Kaleyi Lukoma (1975) and Graham Rees (1977), ran the practical side of the office, which included the mailing list, as well as the print and post room and the stores. Dr Morris Butler provided equally important continuity as Medical Administrator.

The team remained unaltered until 1981 except for the arrival of David Reynolds as the Foundation's Accountant in 1977. This appointment was overdue since the secretarial workload of Denis

The Years of Expansion

Figure 19 *Colonel James Malcolm, Director of Appeals during the years of expansion.*

Blake was as much as he could carry, and Nathaniel Webster, who had assisted him as bookkeeper, was due for retirement. As a qualified accountant Reynolds was well able to cope with the enormous increase in revenue from donations from all sources, and from investment income, as well as the concomitant increase in expenditure, mainly through the various medical committees. He was also able to handle the change to computerization of all the accounts in 1985. He is rightly proud of the fact that Clare Shepherd, who joined him as Cashier in 1979 (succeeding Kathleen Graham), and his assistant, Jill Bayliss, who joined the Foundation in 1976, are still working with him, as was also Louise Levinson (now Blythe), who came in 1981, until, in 1989, she was transferred to the Research Funds Department as Assistant Research Funds Administrator.

Important changes occurred in the personnel at headquarters in 1981. Denis Blake and Frances Neal retired and were replaced by Marion Grainge as Secretary of the Foundation with Pauline Worsfold as her assistant. Mrs Grainge is a chartered accountant, and instigated a number of administrative changes to meet the needs created by the rapid growth of the Foundation's assets and commitments. These included the introduction of computerization for the Finance Department and for staff salaries, a system of departmental budgeting and modernization of office management. Another important change she made was to create a separate Legacy Department to handle the vastly increased legacy income instead of trying to handle it herself as theretofore. Clem Hogan became Legacy Officer in 1982.

Another important appointment was that of Richard Emery as Donations Secretary in 1981; hitherto donations had been handled by the Finance Department as part of the overall responsibility of Denis Blake in his capacity as the Foundation's Accountant; once again the increase in the load made it essential to hive this important work off into a separate department. Furthermore it rightly came, from then on, under the aegis of the Appeals Department, which has the overall responsibility for fund-raising.

Change of address

On 13 March 1982 the headquarters of the Foundation was moved to new and much larger premises at 102 Gloucester Place. The move was unavoidable since the leases of 57 and 59 Gloucester Place were due to run out in 1983 with no promise of renewal, and was long overdue because of the urgent need for more space. The need had been long recognized and, indeed, the first mention of the need is in the minutes of the Finance and General Purposes Committee in April 1977. Thus it took five years to find, purchase and occupy a new home. At first there were high hopes that the Foundation could be accommodated in buildings in St Andrew's Place alongside the Royal College of Physicians and owned by them, but they could not be made ready soon enough. Other sites in the neighbourhood were inspected including a building in Wimpole Street owned by the National Heart Hospital, but none was suitable. The purchase of 102 Gloucester Place was completed on 28 August 1981 at a cost of £790,000; the expenses were £135,000, making a total outlay of £925,000.

The Years of Expansion

Such was the rate of growth of the Foundation, and the increase in its commitments, that it was only three years later that further extension of headquarters became necessary. Attempts were made, without success, to find a building big enough for all needs, so it was decided to purchase 109 Gloucester Place, which lies directly opposite, in spite of the well-recognized disadvantages of having the organization under two roofs. Purchase was completed on 31 January 1986 at a cost of £856,000 including expenses and the building was occupied by the Appeal Department in August 1986, followed by the Education Department in August 1987. When the new building became available the Medical Department moved from the top to the second floor in 102 Gloucester Place, and the top floor was refurbished and let as a prestigious apartment at a suitable rental, which contributes to the Foundation's annual income. This internal rearrangement was necessitated by fire brigade regulations which prohibited the continued use of the top floor as office premises.

The increased availability of space created by these two moves in 1982 and 1986 made possible the reorganization and expansion of several departments.

In the Medical Department, with the appointment of Professor Shillingford as Medical Director in 1983, following the resignation of Dr Butler as Medical Administrator due to ill health, accommodation was found for him and the Medical Spokesman with a shared secretary. At the same time the administration of the main medical committees was reorganized by the appointment of three administrators. Bob Stiller became the Administrator and Buyer for the Cardiac Care Committee and Cary Spink the Administrator of the Education Funds Committee, both in 1982, and Valerie Mason became the Administrator of the Research Funds Committee, the Chairs and Research Groups Committee and the Fellowships Committee in 1983. All three had assistants and secretarial help. A word processor had been installed at headquarters in 1980 at a cost of £10,500 and in 1985 computer terminals were fitted in all departments at a cost of £50,000.

Supporting staff were appointed to the Administration Department, and Sue McNally, who had joined the Foundation in 1983, was officially appointed Assistant Foundation Secretary in 1986. Expansion of the Appeals Department, under the overall direction of James Malcolm, saw the creation of a Press Office with Bernie Lane (1981), followed by Claire Marley (1983) and Elaine Snell (1987), as Press

Officers, assisted by Fiona Barnes (1983) and Jane Landon (1985). The Special Events Department, which was one of the oldest fund-raising departments at headquarters, became a National Appeals Department under the direction of Judy McKeller (1983), who was succeeded by Mary Dunn (1985) and then by Adele Hodgson (1987). The separation of the Donations Department, under the direction of Richard Emery, led to its resiting in 109 Gloucester Place. Throughout the Foundation's entire history those dealing with donations had shared accommodation traditionally known as 'the front room' with the cashiers. Separation gave urgently needed space to the Finance Department in the front room, and allowed Emery's to be self-contained. His secretary is Brenda Mole (1981), who succeeded Betty Appleby on her retirement, and Lakshmi Salvaratnam has been in charge of the filing of all correspondence concerning donations since 1980.

When the headquarters moved into 57 Gloucester Place in 1968 the staff was fortunate to acquire the services of Mary Bransfield, who was employed as domestic helper by the owners of the flats still occupied on the upper floors. She soon began to help with office cleaning and with serving refreshments. She was a quiet reserved person but a keen observer, and knew much about the lives and personal peccadilloes of those she looked after. She stayed with the Foundation until 1986 when she retired to her native Ireland.

In 1978 canteen lunches succeeded the luncheon voucher system previously in use. Not only did this provide a good free meal quickly but it encouraged social intercourse among the staff; this became particularly important after the separation into two buildings in 1986. Sheila Tuson was in charge until 1986 when she retired due to ill health, being followed by Ann Young. Both have done much for the staff by providing excellent meals and by their patience in respecting the whims of individual diets.

The acquisition of 102 Gloucester Place in 1982 gave the Foundation a large versatile conference room, big enough to accommodate all the Foundation's meetings except the annual public meeting. This not only included Council and committee meetings but also medical symposia and workshops. It was calculated that this saved the expenditure of about £3,000 per annum at prices then current for the hire of meeting rooms. The conference room was generously equipped by the Ciba Foundation at a cost of £20,000, in addition to which they gave £2,500 per annum on a three-year basis to pay for the running of

The Years of Expansion

Figure 20 *The conference room at headquarter, used for administrative and medical meetings. Furnished and equipped by Ciba-Geigy Pharmaceuticals.*

medical meetings in it. In this way they have done much to foster the exchange of information and better understanding of problems among research workers and clinicians (Figure 20).

THE FINANCE AND GENERAL PURPOSES COMMITTEE

Meeting every two months this committee has continued to be the executive body responsible for running the Foundation up to the present time. Sir Harry Moore was succeeded as Chairman by Brigadier Cardiff in 1976, and he, in turn, by Nigel Robson in 1985; Brigadier Cardiff and Sir Raymond Hoffenberg becoming Co-Vice-Chairmen. Brian Basset, who became Treasurer of the Foundation in 1983, was also Chairman of the Investment Committee, which advises on the Foundation's portfolio. He was succeeded as Treasurer by Nigel Robson in 1985. The Investment Committee was reconstituted in 1987 with Ian Cameron, of Panmure Gordon, the Foundation's stockbrokers, as Chairman, and was composed of the Treasurer, the Director General, the Secretary and David Beale as outside adviser.

Chapter 4

THE COUNCIL

This is the governing body of the Foundation. It meets twice a year; its fiftieth meeting was in July 1985. It receives reports from the F&GP on the working of the Foundation. It is responsible for policy decisions and it sets out the Foundation's objectives for the ensuing year. These remain essentially the same but there is a change of emphasis from time to time – most notably the acceptance of an increasing responsibility for informing the public on matters concerned with heart disease; in 1984 the policy document also included an obligation for 'improving facilities for cardiac care'. Both are, in some sense, diversions from the primary objective of the Foundation to fund research into heart disease. The Council's policy document for 1975–76 is of special significance as it outlines the objectives to be pursued in the following decade (see p. 65).

Policy decisions

Of the many policy decisions which had to be made by the Council two need special mention; the first is the reduction in the size of the Council and the second the changes in the Constitution regarding membership of the Foundation.

In 1983 Sir Cyril Clarke presented a paper which he had been asked to prepare to seek an appropriate way to reduce the size of Council from 45 to 30 members, which was generally considered to be a more practical number. This was achieved by reducing the number of professional members to 15, the co-opted lay members to 14 and the President. If the President is a layman the numbers are equally balanced. The professional membership is made up as follows:

Chairman	1
Royal Colleges of Physicians of London and Scotland to alternate every 3 years	1
Royal Colleges of Surgeons of England and Scotland to alternate every 3 years	1
Royal Postgraduate Medical Federation	1
Royal College of General Practitioners	1
British Cardiac Society	2
Chest Heart and Stroke Association	2

The Years of Expansion

Other registered medical practitioners or scientists,
to be elected on their personal qualities   6

It was agreed that all chairmen of committees should, ex officio, be members of Council and be included in the six other registered medical practitioners or scientists.

The revised constitution was confirmed by alteration of the Memorandum and Articles of Association at an Extraordinary Meeting of Members on 20 January 1987.

At the same meeting it was also ruled that all Presidents and Vice-Presidents appointed by the Council should retire five years after their appointment, except those currently holding office.

With regard to membership of the Foundation, three categories had been offered in the early days of the Foundation's existence; life, annual and associate. Several hundred members of the public had joined as a way to help and support the Foundation. As late as 1981 the Finance and General Purposes Committee had recommended to the Council that the rates of subscription should be £200 for new life members and £20 for new annual members. At further discussions about the matter, however, in 1982 by the F&GP and Council it became apparent that under the terms of the Memorandum and Articles of Association a detailed record of the name and address of every member in all categories needed to be kept. The bookkeeping involved would be prohibitively expensive and time-consuming, since there were several thousand members in the various categories, and it was unanimously agreed that those who had given money for membership would not want it spent in this way. Clearly they had subscribed with the intention of furthering the Foundation's ability to support research. On the recommendation of the Council, therefore, an Extraordinary General Meeting was called in July 1984 when it was agreed that Article 6 of the Memorandum, which listed the current categories of membership, should be deleted and the following new Article substituted:

6 No person shall become a member of the Foundation unless he is simultaneously elected to membership of the Council in accordance with the provisions of Article 42 provided that any person being a member of the Foundation at the date of the adoption of this Article may continue to be a member until he ceases to be so in accordance with the provisions of these Articles notwithstanding the fact that he is not a member of the Council at the time of the adoption of this Article.

Following the adoption of this Article it was agreed that henceforth all except councillors should be known as subscribers rather than members without altering their privileges; their names would immediately be put on the subscribers list and they would receive the Annual Report, Newsletters and the Christmas Catalogue.

Personnel

Over the years there have been changes in personnel. Lord Tonypandy agreed to become President for five years from 1 January 1984 in succession to Lord De L'Isle and Dudley, who became Vice-President in company with Lords Forte, Cobbold and Samuel. In 1988 Ereld Cardiff was also honoured by his appointment as Vice-President.

Sir Cyril Clarke became Chairman of Council in January 1982, in succession to Sir Ronald Bodley Scott, and was himself succeeded by Sir Raymond Hoffenberg in January 1987.

Many distinguished men served as Council members and assisted the Foundation generously with their own special knowledge and expertise in a variety of ways. It would be invidious to mention some and omit others, but it is right to record the retirement of Dr Lloyd Rusby in 1984 as a representative of the Chest, Heart and Stroke Association, because he had been a member of the governing body of the Foundation since joining the Founding Committee in 1959, a record of service exceeded only by Sir Harry Moore and Lord Forte.

Unhappily, but inevitably, the passage of years saw the deaths of a number of men whose support in the early days of the Foundation had been of vital importance. These included: Dr Graham Hayward (1977), the first representative of the Postgraduate Medical Federation on the Founding Committee, and later Vice-Chairman of Council; Mr Isadore Walton (1980), at some time Chairman of the Scottish Appeal Committee and a major benefactor of the Medical and Surgical Professorial Chairs in Glasgow; Sir Ronald Bodley Scott (1982), Chairman of the Research Funds Committee and of Council, tragically killed in a car accident; Sir Ian Hill (1982), one of the original signatories of the Memorandum and Articles of Association; Mr Leslie Lazell (1982), Chairman of the Appeal Committee; Sir Rudolf de Trafford (1983), who retired from Council in 1980 after 18 years' service including the positions of Treasurer and Chairman of the

The Years of Expansion

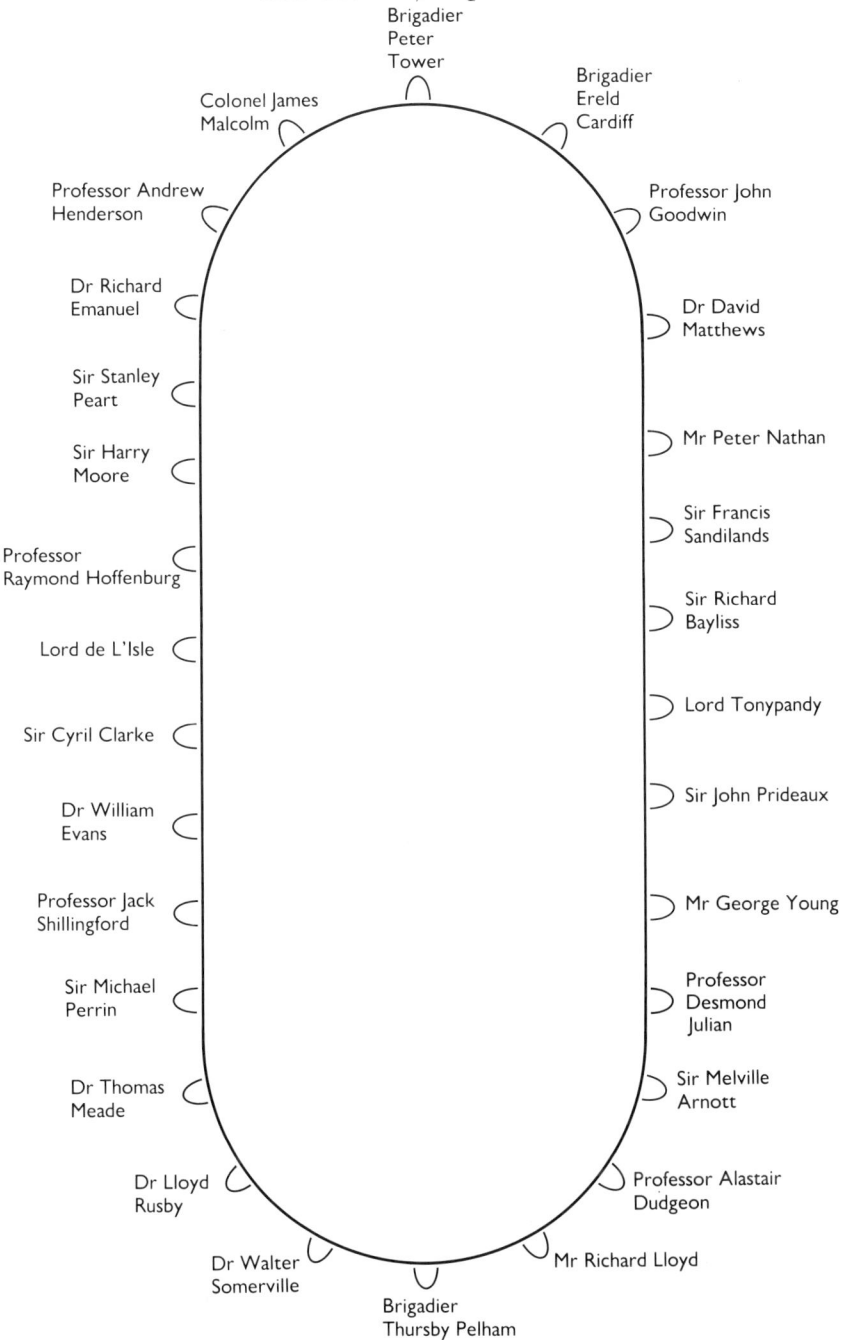

Brigadier Peter Tower
Colonel James Malcolm
Brigadier Ereld Cardiff
Professor Andrew Henderson
Professor John Goodwin
Dr Richard Emanuel
Dr David Matthews
Sir Stanley Peart
Sir Harry Moore
Mr Peter Nathan
Sir Francis Sandilands
Professor Raymond Hoffenburg
Sir Richard Bayliss
Lord de L'Isle
Lord Tonypandy
Sir Cyril Clarke
Sir John Prideaux
Dr William Evans
Professor Jack Shillingford
Mr George Young
Sir Michael Perrin
Professor Desmond Julian
Dr Thomas Meade
Sir Melville Arnott
Dr Lloyd Rusby
Professor Alastair Dudgeon
Dr Walter Somerville
Mr Richard Lloyd
Brigadier Thursby Pelham

Figure 21 *Seating plan showing those attending 25th anniversary dinner at the Cavalry and Guards Club 17 July 1986.*

Finance and General Purposes Committee; Lord Cobbold (1987), the Foundation's first Treasurer and subsequently Chairman of Council and a Vice-President; Sir Thomas Holmes Sellors (1987), a founder member and later Chairman of Council; and Lord Samuel of Wych Cross (1988), Vice-President. In 1988 the Foundation also lost Dr William Evans, the last of the four original members of the Founding Committee, at the age of 94, and Brigadier Cardiff, who became Director of Appeals in 1964, Director General from 1966 to 1976 and subsequently Chairman of the Finance and General Purposes Committee for many years.

On a happier note it is pleasant to record that a Founders Dinner was held in the Jubilee Year, 1986, at the Cavalry and Guards Club on 17 July, which was 25 years to the day since the dinner given by Lord Evans to launch the Foundation's Appeal. Two of those present on the first occasion, Dr William Evans and Sir Harry Moore, were amongst the company (Figure 21).

ANNUAL GENERAL MEETINGS AND PUBLIC MEETINGS

These continued in the same format as during the early and middle years (see pp. 36 and 56) until, in 1982, with the acquisition of a conference room in the new premises at 102 Gloucester Place, it became possible to hold the Annual General Meeting at headquarters. From then on it has been held on the same day as the summer Council meeting. As before, the main business is the presentation of the Annual Report by the President or the Chairman of Council, and of the accounts by the Treasurer, both of which are subsequently published. Apart from discussion of these reports, and any other business a member wishes to raise, the meeting notes retirements and new appointments by virtue of changes in Council membership.

The public meeting, which is as popular as ever, continues to be held in midsummer. It was at the Royal College of Surgeons, where it had been since 1966, until 1979 when it moved back to the lecture theatre at the Royal College of Physicians in Regent's Park. The chairman is either the President or the Chairman of Council. The meeting comprises short talks on subjects related to heart disease in which the Foundation is involved through research programmes, followed by a panel at which the speakers, the Medical Director and

The Years of Expansion

the Director General answer questions from the floor. It concludes with a social gathering for tea.

The full list of speakers and titles during the years of expansion are as follows:

1976	Professor Sleight	Hypertension
	Dr Ann Coxon	Stroke
1977	Brigadier Cardiff	History of the Foundation
	Brigadier Thursby Pelham	The Present
	Professor G.V.R. Born	Biochemical Research
1978	Brigadier Thursby Pelham	The State of the Foundation
	Dr D.M. Krikler	Irregularities of the Heart Beat 24-hour monitoring equipment was on view
1979	Dr M. J. Tynan	Advances in Paediatric Cardiology First public showing of new BHF film entitled, *You've Got to Have a Heart*
1980	Professor M.F. Oliver	Risk Factors in Coronary Heart Disease
	Dr W. Somerville	Heart Transplants: the Facts
1981	Dr D. Southall	Cot Deaths
	Dr D. Chamberlain	First Aid for a Heart Attack First public showing of new BHF film entitled *A Heart Attack – Learn What to Do*
1982	Professor R. Steiner	Nuclear Magnetic Resonance
	Professor A. Maseri	Angiography
	Dr Lindsey Allen	Fetal Echocardiography
1983	Dr R. Emanuel	The Pacemaker
	Dr R. Balcon	Heart Surgery for Angina
	Professor F. Macartney	Modern Treatment for Children's Heart Disease
1984	Dr P. Deverall	New Valves for Old
	Mr T. English	New Hearts for Old
	Professor B. Williamson	Genetic Engineering
1985	'Early Diagnosis of Heart Disease'	
	Dr K. Fox	EEG and the Treadmill Exerciser

	Mr G. Leech	Echocardiography
	Professor G. Radda	Nuclear Magnetic Resonance
1986	'A Generation of Progress'	
	Brigadier Thursby Pelham	A Layman's View
	Professor D. Julian	A Physician's View
	Mr M. Braimbridge	A Surgeon's View
1987	Brigadier P. Tower	The Next Twenty-five Years
	Professor D. Julian	The Way Ahead
	Dr D. Chamberlain	'Save a Life' Campaign
	Dr L. Allan	Fetal Echocardiography

APPEALS DEPARTMENT

In 1976 Colonel Malcolm, as Director of Appeals, assumed responsibility for the attraction of voluntary income from all sources. The ability of the Foundation to fund research depends entirely on the success of this endeavour and he appreciated at once that the secret was to increase public awareness of the existence of the Foundation and its objectives, and to bring home to the public the magnitude of the problems and disasters posed by heart disease. He has always been convinced that the ways to increase awareness are by an ongoing advertising campaign which is professionally orchestrated, and by increasing the number of fund-raising committees nation-wide.

A national opinion poll in 1983 reported an increase in public awareness of the Foundation from 18% to 28% but a poll in 1987 showed that when asked to name a charity only about 20% named the BHF, whilst 41% named cancer research. When prompted, however, over 80% recognized the BHF compared with 90% cancer research. It is noteworthy that heart research charities in Australia and the USA receive at least as much support as cancer, whilst in Britain the Imperial Cancer Research Fund and the Cancer Research Campaign enjoy an income of about £50 million compared with nearly £20 million by the BHF. Reasons for this difference, in spite of the much larger number of deaths from heart disease than from cancer, must include the fact that cancer charities are 50 years older, that they have a joint advertising budget of £1 million, and that they have 2,000 local committees as against the 450 of the BHF. The biggest cause of the disparity is the difference in the size of the legacy income.

ADVERTISING

Before 1976 advertising had been arranged in-house on an *ad hoc* basis without expert help. In 1976 the budget was only £10,000 and advertising had played only a small part in the appeal strategy although it had enjoyed some well-merited successes, particularly with posters. The 'Crossed-out Man' (Figure 22) was an outstanding success and the regular inserts of classified advertisements in national dailies certainly bore fruit.

In these early days the Foundation was indebted to the London Press Exchange for supporting its advertising at little or no cost. This came about through the good offices of Leslie Lazell, the Chairman of the Appeal Committee at the time, because the Exchange handled the advertising budget of the Beecham Group of Companies, of which he was also Chairman.

In 1977, however, the combined enthusiasm of the new Director General and Colonel Malcolm led to a contract with the Westmoreland Advertising Agency. The Foundation paid £30,000 for one year from May 1977, half to be spent in the first six months, and this sum included the costs of artwork, design and layout. Their remuneration above the fixed sum was the customary commission allowed by newspapers and periodicals to advertising agencies. The contract was renewed for a second year, but in 1979 a member of the advertising division of Beechams (Mr Phillips) came by invitation to headquarters to discuss future advertising policy. He recommended asking the Institute of Advertising Practitioners (IAP) to supply a list of advertising agencies from which the Foundation could choose. Five were chosen to make presentations of their proposals to a subcommittee, as a result of which the Barclay Advertising Agency, a subsidiary of J. Arthur Thompson, was chosen with a budget of £100,000 for the year commencing April 1980. The following year this was increased to £150,000, thereafter to be increased by 3% of the increase in voluntary income. In 1982–83 the budget was increased to £175,000, and in 1983–84 to £250,000.

At the end of 1983 several advertising agencies were again asked to make presentations because of increasing and changing needs of the Foundation. As the result Benton & Bowles were appointed as the official agency as from April 1984 with a budget of £350,000. In 1985–86 this was increased to £500,000 and in 1986–87 to £650,000

92   Chapter 4

Figure 22   *The successful poster produced in the early days entitled 'The Crossed-out Man'.*

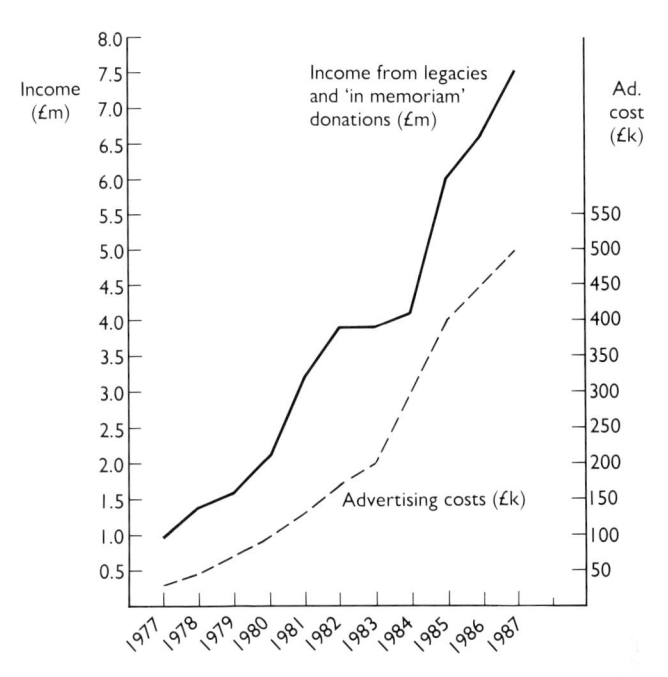

Figure 23 *Comparison of legacy and* in memoriam *income with the advertising expenditure over the period 1977–87.*

with an allocation of an extra £45,000 to be spent on a poster campaign. In 1987 Benton & Bowles became Medicus and continue to serve the Foundation under this name. The chart (Figure 23) shows the relationship between legacies and *in memoriam* donations and advertising expenditure between 1977 and 1987. These two sources of income are chosen because they are the only two which can be directly attributed to the result of advertising.

Figures of the cost-effectiveness of advertising show that the return is still good value but that the ratio is diminishing; the Foundation's income, however, has increased by £6,500,000 at a cost of only £450,000:

1987 £500,000 to raise £7,500,000 = 15/1 ratio
1982 £170,000 to raise £3,900,000 = 23/1 ratio
1977 £35,000 to raise £1,000,000 = 28/1 ratio

It seems likely that in the long term a substantial increase in the budget, even doubling it, would prove financially successful, but it would increase the ratio of expenditure to income in the short term, which might prove embarrassing and attract adverse public comment. It is interesting to note, however, that the ratio would still be well below 20%, whilst our sister charities in Australia and America have no qualms about ratios of 30–40%.

In summary Colonel Malcolm says:

I think 5% of the previous year's total voluntary income is a useful yardstick for the advertising budget, remembering that the BHF's credibility and reputation depends on public confidence. At the same time I am in favour of increasing the basic budget, quite substantially, when obvious targets present themselves. I am as certain now [1987] as I have always been that advertising is the key to the BHF's progress.

THE PRESS OFFICE

The importance of the media as a means of increasing public awareness of the Foundation has been appreciated from the start, and the public appeal in 1963 was heralded by a press conference at the Royal Society. Individual members of headquarters staff have taken every opportunity since those early days to exploit this means of approach to the general public. In the middle years this mostly fell to Geoffrey Davison and later to Bernie Lane, who was the first to be named as the Foundation's Press Officer in 1981.

The need to establish a separate Press Office became urgent with the expansion of the work done for the Foundation by the Joan Scott Public Relations Consultancy. Joan Scott and her partners have increased media coverage by many hundred per cent with the result that the Press Officer is now the most important and most frequently involved member of headquarters staff in this field. The Consultancy makes the contacts with producers and journalists, and the Press Officer has to coordinate the responses of the research workers concerned, or the staff of the Medical Department.

Through her own contacts the Press Officer is also able to find speakers for programmes and to assist regional officers, when required, in their response to invitations by local radio stations. It is her business to generate as much and as wide a coverage of all the Foundation's activities as possible. This involves cooperating with Joan Scott with photocalls and with publicity for national fundraising events. She also has to have at her fingertips statistics on all aspects of heart disease and their trends and pointers; in this the Press

Officer has been ably served for many years by Nick Wells, a statistician in the Office of Health Economics, who has acted as a voluntary consultant to the BHF.

The Press Officer is the voice, and often the face, of the Foundation which greets the media. Hers is a busy, exciting and demanding job, requiring a quick wit, a good memory, patience, tact and endurance. She also has the time-consuming responsibility of editing the *Bulletin* news-sheet, now called *Your Heart*, which is published three times a year, and for the preparation of the Annual Report.

The Foundation has been well served in turn by Bernie Lane, Claire Marley and Elaine Snell. Claire Marley (now Mrs Julian) held the post during the period of most rapid expansion. She was responsible for introducing the system whereby all at head office and in the regions who are likely to be faced with television interviews were sent for special training to the Barry Westwood organization. This was a far-sighted innovation which has paid dividends as the Foundation has become increasingly involved with the media. Claire Marley was well and loyally served by her assistants Fiona Barnes and Jane Landon. She left the Foundation in 1987 to join the Joan Scott organization. Mark Robinson joined the staff of the Press Office at the same time.

THE *BULLETIN*

The *Bulletin* has undergone several changes of format during the decade.

In 1976 the tabloid newspaper style presentation, which contained, almost exclusively, illustrated reports of a large number of fund-raising events, gave way to a journal-style magazine, which included one or two articles of cardiovascular interest, written in lay terms, as well as the continued reporting of activities in the regions, with photographs, as before. Shortly before this change the incorporation of the four-page medical news-sheet seems to have been abandoned.

By the late seventies the magazine-style production had been enlarged to 16 pages, had become glossier in style and had increased the number of articles included. It had also become increasingly expensive and time-consuming to produce, with the result that production became less frequent; to offset this, from 1978 onwards, a four-page supplement was included in one number annually, which was, in essence, a distillate of the Foundation's activities and achievements. It included a message from the Director General, the Annual Report and accounts, details of research grants and awards by the Cardiac Care Committee and a list of BHF lectures. The centre page was so arranged that, when unfolded, it could be used as a poster, showing, each year, a matter of general public interest such as the magnitude of the problems of heart disease and its toll of life, the increase and sources of the Foundation's gross income and how the money was spent.

In 1982 Claire Marley succeeded Sarah Hillard as editor, and the following year she changed the content completely and reduced publication to one annual issue. Accounts and photographs of local fund-raising events disappeared almost entirely, and instead there was a medical editorial by Dr Tony Smith, one lengthy interview of interesting personalities, such as Eric Morecambe by Claire Marley, and articles of topical interest, such as prevention, salt consumption and coronary artery disease. In addition major events were recorded, such as changes of Regional Directors and the award of the Foundation's Gold Medal to Professor Radda for his work on nuclear magnetic resonance. Changes in head office personnel were also reported.

The first issue in 1983 contained a message from the Director General which read:

The style and content of this heart bulletin has been changed, partly through force of circumstances but also by popular request.

Many of our supporters feel that the emphasis should be more on how we spend our money rather than on how it is raised. I must agree. But it saddens me that we can no longer acknowledge all the magnificent fund-raising efforts by our growing army of volunteers. The fact is that local fund-raising efforts have quadrupled in recent years and it has become quite impossible to publish them all without doubling the cost of production and postage. We can make considerable savings and I believe offer you a better service by publishing just one bulletin, normally in late January as a sort of report, the restyled Annual Report in July and the Christmas catalogue.

One of the major spin-offs of any fund-raising event is the local publicity it can generate. Photographs never really achieved this aim because its circulation was restricted mainly to the converted. Fund-raisers can promote our cause, and their own efforts, far more widely by ensuring their events are well publicised by local media. These changes I am glad to say are caused by growing pains. In 1976–1977 we had 150 voluntary committees and our income was one and a half million pounds. In 1983–1984 we had 300 committees and an income of over seven million pounds. Ultimately we need 1000 committees to represent us in every small community; only then will our income match the needs of research.

Meanwhile may I thank every supporter for their voluntary fund-raising, publicity and work which helps so much to bring closer the day when we are no longer threatened by premature death or disabled by heart disease. I hope you will enjoy reading our brand new bulletin; we will be most interested to receive comments from any of our readers.

P.S. Another economy will be to post the publication in bulk to the honorary secretary, or representative, of branches or groups to distribute at their discretion. Twenty of each regardless of membership.

Unfortunately, however, the *Bulletin* continued to prove too time-consuming and expensive to produce. So in 1986 it became a four-page news-sheet again, and resumed the title *Your Heart*, under which it had been published at its inception in 1962; moreover the format was much the same as when Dr Harley Williams had edited it until his retirement in 1969.

The first issue of this new bulletin in 1986 contained an editorial explaining the reasons for the change which read as follows:

This news letter is the first step in a campaign to improve understanding of heart disease and to explain some of the research projects the BHF is now financing to combat Britain's biggest killer.

For the first time the BHF is to send news, information and reports on developments and progress to its 300,000 supporters across the country; by providing better and more regular feed-back to its wide group of friends the Foundation will be ensuring that each of its supporters will have the chance of learning about the achievements their help is making possible.

Your Heart will give statistics and information about the scale and effects of heart disease, will review recent developments of research and will illustrate the Foundation's work through interviews, case histories, and news about fund-raising and education work. Above all, it will illustrate the importance of long-term support of research.

In the past BHF's 16-page magazine has been sent only once a year to a very limited readership. Now the new 4-page *Your Heart* will reach everyone three times a year. The Foundation believes this will lead to better information, better understanding and more support for BHF's essential work.

The Annual Report for 1985 contains a message from the President, Lord Tonypandy, which was reproduced in *Your Heart*, in which he says:

This is my first year as President of the British Heart Foundation. I consider it a special privilege to be asked to pass on a few thoughts to you, our many friends and supporters throughout the country. We sincerely appreciate all that you do. In truth without your efforts we should not be able to do any of the wonderful things which are described in the report. Progress and achievements of heart research are all thanks to you. This report also shows very dramatically the many problems caused by the many mysteries of heart disease and the solutions the researchers have yet to find. It also illustrates the huge cost in financial and human terms of heart disease to our society. The moving stories of the five survivors will have shown you how serious heart disease can be. But they also give great hope, for they prove that research really does save lives. Thank you again for your support and help in the past year, and please do continue in every way you can to give heart research your assistance in the future. It means so much.

JOAN SCOTT PUBLIC RELATIONS CONSULTANCY

Joan Scott's first contact with the Foundation was in 1974 when she was sent by the firm for which she was working to make arrangements for the publicity for a ceremony to launch a new rose called 'Heart Beat', which was being presented by Dickson's, the rose growers. She was unimpressed by the amount of trouble the Foundation had taken in publicizing the event and wrote to Brigadier Cardiff subsequently and told him so with characteristic candour. Shortly afterwards the Foundation was in the process of making changes in the arrangements for their publicity, and the Director General asked his secretary to 'find that girl who told us off; she seems to know her own mind'. By that time Joan Scott had set up her own consultancy and she was invited to attend for interview.

Speaking of the successful outcome she said: 'I was bright enough to turn up on time, which went down well with the military gentlemen; the others were late!' In the light of the happy 14-year partnership which has followed, however, there were doubtless other good reasons for their choice. Her appointment was very fortunate for the Foundation and did much to increase public awareness. Joan Scott and her partners have contacts with most branches of the media and know personally many of the key figures.

She sees her firm's service to the Foundation as threefold. First there is the serious work of informing the public of the way their money is spent in promoting cardiovascular research: the grants and fellowships which are awarded to research workers, and the professorial chairs which are created and maintained, together with the constantly repeated reminder of the need for more money.

The Years of Expansion

Secondly there is involvement in all aspects of fund-raising. These include coverage of national events of all types, securing celebrities to appear at fund-raising events and the organization of photocalls. In many cases the Consultancy is also the originator of the event, either by thinking it up or by securing BHF benefit through sponsorship at an event already known to them. Their task is primarily to secure as much media coverage as possible of fund-raising events, and they were heavily committed in the promotion of 'Heart Weeks' in 1983 and 1985, and in the Jubilee celebration in 1986 to mark the Foundation's 25th year.

Regional events are mostly covered by publicity organized locally but occasionally the help of the Consultancy is sought, particularly in helping to generate interest by local newspapers and radio stations.

The Consultancy has done much to promote the National Slim over the last ten years, including coverage of the prize-giving ceremonies. Similarly it has been on hand to publicize the London-to-Brighton bike ride, and has helped to foster the ride on Hadrian's Wall together with another in Wales and, most recently, another based on Birmingham.

It was due to the Consultancy that the Foundation benefited from the Ladies' Liverpool Half-Marathon, which raised £23,000 in its first year (1987); similarly in 1988 they did much to publicize a golf tournament in which more than ninety heart patients competed, raising £73,000. At present they are working hard to promote coordinated sponsored walks throughout the country in 1989; the emphasis is on the benefits of well-planned exercise, as well as the value of funds raised for the work of the Foundation.

The third role of the Consultancy is in the realm of public education, in which the Foundation is becoming increasingly involved, particularly in schools. The Foundation has always refused to give advice on matters of life-style except when the facts are proven, but it is ready and willing to condemn smoking, to advocate exercise and a balanced diet, and to warn of the dangers of high blood pressure, obesity and over-indulgence in alcohol. To get these messages across to the public needs well-organized publicity campaigns and the Consultancy plays an important part in ensuring that they have maximum impact.

In addition to the benefits the Foundation has enjoyed as a result of the knowledge and skills of the Consultancy it has also benefited from Joan Scott's personal dedication in creating the Westminster

Committee at the suggestion of Bernie Lane, in 1980, and serving as its chairwoman for several years. The committee has raised, on average, over £10,000 per annum for the Foundation.

SPECIAL AND NATIONAL EVENTS

Special and national events are organized at headquarters and put a large burden of work on to a small number of staff. There is, therefore, a limit to what can be done with the resources available. The Special and National Events Department has existed in embryo form almost as long as the Foundation and has two purposes: the first is to collect money for research and the second is to create public interest in, and awareness of, the Foundation. Ideally every event should do this in plenty, and without a disproportionate burden of work. At the beginning of the era of expansion (1976–88) under consideration the department was run by Bernie Lane, later by Judy McKeller and, after her departure, by Mary Dunn, an American, who was in London with her husband because he was on sabbatical leave. It is now under the direction of Adele Hodgson. Recalling her days with Special Events, Bernie Lane said: 'At that stage it was really few people doing an awful lot. We were very small and it was fun.'

The variety of events organized by this small Department is impressive and all are worthy of mention but shortage of space compels selectivity. A sponsored horse-racing day at Ascot in 1977 brought £45,000 to the Foundation and a similar occasion at Newmarket in 1985 £81,000; both were greatly enjoyed. Sponsored angling and cycling also featured in 1977; angling, in spite of enthusiastic publicity by Eric Morecambe, did little more than break even but the 'National Ride a Bike Week', promoted by the British Bike Bureau and launched at Windsor Castle by our Patron the Duke of Edinburgh, brought £5,000; when repeated in 1978 it earned £23,000, and in 1979 £76,000. Two nights of greyhound racing in 1978 and 1979 each brought £7,500.

One of the first sponsored walks on behalf of the Foundation was also organized by the special events team; it was at Wickhurst Castle in Kent in 1979 and produced £3,000. It set a pattern for many similar walks organized by the regions and local committees. In the same year (1979) the *Sunday Times* Fun Run' brought in £10,500. A number of fairs and auctions took place, amongst which was the

The Years of Expansion

Figure 24 *His Royal Highness the Duke of Edinburgh, Patron of the Foundation, enjoying a joke with Eric Morecambe, who did so much to help raise money for the Foundation.*

Belgrave Square Residents Association Fair in 1977, which made a profit for the Foundation of £11,000, wine sales at Christie's in 1978, 1979 and 1983, which earned a total of £10,000, and an art auction at Phillips in 1980, which made a profit of £6,000.

Two events in the theatre world were the première of *Porridge* as a memorial to the actor Richard Beckensale in 1979, which raised £12,500 for the Foundation, and a gala evening at the Palladium, titled 'Bring Me Sunshine', in the presence of the Duke of Edinburgh, as a memorial to Eric Morecambe in 1984; this was promoted by Thames Television and shown on ITV on Christmas Day. It brought over £168,000 to the Foundation (Figure 24).

In 1980 a Festival of Flowers at Westminster earned over £10,000 and in 1981 Harkness, the rose growers, introduced the 'Pacemaker' rose at the Chelsea Flower Show with a benefit to the Foundation for every rose sold. A happy occasion was a charity football match on the Arsenal football ground in 1981 played between children who had been treated for heart disease and the professionals; this was promoted by Jimmy Saville's 'Fix-It' team.

There were many individual sponsored efforts, typified by a

'Round Britain' bike ride by Percy Smith, a heart patient, who rode 2,000 miles and earned a like sum in pounds, and by a Land's End to John O'Groats journey in an 1899 Mercedes Benz car by Richard Smith, which produced £7,500.

The two big national sponsored events which have dominated the decade and involved the Special and National Events Department most heavily are the National Sponsored Slim and the London-to-Brighton Bike Ride.

The National Slim starts early in the year and ends around Easter-time. Those wishing to lose weight get their friends to sponsor them and it has been calculated that several tons are lost every year by those taking part! It started in 1975 and has continued annually without a break. In the first year it was sponsored by Nestlé and the prizes were given by Crosse and Blackwell, but since then it has been sponsored by Cadbury Marvel, who underwrite the expenses and pay for the prizes for the winners; on several occasions they have also hosted a prize-giving ceremony at a prestigious London hotel. As a result of this generosity the Foundation enjoys the income from all the sponsorship money. The total from 1975 to 1987 is little short of £1,000,000.

The London-to-Brighton Bike Ride is not a race. It is a family occasion on a summer day in June. It was started by John Potter, who owns a cycle business in Bath, as a personal effort and at his own expense. The Foundation was first involved in 1980 when, at the last minute, 177 riders took part with sponsorship for the BHF and collected the splendid total of £6,435. By 1981 it had grown so large that it was clearly necessary for the Foundation to contribute to the expenses and the ride came under the promotion of bike events.

There are now 20,000 registered riders every year and the departure site is at Clapham Common instead of Hyde Park, to avoid traffic congestion in central London. The dispatch of riders is meticulously organized by volunteers from the London Fire Brigade and marshalling staff from the BHF. There is close cooperation with the police. There is, however, a problem in that it is impossible to prevent anyone from joining in. It is estimated that there have been as many as 10,000 such unregistered riders who bring no sponsorship money to the Foundation and greatly increase congestion, and with it the likelihood of accidents. In 1986 the ride was promoted by Allinson's and in 1987 by Flora. It is easily the largest earner from sponsorship of all events undertaken on behalf of the Foundation. In 1986 it brought in £784,000, and in 1988 over £1,000,000.

Flora have also supported the Foundation on other occasions. In 1976 they hosted a lunch to launch the Foundation's highly successful cookery book entitled *Cooking for Your Heart's Content*, whose first run of 15,000 copies was exhausted in a few weeks, as was a second run of the same number; and in 1987 Flora undertook a six-week pack promotion of the Foundation on the carton lids of their spread, which raised £179,000.

Another pack promotion was one made by Disprin, which raised £10,000, and there have been others.

The most recent undertaking of the resourceful Special and National Events Department is the sponsored 'Jump Rope for Heart' campaign in schools. It consists of organized skipping sessions in which the children are sponsored singly or as a team. It has proved highly successful as a fund-raiser in Australia and America; although it is too early to say how successful it will be in Britain it seems promising to date, having raised over £200,000 in the first year. An added incentive is the arrangement whereby the schools keep 25% of the money to improve their own sports facilities. It has been promoted by the Cooperative Society.

An account of the lively work of this Department should not, perhaps, end without recalling their powers of persuasion, with the collaboration of the Joan Scott PR Consultancy, in inducing a number of hotels, restaurants and bars throughout Britain to sell a non-alcoholic drink called 'Passion Potion' on St Valentine's Day for the benefit of the Foundation. It is reported to have been pleasant to taste, and to have fulfilled the criteria of making a profit, creating awareness and being easy to sell!

THE DONATIONS DEPARTMENT

All donations received at headquarters were handled by the secretariat until the retirement of Denis Blake in 1981. They were listed by the donations clerks in the 'front room', which they shared with the cashiers, and the money was banked by the Finance Officer and his staff. Letters of thanks were mostly written by hand by a team of part-time volunteers.

The appointment of Richard Emery as Donations Secretary coincided with Denis Blake's retirement, and the administration of the newly created Donations Department became part of the Appeals Department under the jurisdiction of the Director of Appeals. This was a radical change.

It is the responsibility of the Donations Department to write letters of thanks to all donors and this is now done using the word-processor, which provides a standardized framework to which appropriate personal sentences are added. Much care is taken to ensure that all donations are acknowledged individually in this way. Some of the donations are single gifts, others are covenants and others *in memoriam* donations sent by relatives and friends of someone who has died. Legacies are dealt with by the Legacy Department, which is still part of the remit of the Secretary of the Foundation.

The Donations Department works closely with the staff of the supporters' list (Ron Trebell and Steve Johnston), which has grown out of the mailing list. It plays a very important part in fund-raising. In the words of James Malcolm: 'A charity is only as good as its supporters list.'

Starting from the original addressograph machine, which was backed by a hand-written card-index system, the whole supporters' list is now computerized with Southwark Computers. With computerization it is possible to categorize all names according to the type of donation, the amount given, and the year, or years, in which donations have been made. It is also possible to include the names of those who have shown an interest in the Foundation by sending back the form requesting information which they have cut from newspaper advertisements, and indeed the names of those who have been in correspondence with any other department of the Foundation. About 97% of names of donors put on to the supporters list each year are new to the Foundation and the computer takes off any names already there. The list now contains nearly half a million names.

By suitable computer programming it is possible to analyse the percentage response to any mailing; a 5% response is needed to make it cost-effective. The percentage varies greatly between differing categories of donors. For example with *in memoriam* names, which represent about 70% of the names on the supporters list, the response rate is only 7% whereas the response of those who have returned newspaper cuttings is 25%.

When dealing with *in memoriam* donations a card is made out if more than one is received, so that the next-of-kin can be told the total amount. Occasionally a relative writes to say that he, or she, believes more was sent than the total stated; when this happens the information is sent to the Regional Director in whose areas the deceased lived, to check whether some of the donations have been sent to the local office, and the next-of-kin informed accordingly.

In the year 1987–88 a total of 35,000 donations were received of which 24,000 were *in memoriam* donations and 11,000 were general donations. The *in memoriam* donations totalled £550,000, received at a rate of £50,000–£60,000 per month.

Those who have sent covenants are known as key supporters, and are separately listed on the computer. They receive a copy of the Annual Report, the *Your Heart* bulletin twice a year and any other material produced for mailing. At the beginning of 1986 there were 3,000 covenants, with a covenant income of £85,000 including tax rebate. Two years later there were 7,000 producing an income of £250,000.

Every month a schedule is sent to every region analysing the source of head office income in terms of regions; in this way the regions feel that the money received is credited to them. Suitable programming of the computer also makes it possible to send Regional Directors the names and addresses of new donors in their regions so that they can call on them or get in touch by telephone to thank them personally, and to try to enlist their help with fund-raising and in the formation of new committees.

The Donations Department is also responsible for Heart Cards Ltd, which is a trading company, with Richard Emery its managing director. The Foundation has been enthusiastic in promoting BHF Christmas cards since its earliest days when it was managed by Patrick Anderson. In later years its survival was largely due to the efforts of Steve Johnston, who kept it alive almost single-handed.

In its first year the Foundation produced only two cards. The 'Three Wise Men', of which 100,000 were printed and 90,000 sold, and one of a dachshund of which 50,000 were printed and only 2,000 sold. The next year a brochure was printed showing the dachshund because so many dachshunds were unsold. It turned out to be so popular that the dachshund had to be reprinted. As Brigadier Cardiff remarked: 'It goes to show how difficult it is to get things right when it comes to choosing Christmas cards.' The Foundation seems to have overcome the problem, however, since, in 1987, the public bought 5,000,000 BHF cards.

By the terms of the Charities Act a charity cannot be directly involved in the selling of goods; in consequence Heart Cards was set up as a separate company as early as April 1966. Heart Cards can then legally donate its profits to the Foundation. Heart Cards was originally managed by the Delgado Printing Company, which was subsequently taken over by the large mail-order firm of Webb Ivory. Heart Cards has been under their management ever since. They have extended the business for the BHF, which started exclusively as Christmas cards, to include a wide variety of gifts listed in their Christmas catalogue, many of which carry the BHF logo. The Webb Ivory computer is now in electronic communication with Southwark Computers so that they can 'talk to each other'. In this way Webb Ivory can pick out the donors who, from past records, are most likely to be commercially rewarding. By allowing Webb Ivory this discretion the Foundation is freed from all up-front expenses concerned with the catalogue except for postage, and the same applies to the spring catalogue recently introduced. Their expenses are, of course, the first charge on the proceeds of sales, after which the Foundation benefits. The advantage to the Foundation is that it minimizes the risk of losses from a poor trading year.

The catalogue also has an important spin-off in that it attracts donations and covenants as well as money from sales of Christmas cards and other gifts.

Many local committees, or individual members of committees, or friends of committee members act as agents for Heart Cards, as do other members of the public not linked to committees. They all help to increase the sales of Heart Cards Ltd. When local committees act as agents they send 75% of the takings to Webb Ivory and 25% to their regional funds.

There are two other associations of Christmas card charities which sell cards for many charities including the BHF. These are known as the 1959 Group and the Charity Card Christmas Council (the 4 Cs), which produces a catalogue for businesses with a circulation of 20,000.

The Christmas catalogue is sent to all who have ordered in the last four years, all newcomers to the supporters list as well as to key supporters and life subscribers. In addition it is being increasingly sent to people outside the supporters list. These so-called 'cold' names are bought in from other lists by the Donations Department. This new source now comprises nearly 250,000 names.

The Donations Department also started a direct mail appeal in 1986 with a Christmas appeal letter sent out at the beginning of December together with a copy of the *Your Heart* bulletin. It goes to all individuals on the supporters list but not to corporate donors or to key supporters since they have already made covenants. The Donations Department is responsible for this letter, which, to date, has taken the form of a case history; the last was written by the mother of a child who had been successfully treated.

At Christmas 1987 £1,000,000 worth of sales was made by the Christmas catalogue with £124,000 benefit to the Foundation, in addition to which donations worth £55,000 accompanied the orders and covenants and banker's orders for £26,000, making a total of over £200,000.

The success of the Donations Department in turning round a Heart Card enterprise which had been struggling for many years, largely because of under-funding, is a great credit to Richard Emery and his team, consisting of Noel Fisher, who had been with Dr Barnardo's for 15 years, Ken Burnett of Burnett Associates, who are direct mail specialists and print the bulletin, and his secretary, Brenda Mole.

THE LEGACY DEPARTMENT

The Legacy Department was set up in May 1982 with the appointment of Clem Hogan as Legacy Officer; this was a wise choice. Before this legacies were dealt with by Denis Blake, as Secretary of the Foundation; the new Department, although it is autonomous, is still accountable to the Administration through the Secretary, who is currently Marion Grainge. Since 1983 Clem Hogan's assistant has been Ann Whalan, and they run the Department together, with secretarial help (Jocelyne Le Cromps).

The function of the Department is to ensure that the maximum benefit of all legacies due to the Foundation is in fact received. Most legacies are notified to the Foundation by solicitors, either acting in their capacity as executors, or on behalf of executors.

In addition the Foundation is notified weekly by an agency employed by the Foundation of every legacy left to it, as a result of scanning probate registries throughout the country. The agency informs the Foundation, not only of legacies in which it is named as the sole beneficiary, but also of those where the testator has left it a share of the estate, or where a fixed sum of money has been left to the executors to distribute to such charities as they think fit in their discretion.

Notification of this kind of bequest is of great importance to the Foundation since it prompts an immediate response through an appropriately worded letter over the signature of the Director General. Submissions to executors in this way generate a very worthwhile addition to the legacy income.

A further addition is achieved through reclaiming tax already deducted from legacy income prior to its receipt by the Foundation. This is done by obtaining the relevant tax certificates from the executors to present to the Inland Revenue, which generally agrees such claims unless there are valid reasons to disallow them.

There is a good spirit of collaboration and cooperation between the legacy departments of the major medical charities, which makes for fair settlement of complicated claims, and the legacy officers meet annually to discuss matters of mutual and technical interest. The charities with which the BHF most frequently shares a legacy are the Imperial Cancer Research Fund and the Cancer Research Campaign.

Occasionally the Legacy Department comes into potential conflict with relatives of the deceased either through the Inheritance Act, when a relative feels aggrieved at not having received, in his or her view, a proper share to provide support, or when the validity of the will is contested on the grounds of testamentary incapacity.

The Foundation's aim is the settlement of as many as possible of such claims direct without employing solicitors; this is largely achieved in claims relating to the Inheritance Act, but less often when the capacity of the testator is in question.

The Foundation's income from legacies has built up steadily but with a dramatic rise in the last four years. In 1963, two years after the creation of the Foundation, the legacy income was £2,500. This was built up to £500,000 in 1974 and in 1978 the £1,000,000 mark was reached for the first time. The total rose to £3,000,000 by 1982, where it remained steady for three years before starting to rise rapidly in 1984, reaching a total of £7,700,000 for the year ending March 1988.

This dramatic rise is largely due to the increase in the value of the estates of the testators, and the single largest factor contributing to this has been the rise in property prices, but the number of legacies has also risen. In 1982 the Foundation received around 500 legacies and in 1988 869.

As is to be expected the majority of legacies come to the Foundation either from those who have suffered from heart disease, or from relatives of those who have died from it. Since heart disease is commoner in men than in women, except in the elderly, the most frequent testator is the elderly widow or spinster. A relatively small percentage of legacies come from those who have supported the Foundation with covenants or regular donations.

THE REGIONS

The importance of an organization through which to raise money nation-wide has been appreciated as long as the Foundation has existed, and steps were soon taken to set up a regional framework. It was necessarily on an *ad hoc* basis initially, when advantage had to be taken of any promising lead towards the creation of a fund-raising centre. Over the years this good groundwork has been built on by many dedicated men and women until nowadays the regions provide about a third of the Foundation's voluntary income.

Such an important part of the Foundation's effort and success demands the devotion of a separate chapter in the records of its history (see p. 192), but it also needs to be included in the record of the years of expansion.

Colonel Malcolm has had a profound and very beneficial influence on the success of the regions as fund-raisers. Before his arrival Regional Organizers were heavily committed to running and promoting innumerable fund-raising events, which took all their time and left none for advising and directing others in similar endeavours. He appreciated that this was wasteful of time and effort, and that it led to disproportionately high overhead costs.

His conception was of a smaller number of larger regions, each looked after by a Regional Director, whose job it is to direct others in fund-raising activities. He started with 18 regions; now there are 11. Overheads have been reduced by about 33%, mainly by organizational changes involving staff, offices and cars.

Colonel Malcolm's conviction has always been that success in fund-raising depends on the number of voluntary branches working for the Foundation. The Regional Directors have some 25 County Organizers working for them, whose sole role is to start up and nurture voluntary branches. The Regional Directors can be described as 'recruiters' of voluntary fund-raisers, mostly through the intermediation of the County Organizers. Since Colonel Malcolm initiated this policy the number of voluntary branches has increased from 70 to nearly 500.

He described the Regional Organizers he inherited as 'very dedicated and working way beyond the call of duty'; he also thought that they were very poorly remunerated. The remuneration has now been revised, and he has been successful in attracting people to be Regional Directors whose past experience of senior management and delegation of responsibility has made them highly effective. The concept of their management function is devolution to volunteers.

The self-sufficient voluntary branches created in recent years have often, understandably, been increasingly aggressive about fund-raising for local causes such as items of equipment for the local hospital or ambulance service. The collection of money for these purposes has proved to be immensely popular, but it does not benefit research funds directly. However, it is of immense long-term benefit since, by winning recognition and popularity for the BHF, donations and legacies for research continue to grow. Thus these parochial enterprises achieve both aims: local benefit and money for research.

FIVE

THE MEDICAL DEPARTMENT

THE MEDICAL DEPARTMENT, which nowadays bears the responsibility for advising on the allocation of the Foundation's disposable income, amounting in 1987–88 to nearly £17,000,000, started in a humble way with the creation of the Science Committee on 6 February 1961 at the behest of the Founding Committee (see p. 17).

SCIENCE COMMITTEE

The Science Committee served the Foundation for nine years until, in February 1970, it was superseded by the Research Funds Committee, the Postgraduate Medical Education Funds Committee and the Cardiac Care Committee. The committee structure was further subdivided later by the creation of the Chairs and Research Groups Committee in 1978 and the Fellowships Committee in 1983.

The Science Committee had important policy decisions to make in its very early days, and it says much for its members that these decisions have remained basically unaltered. They rejected direction of research as being counter-productive and gave the highest priority, when considering grant applications, to intrinsic scientific merit, irrespective of immediate applicability or value in terms of public appeal. They were not insensitive, however, to the need of the Appeal Committee to be seen to be supporting projects which were of interest to the Foundation's supporters in industry and to an anxious public. They were well aware that without financial support they had nothing to offer to anyone for research of any kind. So, in studying the earliest applications, they listed them into two categories: 'A' with appeal value and 'B' essentially scientific investigations. Before supporting applications in group A they had to be assured not only of their scientific content but also that they were practicable and likely to bear fruit. These decisions are minuted. Professor Melville Arnott, a founder-member of the Committee, put it succinctly when he wrote: 'The more I am associated with research, the more convinced I am of the necessity of supporting adequately those who show that they have scientific ability and have original minds. Projects which are selected because they are attractive, rather than that the investigators themselves are attractive, are not usually fruitful.'

At its second meeting in May 1961 the Committee approved its Proposed Standing Orders, prepared by the Executive Committee. They read as follows:

1 The Science Committee shall consist of such members of the Council as the Council shall appoint, together with co-opted persons from outside, who shall be recommended for such co-option by the Committee itself. The members of the Committee shall hold office for three years and retire in accordance with the rules of the Foundation.
2 The Chairman of the Committee shall be a member of the Council of the Foundation, and shall be appointed by the Science Committee for a period of three years.
3 The Committee shall advise the Council upon research and postgraduate medical education, and may initiate, promote and support such research, and shall adjudicate upon all research proposals presented to the Foundation, and advise on other questions of scientific interest.
4 The Committee may establish from its own membership, including co-opted members, such subcommittees as it shall think fit, with power to consult persons other than members of the Science Committee.
5 The Committee shall report to each meeting of the Council, which shall, as it thinks fit, establish a budget of expenditure within which the Science Committee shall have powers of allocation.
6 The Science Committee may appoint such Consultant Advisers in special departments as it thinks fit, and such Consultant Advisers may be invited to attend any or all of the meetings of the Committee, and when they so attend they shall have power to vote.
7 All applications for grants to undertake research or investigation shall be presented through the Secretary to the Committee, or subcommittee, in the manner which the Committee shall decide.
8 The Council, upon the recommendation of the Committee, shall authorise the manner of disbursing the funds of the Foundation, upon research and postgraduate medical education, either as a lump sum, or by instalments.
9 The Science Committee shall, within the budgetary powers laid down by the Council, have power to notify acceptance of research proposals.

In January 1963, prior to the launch of the public appeal in June, the Committee had a lengthy discussion about its objectives and policy, which was summarized by its Vice-chairman, Professor Sir John McMichael, in the following terms: 'To seek improved understanding of the heart and circulation in health and disease; the prevention and cure of heart and blood vessel disease through the financial support of skilled investigators; the provision of special equipment; the promotion of international co-operation in pursuit of these objectives.'

There was pressure on the Science Committee from the Appeal Committee to finance some projects from the income derived from the appeal to industry before the launch of the public appeal, so that this could be backed by evidence that the Foundation was already active in funding research. Clearly, however, it was inadvisable to publicize the availability of money for research in advance of the launch of the public appeal, and the members of the Science Committee were adamant that they would not recommend the acceptance of applications received before notification of medical schools and through the medical press. This was because to date, no one except members of the Committee, and the few others closely associated with the Foundation, knew of the likely availability of funds and in consequence no one else had been in a position to submit applications. They rightly refused to take advantage of this situation although they understood the Appeal Committee's needs.

At their meeting in July 1961 the Committee recorded the following minute:

The Chairman and other members expressed doubts as to the desirability of considering specific research projects at the present time, when only members of the Science Committee, and a few others closely associated with the Foundation, were in a position to submit proposals. It was felt that the applications already before the Committee should be considered again, in open competition, after the Foundation's willingness to accept applications had been published. It was felt, however, that time might be saved subsequently if preliminary consideration were now given to current applications.

So, as a compromise, they agreed to study the applications and grade them as suitable or unsuitable, and, if suitable, to categorize them as 'A' or 'B', so that they would be able to recommend some funding soon after public notification to the medical profession, which was timed to coincide with the launch of the public appeal. They went to much trouble in this connection, in preparing a letter for circulation to the deans of medical schools, explaining the intention to fund research and inviting applications. In the event the Committee disbursed a little under half the £40,000 made available by the Council for the year 1962–63.

The Committee was also much exercised in deciding how to handle the applications it received, both because of the volume of work and because of the diversity of specialist expertise required to make proper judgements. Many alternative suggestions were considered to resolve both difficulties.

There was considerable support for the creation of multiple specialist subcommittees, but others argued that this would add to the workload since members of the Committee would have to serve on the subcommittees without absolving the main Committee from making the final decisions. It was ultimately decided to appoint Consultant Advisers to the Committee from well-known experts in particuar disciplines without making them full members of the Committee, which would have required them to attend Committee meetings; they combined the roles of external advisers and referees. Departments involved in this way included biochemistry, epidemiology, pathology, physics, electronics, physiology, radiology and paediatrics. The arrangement worked well, particularly after the inclusion of eminent industrial scientists, such as Dr Popjak from Shell, Dr Woodroofe from Unilever and Dr A. Spinks from ICI, and a representative from the Royal Society, Professor W.D.M. Paton (later Sir William) and later Professor A.S.V. Burgen (later Sir Arnold).

PROJECT GRANTS

After a few years the number and wide diversity of the applications for grants made it necessary to enlarge the Committee to include, on a full membership basis, experts from many of the disciplines hitherto covered by advisers. Within two months of the announcement of the availability of money to fund research the Committee received 75 applications for grants. Of these, 31 were approved and 12 deferred for further consideration. Some of the applicants who were rejected were advised to seek support from other research bodies which were felt to be more appropriate.

When the Committee met three months later, in October 1963, 34 applications were supported at a total cost of £180,980, of which £93,000 would be spent in the first year; of this £41,000 was for apparatus and therefore non-recurrent. The following year 33 grants were awarded at a cost of £95,000, with an annual expenditure of £24,500 and £27,000 for apparatus.

The Finance Committee allocated £100,000 to the Science Committee for disbursement in 1965, by which time the Committee urged a system of forward budgeting so that they would be better able to decide which applications they could support and by how much. As a result £150,000 was promised for 1965–66 and the same amount for 1966–67. This was raised to £175,000 for 1967–68. In a review by Dr Harley Williams at his last attendance he said that to date the Committee had disbursed £875,000 in grants, £25,000 to the appeal for the Hospital for Sick Children, and £40,000 to support the professorial chair at the Institute of Cardiology, making a total not far short of £1,000,000.

It is interesting to record that the Committee continued to be under such pressure from the volume of work with which it had to deal that in 1968 it was forced to accept the concept of subcommittees previously rejected. At the suggestion of Melville Arnott the Committee was divided into two panels, one under his chairmanship and the other under Professor Shillingford. Each panel reviewed half the applications and subsequently reported to a full meeting of the Committee. The system was still in operation when the Committee was disbanded in 1970 but the anticipated disadvantages of reduplication of work had by then already become manifest.

At their meeting in May 1964 the Committee first discussed the possibility of funding professorial chairs, and it was followed a year later by a submission by Professor Melville Arnott for £100,000 to finance a Chair of Cardiology at Birmingham. The Committee responded by setting up a subcommittee to advise on how to deal with applications for large sums; further urgency was given to this by the gift of £200,000 by Lord Marks, the income from which was to fund a professorship at the Institute of Cardiology. The subcommittee reported favourably on the concept of academic chairs as centres of excellence in universities to attract research workers in cardiology.

The Committee also discussed and approved the creation of Fellowships and suggested initially that these should be for seven years and tenable by experienced researchers. They received a report of a satisfactory meeting with members of the American Heart Association, which resulted in the establishment of British/American Exchange Fellowships to which the Americans subscribed $10,000 and the BHF $5,000. These were advertised in 1966 and the first two British Fellows went to America for the academic year 1967–68:

Dr Michael Lee went to the National Heart Institute in Bethesda to work on the immunoassay of hormones and Dr B.M. Rifkind to work at the same institute on lipoprotein metabolism.

At this time applications for project grants were considered from those engaged in cardiovascular research in Commonwealth countries and several were successful. For example in 1964 £2,000 per annum for three years was awarded to a worker in Jamaica to supplement support he was already receiving from the Canadian Heart Association. Later the increasing demands on BHF funds necessitated the restriction of awards to those working in Britain.

From time to time the Committee, or a member individually, was approached by a commercial firm offering to support a research project concerned with their particular product. The Committee's reply to such enquiries was that no donation could be automatically channelled in this way. An exception, however, was made to an approach on similar, though not identical, lines by the Tobacco Research Council, which was prepared to consider applications referred to the Committee concerning the possible relationship between nicotine, lipid levels and heart disease.

Following talks between the Chairman, Sir Philip Rogers, and Sir Charles Dodds and Sir John McMichael, the Tobacco Council supported a number of appropriate applications forwarded to it by the Science Committee over a period of several years. The first was for £10,000 over three years to Dr R. Mahler at Guy's Hospital in 1965. In 1967 the Council supported an award of £7,500 over three years to Professor Lawrie in Glasgow and of £13,000 to Dr J.D. Billimoria of Westminster Hospital Medical School over the same period of time.

From the earliest days the Committee was conscious of the importance of honouring its objective of 'the promotion of international cooperation', and to this end it agreed to the loan of £1,300 per annum for four years to the British Cardiac Society, which, through its Secretary, Dr P. Mouncey, was organizing the Sixth World Congress of Cardiology in London in 1970. When this took place the Foundation also supported the meeting with a concert at the Festival Hall, at which Sir John Barbirolli conducted the Hallé Orchestra.

During its nine years of existence the Committee saw many changes of personnel. Its first Chairman, Sir Charles Dodds, the eminent biochemist, and, at the time, President of the Royal College of Physicians, was succeeded by Sir Ronald Bodley Scott in

1968. Following the death in 1962 of Dr Paul Wood, who was Vice-Chairman, Professor Sir John McMichael took over and was, in turn, succeeded in 1967 by Professor Melville Arnott.

Initially the Committee was composed, for the most part, of members of the Founding Committee, including Sir Harry Moore and Lord Forte as lay members; in 1968 Sir Michael Perrin and Mr B.W. Goodman joined as lay members.

In 1963 Sir Ernst Chain, Professor of Biochemistry at Imperial College, joined the Committee and in 1966, following retirements in rotation, newcomers were Dr John Hay of Liverpool, Professor Peter Harris, Institute of Cardiology, Dr Linden, Leeds, Dr Shillingford, Hammersmith, and Dr Peter Stock, Stoke-on-Trent. Dr A. Spinks, Medical Director of ICI, who had been an adviser for some years, also joined the Committee at this time. In 1967 Professor K.W. Donald, Edinburgh, Professor J.F. Goodwin, Hammersmith, Dr Somerville, Middlesex, and Dr Popjak of Shell, who had been an adviser, joined the Committee: Dr Woodroofe of Unilever, who had been a member of the Committee for some time, agreed to continue to serve. In 1968, when Dr Maurice Campbell and Dr Evan Bedford were due for retirement, they were made honorary members of the Committee in recognition of the great contributions they had made throughout the lifetime of the Committee.

New members appointed at this time were Professor K.A. Porter, St Mary's, Mr W.P. Cleland, Brompton, Dr Oliver, Edinburgh, Dr A.M. Johnson, Southampton and Professor H. Ford (later Sir Hugh), Professor of Applied Mechanics at the University of London.

In 1968 Dr F.H.K. Green, who had been scientific adviser to the Committee from its inception, retired because of ill health and in 1969 Dr Harley Williams retired on completion of his appointment as Administrative Medical Director, a title he had been given on his resignation as Secretary of the Foundation in 1966. As in all matters pertaining to the Foundation he had a fine record of service to the Committee and did much hard work in helping to formulate its policies and working methods. At his last appearance at the Committee he announced the appointment of Dr Margaret Haigh as Medical Administrator. He also paid generous tribute to Mrs Davis and Miss L.M. Glasse, two members of the secretariat of the Chest and Heart Association, who had serviced the Committee throughout. It was Dr Harley Williams who first suggested to the Committee in

1966 that it would be more appropriately renamed as the Research Committee. It last met as the Science Committee on 27 October 1969.

MEDICAL DEPARTMENT COMMITTEE STRUCTURE

At its meeting on 4 February 1970 the Council accepted the recommendations of the Finance and General Purposes Committee, which read as follows:

The Finance and General Purposes Committee, after much consideration, recommend the allocation of funds should, in future, be made in the following ways:
(a) In the first place, the Finance and General Purposes Committee will decide each year what funds are available for distribution to each of the following three committees during the following year:
    1 The Research Funds Committee.
    2 The Post Graduate Education Funds Committee.
    3 The Cardiac Care Committee.
(b) These Committees will have full discretion to distribute the funds provided by the Finance and General Purposes Committee subject to any restrictions imposed by the latter body.

The Medical Administrator will be the full-time secretary of all three committees and will be responsible for receiving, processing by consultation and submitting proposals to the committees.

Research Funds Committee

(a) There will be between eight and twelve members, of whom the Chairman will preferably be non-medical or at least non-cardiological. One other member of the Committee will be a layman. In appointing members, regard should be had to the desirability of representatives from Scotland and the Provinces.
(b) The Vice-Chairman, who will be medical or scientific, should be available in London. He will have important advisory functions in the detail of awards and should be readily accessible to advise the Medical Administrator.
(c) A Chairman will be elected every five years: after the fourth year two members will retire and two others will be elected in their place. Thereafter, every year, two members will retire in rotation and two others will be elected in their place. The Director General or his deputy will attend every meeting.

Postgraduate Education Funds Committee

This will consist of four members. The Chairman should be actively interested in postgraduate education, and, of the other three, two will be medical

The Medical Department

members and the other the Director General. Its purpose will be to encourage expert instruction in cardiovascular disease in peripheral centres.

Cardiac Care Committee

This will consist of a Chairman and two members of whom the Chairman and one other will be medical and the third the Director General. Its purpose will be to give aid in cardiac care, especially where needs are too urgent to be met by National Health Service resources.

Members of Committees

(a) The Finance and General Purposes Committee will be responsible for suggesting names to the Council to fill vacancies arising on the Committees.
(b) The Finance and General Purposes Committee recommend the following initial composition of the Committees:

1 Research Funds Committee
Chairman   Sir Ronald Bodley Scott

Vice-Chairman   Professor Shillingford

Members   Dr Bonham Carter
                    Professor Sir Ernst Chain
                    Mr W.P. Cleland
                    Mr B. Goodman
                    Professor Harris
                    Professor Lawrie
                    Professor Linden
                    Professor Porter
                    . . . .
                    . . . .

2 Postgraduate Education Funds Committee
Chairman   Professor Shillingford

Members   Dr A.M. Johnson
                    Professor Goodwin
                    Dr Aubrey Leatham
                    . . . .
                    Director General

3 Cardiac Care Committee
Chairman   Dr W. Somerville

Members   . . . .
                    Director General

The existing Science Committee, to be renamed the Scientific Advisory Committee, will have the same membership and rules as to retirement and election as at present. Professor Arnott has agreed to be this Committee's Chairman. It will act as an advisory body to the Research Funds Committee. It will meet once a year to receive reports from the Research Funds Committee and to discuss matters of interest. The Chairman will always be a medical member.

It is further recommended that the above changes should take effect as early as possible.

PERSONNEL

Professor (later Sir) Melville Arnott remained Chairman of the Scientific Advisory Committee during the two years of its existence, until it was disbanded late in 1972 because it was found to be superfluous to the satisfactory working of the other committees.

Sir Ronald Bodley Scott, who had been Chairman of the Science Committee, continued as Chairman of the Research Funds Committee until 1975 when he became Chairman of Council. Professor Shillingford remained Vice-Chairman of the Research Funds Committee until he was succeeded in 1976 by Professor Linden, on becoming Vice-Chairman of Council. Professor Shillingford also remained Chairman of the Postgraduate Education Funds Committee until 1976 when he was succeeded by Dr Elliott Shinebourne.

Sir Cyril Clarke, lately President of the Royal College of Physicians, took over the chairmanship of the Research Funds Committee from Sir Ronald Bodley Scott in October 1975, and followed Sir Ronald as Chairman of Council in 1982; his position as Chairman of the Research Funds Committee was taken by Professor Alastair Dudgeon in 1982, and he, in turn, was succeeded by Sir Philip Randle in 1987.

Professor Desmond Julian became Vice-Chairman of the Research Funds Committee in succession to Professor Linden in 1983 and he was succeeded by Professor J.L. Reid in 1987.

Dr Margaret Haigh became Medical Administrator to the Foundation on the retirement of Dr Harley Williams in 1969, and was succeeded, on her resignation towards the end of 1972, by Dr Morris Butler. His first attendance at the Research Funds Committee was in October 1972 and his last in June 1983. At the time of his appointment he was Consultant Physician to the British United Provident

Association and medical adviser to a number of industrial concerns and insurance companies. His appointment to the Foundation was, at first, on a part-time basis for three mornings a week. In summarizing his work he said: 'My task really was spending the money and seeing that it went in the right direction. We were spending at that time something like 90% of available income on research. The three main committees made the decisions.' As Medical Administrator Dr Butler was the secretary of all three. He retired in 1983 because of ill health and was assisted during his last 18 months with the Foundation by Professor Shillingford, who became part-time Medical Director in 1981; his initial appointment was for two years. In the succeeding six years, however, this appointment took an ever-increasing amount of his time until, at his retirement in 1987, he was working for the Foundation virtually full-time.

PROFESSOR SHILLINGFORD

Professor Shillingford gave over 23 years' continuous service in various capacities as a member of the Foundation's committees, and he did more than anyone else to shape its medical policies, expand its influence in national and international medical cardiological circles, and to guard its integrity as a source of unbiased information concerning current knowledge of proven and unproven risk factors of importance in heart disease.

He was the guide and counsellor of Brigadier Cardiff and Brigadier Thursby Pelham, during their periods of office as Directors General, on an infinite variety of medical questions encountered in day-to-day business, and his advice greatly influenced the Council in its policy decisions on all matters relating to the funding of research and its ancillary activities in the fields of education and cardiac care. Dr Butler put it very simply: 'On the medical side Jack Shillingford has been the "king-pin" for the Foundation.'

It is impossible to overstate his contribution to the success of the Foundation as the heart research charity of the United Kingdom. He strove ceaselessly to increase the scope of the research funded by it, and championed the support of many new developments hitherto untried in the field of cardiology including, for instance, magnetic resonance and genetic engineering; at the same time he resisted, with passionate conviction, the many pressures put on the Foundation to climb on popular bandwagons of the day. In this way he saved it the embarrassment of being aboard several whose bands finished in discord as they were overtaken by bigger newer models. This farsighted policy redounded greatly, in the fullness of time, to the credit of the Foundation, and established it as a world leader in cardiovascular research. On such occasions he justifiably enjoyed the rewards of his prudence which had sometimes cost him dear in firmness of resolve.

By the time Professor Shillingford was appointed in 1981 as part-time Director the Medical Department was in difficulties because of the enormous increase in the volume of work. Processing the applications for grants was very time-consuming, as were also correspondence with referees and notification of the results to applicants. Besides these commitments the Department had to investigate applications from universities for the establishment of professorial chairs, and from research workers for Fellowships, in addition to running the postgraduate education programme of lectures, symposia and publications, and implementing the awards recommended by the Cardiac Care Committee.

The situation was made worse by Dr Butler's illness in spite of the hard work of his competent secretary, Shirley Jacobs, and the assistance of Brenda Mole. It gave Professor Shillingford much anxiety as he readily admits. Clearly the staff was too small to cope with so many demands. He solved the problem by splitting the administration into three sections and appointing an Administrator to each.

In 1982 Cary Spink was appointed Administrator to the Education Funds Committee and Bob Stiller Administrator and Buyer to the Cardiac Care Committee; and in 1983 Valerie Mason was appointed as Administrator to the Research Funds Committee, the Chairs and Research Groups Committee and the Fellowships Committee. All three appointments were highly successful and gave the Medical Department the personnel with which to meet the challenges which were already evident and which were, so soon, to become much bigger still. All three did wonderful jobs for the Foundation and an appreciation of their individual contributions is to be found in the appropriate sections of this chapter.

The Foundation was fortunate that Professor Desmond Julian was available in 1987 to succeed Professor Shillingford as Medical

The Medical Department

Figure 2.5 *Medical Directors of the Foundation: (a) Professor Jack Shillingford; (b) Professor Desmond Julian.*

Director. He knew the organization well, having been a member of Council as well as Vice-Chairman of the Research Funds Committee and the holder of the BHF Professorial Chair in Newcastle. He was also, at the time, President of the British Cardiac Society (Figure 25).

He is held in universally high regard in cardiovascular circles nationally and internationally, and is a popular figure with colleagues, both lay and medical, being blessed with a ready sense of humour. He has excellent rapport with the media, and much enjoys radio and television work, at which he excels.

He brought a new approach to several matters of medical policy. These included changes of emphasis to encourage greater involvement in public education, the widening of the scope of funded research to include clinical trials and their scientific evaluation, and an attempt to set up a programme to determine if and how rehabilitation could best help after a heart attack.

SCIENTIFIC ADVISORY COMMITTEE

From the records it seems that the Scientific Advisory Committee met three times: on 15 July 1970, 21 June 1971 and 12 July 1972. Being composed of members of the pre-existing Science Committee it was well-versed in the affairs of the Foundation, particularly in relation to the funding of research.

At its first meeting it defined the qualifications necessary for applying for a research grant and detailed the regulations governing the award of a grant. It also summarized the current position by stating that, since the first grants were awarded in October 1963, 250 grants had been made, totalling nearly £2,000,000 up to 1970.

At its second meeting on 21 June 1971 it suggested to the Research Funds Committee that there might be a need for a research post between senior fellows and university chair-holders at consultant level and was the first to suggest the title 'personal chair'; it recommended inserting into the Grant Regulations the wording: 'The Foundation will be able to endow University or Personal Chairs, Readers, or Senior Fellows in Cardiology, Cardiovascular Disease or Cardiovascular Surgery.'

It also suggested to the Research Funds Committee that it should advise the Council against financial support of the College of Physicians' request for money for their anti-smoking campaign (ASH), which was to be under the auspices of Lord Rosenheim, the President of the College.

The Committee also advised the Research Funds Committee in favour of setting aside £2,000 per annum to satisfy requests for the funding of travel by grant-holders.

At the last meeting the Committee debated the issue of 'bricks and mortar' at length and advised the Research Funds Committee against spending money on setting up an institute. The Committee also proposed to the Research Funds Committee the award of junior research Fellowships for a trial period of five years in epidemiology, physiology, paediatric cardiology, biochemistry and cardiovascular disease. They were to be held for one year, renewable for a second.

THE RESEARCH FUNDS COMMITTEE

The main function of the Research Funds Committee is, and always has been, the assessment of applications for research grants and making awards within the budget allocated to it by the Council.

In the early days, however, it was the authority through which all medical matters were channelled, including the recommendations of the Postgraduate Education Funds Committee and the Cardiac Care Committee.

The need for decisions about proposals put to it for the endowment of professorial chairs soon became urgent and the Committee responded by setting up a subcommittee to explore these requests and report back. This system continued for eight years until, in 1978, the Chairs Committee was formally established. Within a short time its title was enlarged to Chairs and Research Groups Committee, and its terms of reference altered to include the funding of groups, mostly for a five-year period, to keep a team together on a special project. The first group award was made in 1980.

Ever since the earliest days the Foundation has been receptive to suggestions that it should support Fellowships to encourage young doctors to follow careers in research, and had instigated British/American Exchange Fellowships by the mid-sixties.

It is not clear from the records whether recommendations for Fellowships were handled, in the early days, primarily by the Postgraduate Education Funds Committee as part of postgraduate medical education in cardiology, or whether they were handled directly by the Research Funds Committee. On the evidence the former seems the more likely but the recommendations certainly also came before the Research Funds Commitee. It was not, however, until 1983 that the award of Fellowships at varying grades of seniority became such an important part of the Foundation's strategy in fostering research that a separate Fellowships Committee was created.

In a very short while the 8–12 members of the Research Funds Committee, as laid down by the Council recommendations in 1970, were increased to the present number of 18 in order to cover a wider spectrum of research specialities.

The Committee meets quarterly in all-day session, all members having had all the papers circulated to them some days in advance. A member of the Committee who is an expert in the discipline of the application under consideration is asked, beforehand, to act as the internal referee and speaks first; then all Committee members who wish add their views, after which the Vice-Chairman reads the report of an external referee. The external referee to whom the application was sent for opinion has no communication with any member of the Committee before the meeting, including the internal referee.

After further discussion the application is graded and thus comes into open competition with all the others before the Committee. It has always been the policy of the Foundation to judge every application entirely, and only, on its scientific merit without reference to the existing level of support of the particular subject by the Foundation.

It can happen that as a result of debate the Committee feels that an adjustment of the request is desirable, either in the level of technical help or equipment needed, or in the proposed length of time the project needs. In such cases an award with these amendments can be offered.

In other cases it is felt that further information is needed before a decision is made, and the usual way of obtaining this is by a site visit, either by two members of the Committee, or by one member with an expert from outside the Committee with special knowledge of the problem. When applications are deferred for this purpose they come up for reconsideration at the next meeting.

When deferment is for some relatively small query which needs to be answered before approval is given, the Committee allows settlement of the matter by Chairman's action to avoid unnecessary delay.

Periodically, over the years, the Committee has noted damaging inexperience in the presentation of an application by some young applicants and has exhorted those in senior teaching posts to guide them, and where appropriate to revise what they have written; similarly the Committee has exhorted the applicants to seek advice. It has also published detailed guidelines for applicants on how best to prepare a protocol in the booklet containing the Grant Regulations (see p. 150).

There have been a number of attempts to assess the quality of the research work the Foundation has funded. It is clearly difficult, if not impossible, to assess value for money in research, but it is equally clearly desirable that the public, which has given the money, is assured that all possible steps are taken. To this end, in the early days, Dr Haigh asked all grant-holders to write two short annual summaries of their progress; one, in scientific terms, was for information to colleagues, and not for publication, whilst the other, in lay terms, was for publication; for a time some of the information obtained in this way was made available as a booklet with the Annual Report and was also included in the medical news-sheet distributed with the *Bulletin*.

Another assessment was obtained by asking BHF professors to visit grant-holders in their neighbourhood, towards the end of the project, to assess the results and help the research worker to prepare a paper for publication. Later still, in response to the need of the Appeal Department and the Regional Directors for stories about the results of funded research, the Medical Spokesman obtained a good response to a request for information, which led to increased press and media coverage.

Overall the quality of the project applications has been high, and whenever disquiet has been expressed as to quality or quantity, or both, by the Research Funds Committee the Finance and General Purposes Committee has responded by backing generously any measure suggested by the Committee to improve the situation (Figures 26 and 27).

Of the many matters which occupied the Research Funds Committee other than the assessment of applications for grants, the policy of promotion of professorial chairs by the Foundation, as centres of excellence and magnets to attract young doctors into cardiovascular research, was the most important.

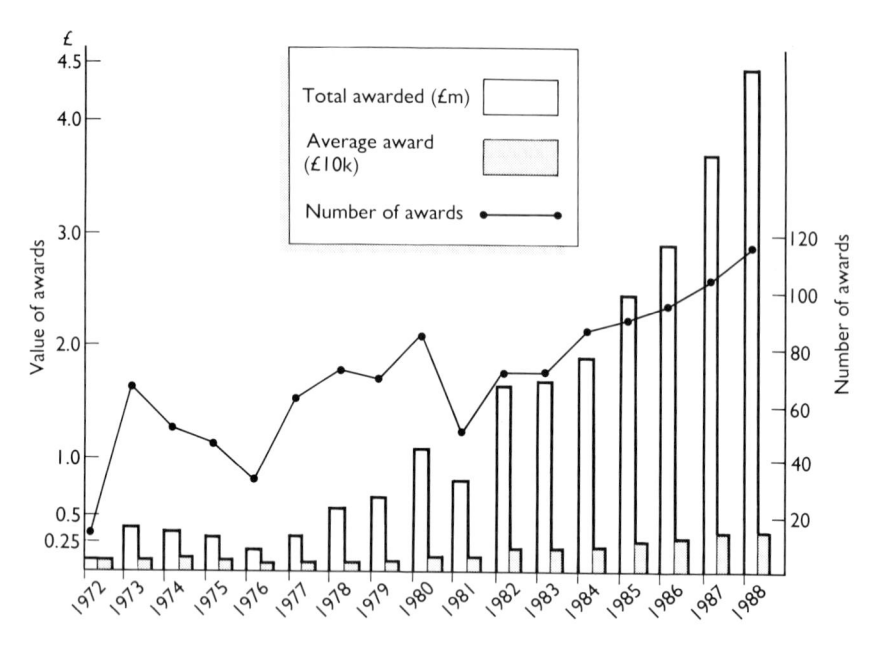

Figure 26 *Analysis of expenditure on research grants 1972–88.*

Through the subcommittee which it set up the Research Funds Committee received a letter from Professor Beeson in Oxford at its first meeting in March 1970 seeking the creation of a chair. This was followed by correspondence and meetings with Professors Doll and Beeson and resulted in the Field Marshal Earl Alexander Professorship of Cardiovascular Medicine, created in 1973 with Peter Sleight as Professor.

In June 1971 the Committee recommended to the Finance and General Purposes Committee an increase of £100,000 in the endowment of the Simon Marks Chair at the Cardiothoracic Institute. This was agreed and the thanks of Sir Douglas Logan, the Principal of the University of London, are recorded in the minutes of the meeting of the Committee in December.

In June 1971 Dr Bonham Carter, a member of the Committee, proposed the creation of a Chair of Paediatric Cardiology at the Hospital for Sick Children, Great Ormond Street. This ultimately resulted in the establishment of the Vandervell Chair of Paediatric Cardiology in 1975. The Vandervell Trust, of which Sir Rudolph de Trafford, the Foundation's Treasurer, was a Trustee, offered £100,000,

The Medical Department

Speciality	1979	1980	1981	1982	1983	1984	1985	Total (7 years)	%
Biochemistry	138,400 (15)	176,500 (9)	251,400 (13)	293,000 (11)	414,400 (12)	284,800 (9)	623,400 (21)	2,181,900 (90)	16.9
Clinical cardiology and diagnosis	176,000 (5)	78,200 (5)	156,400 (7)	214,100 (10)	166,400 (9)	320,000 (11)	210,300 (6)	1,321,400 (53)	10.2
Epidemiology	103,800 (6)	356,400 (9)	30,400 (1)	92,500 (4)	69,300 (2)	—	114,800 (4)	767,200 (26)	5.9
Genetics	—	—	145,200 (2)	36,800 (2)	79,400 (2)	97,600 (2)	42,300 (1)	401,300 (9)	3.1
Hypertension	27,400 (3)	53,900 (4)	101,100 (9)	105,700 (6)	81,500 (5)	136,100 (8)	395,500 (13)	901,200 (38)	7.0
Immunology	45,900 (2)	29,500 (3)	39,300 (3)	184,100 (6)	5,200 (1)	169,400 (6)	155,400 (5)	628,800 (26)	4.8
Paediatric cardiology	25,400 (3)	75,500 (3)	89,000 (5)	15,300 (1)	119,000 (4)	34,300 (1)	119,600 (3)	478,100 (20)	3.7
Pathology	118,200 (9)	11,300 (1)	61,200 (4)	18,700 (1)	158,600 (5)	199,300 (8)	40,400 (1)	607,700 (29)	4.7
Physiology, electro-physiology and anatomy	49,000 (6)	125,800 (9)	217,300 (12)	254,800 (10)	149,700 (7)	164,100 (6)	418,000 (13)	1,378,700 (63)	10.7
Surgery	29,800 (5)	75,700 (4)	152,900 (5)	59,100 (3)	67,900 (4)	183,000 (8)	165,900 (7)	734,300 (34)	5.7
Treatment and pharmacology	35,300 (2)	91,300 (10)	62,800 (4)	90,800 (7)	416,200 (13)	483,300 (18)	196,200 (6)	1,375,900 (60)	10.6
Techniques and instrumentation	168,900 (12)	8,300 (2)	90,100 (5)	52,500 (2)	117,400 (5)	41,700 (2)	—	478,900 (28)	3.7
Thrombosis and atherosclerosis	106,300 (10)	117,300 (7)	347,000 (17)	143,200 (8)	349,000 (15)	261,800 (12)	356,700 (14)	1,681,300 (83)	13.0
Total	1,024,400 (78)	1,209,700 (66)	1,734,100 (87)	1,560,600 (71)	2,194,000 (84)	2,375,400 (91)	2,841,500 (94)	12,939,700 (571)	100.0

Figure 27 Analysis of distribution of funds on research grants 1979–85.

to which the Foundation added £150,000. Fergus Macartney was appointed Professor.

At the meeting in December 1971 there was a long discussion about professorial chairs and Peter Harris, the Simon Marks Professor, suggested the Committee give serious thought to the fields of interest they should support, and advocated physiology and epidemiology, with which Professor Shillingford agreed. At the same meeting Donald Ross and William Cleland put forward, for the first time, the suggestion that a Chair of Cardiac Surgery should be established at the Brompton Hospital: it was subsequently made known that an anonymous donor (later revealed as the Prudential Assurance Company) had promised £100,000 in support.

In October 1972 the subcommittee reported protracted negotiations with the Postgraduate Hospital, Hammersmith, which resulted in the Foundation taking over Professor Shillingford's personal chair, currently funded by the University of London and the Medical Research Council, and creating the Sir John McMichael Chair in 1977, endowed in perpetuity in the sum of £250,000, with Jack Shillingford as Professor until his retirement in 1979. He was succeeded by the current holder, Atillio Maseri.

Also in 1972 discussions were started with the University of Edinburgh. These took several years because the University, at first, was unable to provide the necessary accommodation. These difficulties were finally overcome and the Duke of Edinburgh Chair of Cardiology was inaugurated on 10 November 1978 when Sir Ronald Bodley Scott, the Chairman of Council, presented a cheque for £350,000 to the Duke of Edinburgh. Professor Michael Oliver, who had already been awarded a personal chair by the University, was appointed British Heart Foundation Professor.

Two other developments in 1972 were the proposal by Professor Goodwin for a Chair of Cardiology at St George's Hospital and a recommendation for additional funding of the chair in Birmingham. Professor Goodwin's proposal was rejected because the buildings in Tooting, whither the hospital had recently been transferred, were not yet ready; in the event it took 15 years before his proposal was implemented. At Birmingham, where a chair had been inaugurated in 1971 with an anonymous donation of £100,000, the Foundation agreed to supplement this with £15,000 per annum for ten years provided the Birmingham University assumed responsibility for its continuation thereafter; subsequently, however, in 1980, the Foundation provided £200,000 for the chair's continuation. In 1971 Sir Melville Arnott was appointed to the professorship, and on his retirement in 1974, he was succeeded by Professor W.A. Littler. In 1986 the Foundation agreed to the University's request that the chair should be known as the Sir Melville Arnott Chair.

The following year, 1973, saw meetings with the University of Leeds which resulted in the same year in the creation of the Chair of Cardiovascular Studies under Professor Linden; he was succeeded in 1986 by Professor Stephen Ball, who had previously been a British Heart Foundation Senior Research Fellow.

The same year saw the development of the Foundation's presence in the academic life of the University of Glasgow with the inauguration of the Walton Chair of Medical Cardiology, followed the next year, 1974, by the British Heart Foundation Chair in Cardiac Surgery supported by the Isadore and David Walton Charitable Trust. Mr Isadore Walton had already financed a Personal Chair in Cardiology which was held by Professor Lawrie. This was endowed in perpetuity by contributions of £35,000 each by Mr Walton and the Foundation. When Professor Lawrie retired in 1985 he was succeeded by Professor Cobbe.

The Chair in Cardiac Surgery at the Glasgow Royal infirmary was created by a gift of £100,000 by Mr Walton and of £75,000 by the Foundation. Its first occupant was Philip Caves, who had held a British/American Exchange Fellowship and was working at the Brompton Hospital when he was appointed. Tragically he died of a heart attack in 1978, at the age of 38, when playing squash. He was succeeded by Professor David Wheatley.

In 1974 negotiations were concluded with the University of Newcastle to establish a British Heart Foundation Chair of Cardiology with an initial gift by the Foundation of £120,000; this was followed by £40,000 from Mr Bell towards building costs and by £100,000 from the Foundation to establish a senior lectureship. Both were treated as part of the endowment. Professor Desmond Julian, who is now the Medical Director of the Foundation, was the first incumbent, and he was followed in 1986, upon retirement, by Professor Ronnie Campbell.

Thus the Research Funds Committee was wholly responsible for the medical decisions involving the creation by the Council of nine

	Research* (£)	Education (£)	Cardiac care (£)	Total (£)
1986	9,003,000	339,000	1,668,000	11,010,000
1985	8,592,000	141,000	1,605,000	10,338,000
1984	6,213,000	263,000	1,203,000	7,679,000
1983	5,513,000	138,000	859,000	7,210,000
1982	5,095,000	73,000	479,000	5,647,000

Notes: * Including provision for project grants, Chairs, research groups and fellowships

Figure 28 *Analysis of expenditure 1982–86.*

professorial chairs, before a separate Chairs Committee was formed in 1978.

During this time it had also been responsible for recommending to the Finance and General Purposes Committee the level of funding needed for maintenance. In 1976 an annual increment of £8,000 for the next three years was agreed. In a review of policy put to the Council in July 1977, however, it was recommended that:

Between 1977/78 and 1980/81 the ten university Chairs to which the Foundation is committed, should be funded with a further £100,000 each in order to make them self-supporting. This would be achieved by building up a total fund of £1,000,000, which would be retained and invested by the Foundation. The income from this fund would be distributed to Chairs, to be spent by them at their discretion; and as Chairs were funded in this way, the existing annual contribution of £8,000 would be discontinued.

It should be emphasised that this additional funding is regarded as a long-term supplement to Chairs. The Foundation will, however, retain the right, at its sole discretion, to cease this supplement in any particular case if it feels that the Chair is not adequately performing the function for which it was originally set up.

The tenth Chair which the Foundation is committed to establish by 1980, should be established in 1979/80 and funded with a further £100,000 to bring it into line with the other nine Chairs.

The same document also states: 'Some provision should now be made for general education in addition to postgraduate education.'

The resources and proposed distribution, on the expectation that £1,000,000 would be available, are listed as follows:

'Research Funds Committee   50%
Chairs   26%
Fellowships   8%

The Medical Department

'(Postgraduate Education Funds Committee 2%, General Education 1%, Cardiac Care Committee 8%, Reserve 5%)' (Figure 28).

In January 1978 the Treasurer reported to the Finance and General Purposes Committee that the value of the Chairs Maintenance Fund was £924,000 (Figure 29).

In 1977, at the request of the Finance and General Purposes Committee, Professors Shillingford and Linden drew up proposals for the optimum staffing of university chairs, which they recommended should be a professor, senior lecturer, lecturer, technician and secretary. The Research Funds Committee endorsed these proposals.

In September 1978 the Finance and General Purposes Committee accepted the recommendation of the Research Funds Committee that £350,000 should be considered the likely requirement to endow a new chair in perpetuity, and that £100,000 should be allocated to each chair for the appointment of a senior lecturer. Similarly it was agreed that up to a total of £100,000 per annum was likely to be needed for equipment, and that this sum should be set aside for this purpose.

As a background to these sizeable commitments it is necessary

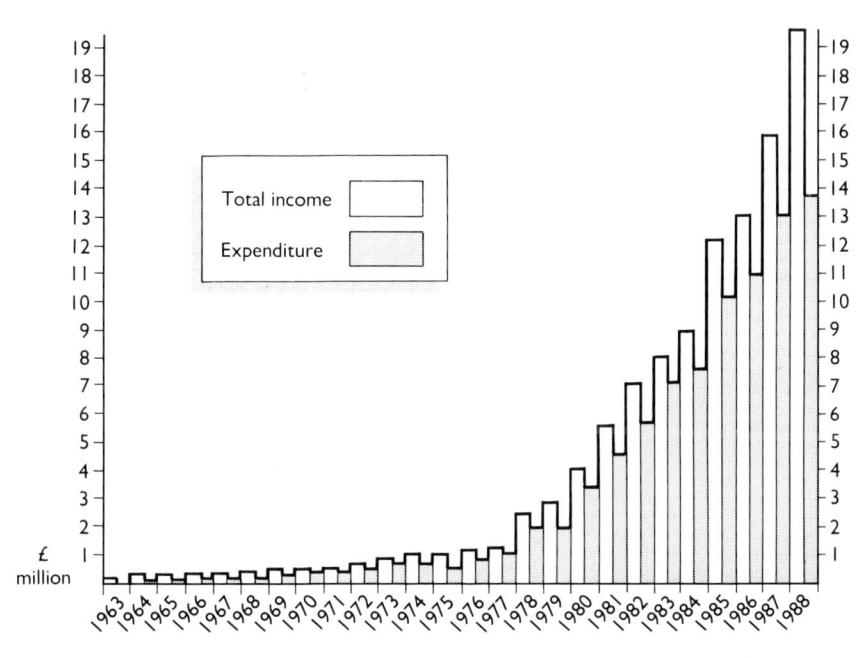

Figure 29 Total income, and expenditure on research, chairs and education 1963–88.

to remember that the Foundation, and consequently the Research Funds Committee, was always at the mercy of the vagaries of national financial well-being, and had to contend with several crises which threatened its ability not only to expand, but also to meet its existing commitments. In one such crisis a special meeting of the Research Funds Committee was called on 20 January 1975 'to discuss the situation which had developed as the result of inflation'.

The meeting decided that the chairs must have the top priority and that the Foundation should try to satisfy the needs of existing chairs at the temporary sacrifice of the expansion programme. It also decided that the continuation of the award of senior and junior research Fellowships to suitable applicants was a high priority.

After satisfying these two prime needs it was generally agreed that worthy applications for project grants should continue to be met as fully as the budget allowed. It was felt that the use of the Foundation's money for this purpose had been right and the research profitable, but concern was expressed that some grant-holders might not be making sufficiently good use of the opportunities created for them by the Foundation to justify continued support. The difficulty of assessing this was fully appreciated, and it was agreed that the best solution was a site visit in all doubtful cases, after which the Committee could curtail or withdraw support as appropriate.

The meeting resisted renewed requests from unsuccessful applicants for grants to be told the reason for failure, except when it was because the Committee felt that application elsewhere was more appropriate.

This meeting also discussed at length the problems of attracting suitable people into the research structure and threw up a number of suggestions to improve the situation, amongst which was the suggestion by Professor Shillingford to establish senior lectureships at BHF professorial centres.

CHAIRS AND RESEARCH GROUPS COMMITTEE

Personnel

A Chairs Committee was created in 1978 and met first on 8 March. The full membership consisted of Sir Ronald Bodley Scott, Chairman of Council, Sir Cyril Clarke, Chairman of the Research Funds Com-

The Medical Department

mittee, Brigadier Cardiff, Chairman of the Finance and General Purposes Committee, Brigadier Thursby Pelham, the Director General, Professor Shillingford, and Dr Butler, the Medical Administrator. In 1980 the Committee was joined by Sir Richard Bayliss.

The minutes of the meeting on 15 April 1981 include the words 'Research Groups' in the name of the Committee for the first time. At its meeting in November it was agreed to invite Professor T.J. Peters of Hammersmith Hospital to join the Committee and in September 1982 Professor J.R.A. Mitchell of Nottingham University. Mrs Grainge, as Secretary of the Foundation, joined the Committee in June 1982, as did Professor Dudgeon on becoming Chairman of the Research Funds Committee. Shirley Jacobs was the minutes secretary until the arrival of Valerie Mason as Administrator in 1983.

In September 1985 the Committee welcomed Professor Julian as Medical Director Designate; his appointment as Medical Director started in April 1987.

In February 1987 Professor C.J. Dickinson, St Bartholomew's Hospital, was welcomed to the Committee upon the retirement of Professor T.J. Peters following his appointment as Regius Professor of Physic at Cambridge University. Also in 1987 Professor C.R.W. Edwards, Edinburgh University, replaced Professor Mitchell on completion of his term of service. At the same time Sir Raymond Hoffenberg, the new Chairman of Council, replaced Sir Cyril Clarke on his retirement, and Sir Philip Randle, the new Chairman of the Research Funds Committee, joined the Committee, whilst Professor Dudgeon agreed to serve for a further year.

In 1985 Valerie Mason tabled a paper on current membership and terms of service of the Committee as a result of which it was decided that the Vice-Chairman of Council should be invited to attend meetings. But with the passage of time it became clear that the ever-increasing workload could not be carried by such a small committee, all of whose members had other important commitments. In 1987, therefore, again at the instigation of Valerie Mason, the Committee was reconstituted and enlarged, and its duties defined.

Its Standing Orders and composition read as follows:

Reconstitution of the Chairs and Research Groups Committee, 31/1/87.
1 The composition and function of the Chairs and Research Groups Committee is defined in the attached document.

2 Over the last year it has failed to achieve a quorum on two of the four occasions on which it was intended to meet.

3 The Council and F&GPC have approved the concept of a periodical formal review of research supported by the BHF and have agreed that this should be a function of the reconstituted Chairs and Research Groups Committee.

4 The Council and F&GPC have approved the concept that there should be support for research resources (e.g. data-banks) and co-ordinated research projects (e.g. the task force on Blood/Arterial Wall Interface), and that they should be under the aegis of the reconstituted Committee.

5 The Council and F&GPC have approved that a Clinical Trials organisation should be set up under the aegis of the Committee.

6 It may also be considered appropriate to refer some large applications sent to the Research Funds Committee to the reconstituted Committee.

7 The Committee at present appears too small and should be enlarged by adding a basic scientist, the Chairman of the Fellowships Committee and (if there is one) the Chairman of the Clinical Trials Working Group.

8 A suitable title, which would not be too similar to that of other committees, needs to be chosen. Suggestions include Research Board and Research Advisory Committee.

The Constitution of the Committee

Chairman	Chairman of Council
Members	Vice-Chairman of Council
	Chairman of F&GPC
	Chairman of Research Funds Committee
	2 Professors of General Medicine, one with an interest in cardiovascular disease
	1 Consultant Cardiologist (Term of service 5 years)
	Director General
	Consultant Medical Director (*ex officio*)
	Medical Public Relation Spokesman (Observer)
Meetings	3-monthly

The Committee is responsible for all recommendations relating to the establishment and maintenance of Chairs and Research Groups (excluding specific research projects considered by the Research Funds Committee). It can co-opt members for specialist advice.

The Committee is responsible to the Finance and General Purposes Committee. Agenda to be sent out 2 weeks before the meeting.

Administration of this Committee is the responsibility of the Research Funds Organiser.

The Committee met for the first time on 1 September 1987 with its membership enlarged from six to nine members. Sir John Badenoch attended as Chairman of the Fellowships Committee, Sir Stanley Peart as Chairman of the Clinical Trials Working Party, Professor K.M. Spyer as the new scientist member, Professor Edwards replacing Professor Mitchell, Dr D.J. Coltart replacing Dr Emanuel as cardiologist and Mr Nigel Robson as Chairman of the Finance and General Purposes Committee.

Since no generally acceptable new name had been put forward it was decided to retain the old name *sine die*.

Professorial chairs (personal and endowed)

It fell to the Chairs Committee to finalize the negotiations started by the Research Funds Committee to create the first BHF personal chair, as opposed to endowed chairs which had been established hitherto. A personal chair is a career post for an individual with exceptional talents and ceases with the retirement or death of the holder. The Foundation alone has the power to renew it on the same site or elsewhere, and in the same or another discipline as it chooses. In contrast, an appointment to a chair endowed in perpetuity is made by a university appointment committee, which could, possibly, choose someone other than the Foundation's first choice; in practice, however, the likelihood of a serious problem arising is small. Perhaps more importantly, the initial outlay for the Foundation is smaller for a personal chair than for an endowed chair, although the subsequent costs of maintenance are very similar.

In 1980 a personal chair was awarded to Dr Robert Anderson at the Cardiothoracic Institute, where he was already a Reader funded by the University of London, to be known as the 'Joseph Levy Chair of Paediatric Cardiac Morphology supported by the British Heart Foundation'. The Joseph Levy Foundation put up £150,000, of which the Foundation provided £50,000 repayable over ten years.

In 1981 the Foundation was approached by the Medical Research Council for assistance in the funding of a Personal Chair in Cardiovascular Pathology at St George's Hospital Medical School Department of Histopathology, for Dr Michael Davies, when it was agreed to share the cost of £446,000 equally.

The Bodley Scott Chair of Cardiovascular Medicine at St Bartholomew's Hospital was awarded to Dr John Camm in 1983, and inaugurated at a ceremony at the hospital on 26 September during the Foundation's 'Heart Week' for fund-raising. The initial cost for the first year was £54,000 and the current cost is £70,000 per annum. The initial cost of all subsequent personal chairs was £60,000 for the first year, and all now cost the same annual amount of £70,000.

In 1984 a personal chair was awarded to Dr Denis Noble at Oxford to be known as the 'Burdon-Sanderson Chair of Cardiovascular Physiology', and Dr Trevor Powell was appointed as Reader to work with him; this is known as the 'Winston Readership', having been funded by a legacy of £300,000 from the estate of the late Mr Philip Winston.

Also in 1984 the Foundation awarded a personal chair to Dr George Radda, to be held at the Clinical Magnetic Resonance Laboratory at the University of Oxford and known as the 'Chair of Molecular Cardiology'. The following year (1985) saw the award of a Personal Chair of Cardiovascular Immunology to Professor C.J.F. Spry, tenable at St George's Hospital Medical School.

At the same time the establishment of endowed chairs was continued with the creation of the Sir Thomas Lewis Chair of Cardiology at the University of Wales College of Medicine at Cardiff in 1980. A cheque for £300,000 was handed to the University at an inaugural ceremony on 24 November, when Professor Andrew Henderson was appointed to the chair.

An Endowed Chair in Cardiothoracic Surgery was inaugurated on 1 August 1983 at the Royal Postgraduate Hospital, Hammersmith, at a cost of £500,000; Professor Kenneth Taylor, who had been a BHF Senior Research Fellow, was appointed to the chair.

Negotiations had been in progress for some years about the establishment of an endowed chair at St George's Hospital, where problems concerning space, facilities and clinical workload had had to be overcome. These were successfully resolved and the chair was established in 1986 at an inauguration ceremony on 17 June. With the agreement of the Prudential Assurance Company the money originally provided by the Prudential to establish a Chair of Cardiac Surgery at the Brompton Hospital, but which had not proved possible, was used to finance the 'Prudential Chair of Cardiology' at St George's Hospital instead, and a cheque for £500,000 was handed to the University of London. Professor Camm moved from his personal chair at St Bartholomew's Hospital to accept the appointment, and the Bodley Scott award to St Bartholomew's Hospital was continued as a senior lectureship, to which Dr A.W. Nathan was appointed.

The senior lectureship at St George's Hospital was funded with a legacy of £300,000 from the estate of the late Mr A.E. Sugden and bears his name.

The most recent professorial appointment was to Professor Magdi Yacoub, who became Professor of Cardiac Surgery at the Brompton Hospital in 1986. The inaugural ceremony, at which a sum of £500,000 was presented by the Foundation, took place on 2 September 1986.

Both the Chairs and Research Group Committee, and the Research Funds Committee before it, have spent many hours deliberating the financial needs of the professorial chairs. Rising prices and salaries caused by inflation, and the nation-wide demand for ever higher standards of living as the norm, have led to the insidious and continuing devaluation of the pound. In consequence the money accepted by the universities in good faith to endow a chair in perpetuity has proved inadequate and all have needed substantial further support. In 1965 the 'Simon Marks Chair' was created with a gift by the Foundation of £40,000 spread over eight years at £5,000 per annum. In 1986 the inauguration of the chair at St George's Hospital needed an initial gift of £500,000.

Enormous sums are also needed for equipment to set up new chairs, and to meet the research requirements of new professors on their appointment to existing chairs upon the retirement of their predecessors. In addition all chair-holders, endowed and personal, receive an equipment grant of £13,000 per annum as well as a discretionary fund of £27,000 per annum for the running costs of their departments; both are guaranteed for five years.

Endowed chairs also have a senior lecturer, supported by the Foundation, if they have a need for them.

Support of the 20 professorial chairs is a gigantic commitment by the Foundation and it is achieved by the income from a Chairs Maintenance Fund which is currently valued at over £20,000,000. The average cost of maintenance of each chair is £70,000 per annum. The Foundation is very conscious of its responsibility to its supporters to be sure that it and they are getting value for money, and one of the important ways by which this is evaluated is by regular site visits to all its professorial establishments by a team consisting of the Medical Director, the Chairman of the Chairs and Research Groups Committee, the Director General, an overseas assessor, a UK assessor and a Committee member, together with the Research

Funds Administrator. The UK assessor is sometimes a Committee member. The overseas assessor is a distinguished scientist from Europe or America.

Until 1985 visits were made every two years but since then at intervals of three to five years. This change was partly to save expense but principally because it was agreed that longer intervals would be more productive in judging the progress of research activities. The overseas assessor stays in Britain for a week and is invited to lecture at BHF units. He is given a form on which to report on site visits on research, teaching, patient care and administration, besides making his personal summary on the performance of the unit. The home team prepare similar reports; criticisms, suggestions and praise are passed on to the professor by the Committee after studying all the reports. The visit is aimed to be a detailed survey of the work of all the staff under the professor's direction.

Recently Professor Julian, the Medical Director, has asked for two annual summaries of work from all units; one in technical terms for the benefit of other research workers in the same field and the other in lay terms for printing and circulation to supporters with the Annual Report. This is, in fact, almost identical to the scheme started in 1970 by Dr Margaret Haigh when she was Medical Administrator, but which did not survive long after her departure.

Research groups

A research group is a team dedicated to researching a special subject of current topicality in cardiovascular research, and funding is aimed to keep the group together for a long enough period to produce results; most groups are funded for five years with a critical review after three. Like professorial centres research groups receive site visits from a team organized by head office.

At its meeting in March 1983 the Chairs and Research Groups Committee issued a directive to research workers about the composition of research groups, stating that in addition to the head of the group the staff nucleus was to be a part-time secretary, a senior technician and a junior laboratory attendant where necessary.

The cost of a research group varies, but averages between £300,000 and £400,000 over five years. With an increasing number of applications for large amounts for project grants to the Research Funds

Committee there is some potential overlap between the responsibilities for funding between it and the Chairs and Research Groups Committee. To date there has been a rough, but undefined, working rule that the Research Funds Committee limits a single award to £100,000, although this has been exceeded occasionally. The Research Funds Committee, however, considers all applications for amounts of this size, and, if they are worthy of support, either accepts them or advises the applicants to make a fresh submission to the Chairs and Research Groups Committee if this is more appropriate.

The first research group was set up in 1980 at the Papworth Hospital Transplant Unit under the direction of Mr Terence English to investigate the causes of tissue rejection and was instrumental in the introduction of cephalosporin. The title of the group is the 'BHF Cardiac Transplantation Research Group'. On the expiry of the five-year period of the grant it has been renewed.

This group was followed in 1982 by the research group in Oxford, headed by Professor George Radda, which investigates the use of nuclear magnetic resonance in the study of the biochemistry of cells at molecular level and has proved of immense importance in the fields of biochemistry, spectroscopy and imaging. The title of its project is 'The Study of Heart Disease by Phosphorus NMR' and it has been renewed for a second five-year period.

In the same year the Foundation funded the 'Cardiovascular Epidemiology Research Group' under the direction of Dr Tom Meade at the Epidemiology and Medical Care Unit at Northwick Park Hospital. One of its principal preoccupations has been the study of factors responsible for blood clotting in ischaemic heart disease, to which it has made major contributions, especially in relation to factor VII. It has worked in close association with the Medical Research Council, and has had a two-year extension of support by the BHF.

At the meeting in December 1983 the Committee agreed to the proposal by Professor Tynan to set up the 'Research Group in Fetal Echocardiography'. This work is headed by Dr Lindsay Allen, who, after pioneering this advance, has become an accepted world leader in this speciality, which has proved to be of great clinical value.

In 1984 a proposal by Professor Williamson to establish a genetic engineering group at St Mary's Hospital was accepted. The work was under the direction of Dr Steven Humphries, who also became an acknowledged world leader in his speciality and has already advanced knowledge of the role of 'sick' genes in familial hypercholesterolaemia. In 1985 Dr Humphries was appointed to the Bernard Sunley Research Centre at Charing Cross Hospital, and, with the agreement of Professor Williamson and the Foundation, took the group with him and the funding to support it; the original sum provided by the Foundation was £450,000 over five years. The title of the group is 'The BHF Molecular Biology Research Group'.

The Committee agreed in 1985 to an application by Professor A.G. Shaper for a research group at the Royal Free Hospital to continue his epidemiological study, which had been supported until then by a five-year grant from the Medical Research Council. It is now called the 'BHF Regional Heart Study Research Group'. Amongst other interests Professor Shaper is researching possible explanations for the difference in incidence of heart disease in 26 British cities. His unit has produced a number of interesting and informative papers on this subject, and on the epidemiology of risk factors, which have excited much media interest and coverage.

In the last two years, with an increase in the funds available, the Committee has been able to approve five new groups at an estimated cost of more than £1,750,000.

Professor Spyer's group at the Royal Free Hospital is to study the 'Central Nervous Control of Cardiovascular Function'. Dr Peter Cummins's group at the Department of Cardiovascular Medicine in Birmingham is to study 'Contractile Proteins in Normal and Abnormal Cardiac Function'.

In 1987 Dr S.J. Pocock was awarded a 'Clinical Trials Research Group' at the Royal Free Hospital and Dr Sowton a 'Clinical Trials Group' based at Guy's Hospital, the project being entitled 'Angioplasty versus Bypass Surgery Assessment', whilst in 1988 three more groups were approved. Dr A.J. Williams, at the Cardiothoracic Institute, started work on his study of 'Cardiac Membrane Ion Channels in Reconstituted Systems', Professors J.R. Hampton and A.F.M. Smith set up the 'BHF Cardiovascular Statistics Group in Nottingham' and Professor G. Burnstock at University College, London, began work with his group on a project entitled 'Mechanisms of Local Control of Blood Flow – Physiological and Pathophysiological Implications'. None of these groups has been at work long enough to have published results.

The Medical Department

Other activities of the Committee

The Chairs and Research Groups Committee has had to consider many more applications for both professorial chairs and research groups than those which have been approved. Each application creates much hard work and necessitates the expenditure of a lot of time before a decision can be taken. It is often necessary to visit the site and always to engage in consultations with experts in the particular discipline under review.

The Committee is also the watchdog of the needs of the professorial chairs, advising the Finance and General Purposes Committee on all matters relating to their funding. This includes the need for increased capital funding and for increases in the annual discretionary and equipment funds. In 1985 the Committee also recommended that the senior lecturer fund should be increased from £30,000 to £35,000.

Besides these blanket payments the Committee is frequently asked to review, modify or endorse individual requests for large sums of money to reequip a unit, either to update it or to set up the work of a new incumbent of a chair. To do this well needs expert knowledge and much time from Committee members.

From time to time decisions are needed on unique specific requests which fall into no known pattern. As examples, in 1983, the proposal to set up the Walton Surgical Research Unit in Glasgow at an initial cost of £50,000 and the employment of a senior lecturer had to be decided upon, and in 1985 a request from Sir Patrick Forrest, the Chancellor of the University of Edinburgh, to give core support to the creation of a Professorship of Cardiac Surgery by the Lothian Health Board costing £75,000 over three years needed an answer. Both were agreed by Council on the advice of the Committee to the Finance and General Purposes Committee. Professor I.D. Hamilton was appointed to the Chair of Cardiac Surgery in Edinburgh.

On another occasion the grateful father of a child treated at the Hospital for Sick Children, Great Ormond Street, offered a gift of £200,000. The hospital approached the Foundation for £100,000 to add to this in order to create a senior lectureship in perpetuity; as a result of a report by the Committee in favour of this proposition the Foundation made possible the Al-Maktoum Senior Lectureship.

Similarly in 1986 the Committee recommended matching a

legacy of £250,000 to establish in perpetuity a senior lectureship at Professor Ball's unit in Leeds. This is to be known as the Mauntner Lectureship in memory of the testators, Dr and Mrs Mauntner.

The Royston Fellowship

In 1974 the Foundation was approached by the trustees of the board set up to administer the £60,000 raised by the friends of the late Viscount Royston through the Royston Memorial Fund. The purpose was to set up a Royston Fellowship to research cardiomyopathy, from which Viscount Royston had died at an early age. The Foundation agreed to add £40,000, provided the Fellowship was in perpetuity and was administered jointly by the trustees and the Cardiothoracic Institute, with the Fellows under the supervision of a senior member of the Institute staff.

There was a provision written into the agreement that if the work on heart muscle came to an end the trustees could continue the Fellowship in some other aspect of cardiovascular research. It was normally held for three years.

The trustees are two members of the Royston family, the Chairman and Dean of the Institute and one other.

The Fellowship has been continuously held since 1975. The first three Fellows were Ph.D. students: Miss E. Barry, 1975–77 (supervisor Professor Harris); Miss S. Grieve, 1978–81 (supervisor Professor W. Naylor); and Dr M. Tones, 1982–85 (supervisor Professor Poole-Wilson). The fourth was Dr R. Underwood, 1985–88, (supervisor Mr D. Longmore) studying magnetic resonance with senior registrar/lecturer status.

The Blood/Arterial Wall Interface Task Force

The Foundation had long recognized the importance of research into the nature of the changes and interactions between the blood and the arterial wall which could lead to heart attacks, and held a symposium on this subject in 1981.

The Blood/Arterial Wall Interface Task Force was created in 1985 at the instigation of Professor Shillingford, who was its chairman throughout. At first it was administered by the Education Committee but responsibility for it was later transferred to the Chairs and Research Groups Committee.

The need for a Task Force was born of concern about the fragmentation of research on this important subject, to redress which, it was felt, the Foundation was in a position to assist. There was general agreement that a multidisciplinary attack was needed and, most importantly, a need to collect information before forming hypotheses. It was accepted that there existed damaging ignorance by cardiologists of what biochemists knew and vice versa, and that a way ahead would be to promote workshop-like meetings to encourage collaboration and facilitate exchanges of information, with adequate time for unhurried discussion.

The Task Force included specialist research workers in biochemistry, immunology, pharmacology, molecular biology, epidemiology and haematology as well as clinicians.

The first meeting at BHF headquarters was in June 1985, and besides further meetings at headquarters, others have been held at Charing Cross, Northwick Park and Hammersmith Hospitals, with presentations by the directors of research at these institutions.

The following talks have been given: Professor Born on bleeding and plaque fissuring; Dr Meade on thrombolysis; Dr Humphries on the place of molecular biology in cardiovascular research, with special reference to hyperlipidaemia; Professor Spry on immunological factors; Professor Davies on varieties of pathological obstruction of arteries; Dr N.E. Miller on factors which underlie sex difference in coronary disease; and Professor Maseri and Dr J. Gordon on coronary spasm.

The members of the Task Force agreed that a project should be started to collect and computerize, as a family data-base register, information concerning 50 hyperlipidaemic families with heart disease, under the direction of Dr Ann Child at St George's Hospital and the Foundation has provided £120,000 to fund this work over three years. The work is ongoing, with the co-option, when advantageous to discussion, of additional experts in relevant fields, for example, thrombolysis.

Rolling tenure

Later the Chairs and Research Group Committee gave much time and thought to the need and desirability of 'rolling tenure' of senior lecturers on the expiry of their five-year appointment. The problem was particularly urgent for non-clinical scientists, where professorial posts are especially scarce, as are also appointments in the Health Service. Clearly it was important to cardiovascular research that these talented and experienced people should not be lost to research. Equally clearly, however, it was important that these important posts should not be blocked indefinitely. A wise decision on limited 'rolling tenure' with safeguards for future aspirants was reached.

Policy reviews

The reconstituted enlarged committee was soon faced by two important matters of policy. The first was a review by a subgroup chaired by Sir Raymond Hoffenberg, the new Chairman of Council, containing important observations and recommendations, and the second, a short while later, the report of a working party on clinical trials organization chaired by Sir Stanley Peart.

The subgroup's recommendations which were accepted in full by the Committee, can be summarized as follows:

1 To continue to take applications from research workers, and not to start directing research.
2 The only possibility of departing from this policy would be if a specific area presented itself such as an epidemic.
3 The Foundation should not create its own units or institutions of research other than the endowed chairs it supports.
4 Whilst recommending against the funding of buildings because of the expense of erection and maintenance, the Foundation should be prepared to consider covering the cost of modifying existing buildings if this is essential to a research project.
5 The Foundation should continue to provide a senior lecturer if the professor made a good case for such an appointment.
6 The Foundation should be more generous in supporting the substructure in the form of technical and secretarial salaries in its own departments and in research grant applications.
7 The Fellowships scheme should be continued and the Overseas Visiting Fellowships extended.
8 To initiate Travelling Fellowships of up to six months' duration to UK citizens in the research field, rather like sabbaticals, for established research workers of outstanding talent.
9 The Foundation should fund the salary of a locum for a lecturer at Senior Registrar level during the lecturer's absence for general

medical training in the National Health Service. It was noted that, in these circumstances, the locum would have to be a foreign graduate.

Clinical trials

The chairman of the working party looking into the desirability of involvement by the Foundation in clinical trials reported favourably. In debate, however, several members expressed disquiet at the size of the investment likely to be needed, and the Medical Director was urged to continue his endeavours to get the Department of Health to share the cost in spite of their inability to do so in the immediate future. He was also asked to monitor the costs closely and keep the Committee informed. With these reservations it was agreed to support Dr Pocock at the Royal Free Hospital and Dr Sowton at Guy's Hospital at a total estimated cost in excess of £600,000, both being categorized as research groups.

Sabbatical leave

In 1987 the Committee also clarified and updated the policy on sabbatical leave applicable to BHF professors and on the appointment of senior lecturers attached to BHF chairholders.

The policy on sabbatical leave reads as follows:

1 Chairholders may take twelve months sabbatical leave in every seven years, or six months in every three and a half years.
2 The travel expenses (economy) of the Chairholder and one dependant will be paid by the Foundation.
3 Where the Chairholder arranges an exchange, the BHF will pay the travel expenses (economy) of their replacement (but not of dependants).
4 A locum will not usually be paid for, but if the Professor submits research proposals to be reviewed by the Committee and which are adjudged to be of high merit, funds for a locum may be provided in so far as the Professor's absence from the Department requires such replacement on service grounds (e.g. teaching and clinical responsibilities).
5 The BHF will not be held liable for any additional expense.

The policy on the appointment of senior lecturers attached to BHF chairholders reads as follows:

1   Senior Lecturers are appointed for five years in the first place.
2   Senior Lecturers are not regarded as career posts; Senior Lecturers are expected to move to more senior permanent positions.
3   One or more extensions of three years may be applied for; extensions will only be granted after a critical review of the applicant's achievements.
4   The Chairholder of the Department in which the Senior Lecturer works is responsible for applying for any such extension at least two years before the current appointment terminates.

The use of animals in research

The Foundation accepts the need for using animals in some research projects, but is committed to the use of alternatives, such as cell cultures, whenever possible. To this end the Medical Director and the Director General met representatives of the Lord Dowding Fund for Humane Research in 1981 and agreed to support, with joint funding, any research project capable of execution with alternative methods as a substitute for the use of animals. The Foundation has also been in touch with FRAME (Fund for the Replacement of Animals in Medical Experiments) with the same objective.

The Foundation is very conscious of its responsibilities in this important matter and charges its committees with the obligation to be satisfied that there is no alternative to the use of an animal in a research project, and also that the likely benefits to humans (and often animals) are sufficient to justify the work. The work must also be new. These stringencies result in the use of animals in only a small percentage of the work funded by the Foundation, which, in turn, does not feel that the use of animals needs justifying when the evidence of benefit is overwhelming. An example in surgical cardiovascular research is the transformation of an 80% death rate in children with serious congenital cardiac defects into an 80% survival rate, consequent upon the introduction of new operations which could not have been done without animal experimentation. In medical research the introduction of drugs, which would have been illegal without animal testing for toxicity, for the treatment of high blood pressure has transformed the lives of a multitude of sufferers, and greatly reduced the incidence of strokes, with all the distress these bring to victims and relations; it is hard to remember that these drugs, accepted nowadays as routine treatment by every sufferer, did not exist 30 years ago.

The instructions to research workers and fund-raisers regarding the use of animals drawn up by the Finance and General Purposes Committee in 1985 and approved by Council read as follows:

1 The British Heart Foundation recognises the need for animals to be used for research purposes, particularly where no alternative procedure such as tissue or cell culture exists. It is implicitly understood in any research application that the grant-holder or applicant is in possession of the necessary animal licence or certificates issued by the Home Office, and that any experiment carried out is strictly in accord with the Provisions of the Cruelty to Animals Act 1876 or such other Act as Parliament may from time to time approve. The Home Secretary has recently announced that it is the intention of the Government, when Parliamentary time permits, to introduce new legislation. But until a new Bill has been enacted, the provisions of the 1876 Act prevail and must be adhered to.

2 The onus is upon the Heads of Schools or other scientific institutions to ensure that any research grant involving the use of experimental animals approved by, and financed by, the BHF is carried out in strict accord to the conditions and licences and certificates held personally by the individual(s) undertaking the research.

3 The BHF scrutinises carefully all research applications involving the use of animals and makes certain that:

(a) applicants/grant-holders pay special attention to the need for survival experiments or any other procedure where pain may result.
(b) the results of experimental work on animals already done elsewhere are taken note of. Unnecessary repetition is avoided.
(c) the use of experimental animals as part of the research project is vital in order to advance knowledge in the control or treatment of cardiovascular disease.
(d) there is no acceptable alternative.
(e) the design of the proposed experiment is such that the validity of the results can be determined by statistical analysis on the conclusion of the experiment.

4 Under all circumstances the BHF strictly acts in accordance with the Act of Parliament – 'All experiments on animals must be strictly in accord with the Provisions of the Cruelty to Animals Act 1876 of the appropriate Certificates A, B and C or E and F, depending on the types of animals being used.'

5 All points regarding pain, the use of anaesthesia and termination of the experiments are specifically covered by the appropriate Certificate.

Budget

The budget of the Chairs and Research Groups Committee for 1988 was £2,500,000. It has increased annually without interruption in the ten years since the Committee was set up.

Research Funds Administrator

Miss Valerie Mason joined the Foundation in September 1983. She had previously worked for the Royal College of Obstetricians and Gynaecologists.

When she arrived the work of the Medical Department was expanding rapidly because of the increased amount of money available to the Foundation with which to support research.

Hitherto Dr Butler had been responsible for the administration of all the committees of the Medical Department but this was no longer possible. Miss Mason became responsible for the administration of the Research Funds Committee, the Chairs and Research Groups Committee and the Fellowships Committee, whose total budget in 1988 was £13,000,000; she does this with a staff of two to help her. She is held in universal high regard by head office staff and by the grant-holders, who number nearly 400 and depend on her for the smooth operation of their funding. She also has the delicate task of informing those whose applications have not been successful. Her ability to do all this with outwardly unruffled calm, speed, accuracy and efficiency contributes much to the success of the committees she administers and the good public relations which exist with those who depend on the Foundation for their research funding. (In 1989 she was appointed Manager of the Research Funds Department.)

Project Grant Regulations 1988 (laid down by the Research Funds Committee)

Grants are awarded by a committee of 18 eminent members of the medical and allied professions, which meets quarterly to consider applications. Its Chairman is a physician or scientist who is not a cardiologist.

Applications are considered for basic or applied clinical science, and grants, which are not transferable, must be taken up within six months of the award, may be for remuneration of personnel, equipment and expenses. Grants are given on scientific merit only, and no reason is given for rejection unless specifically requested by the Committee.

Applicants should normally be graduates and the work must be undertaken in the United Kingdom. The period of support is from

The Medical Department

one to three years. All research projects involving investigations in man must have received appropriate clearance, in writing, from the host institution's ethical committee prior to submission of an application. The use of animals must fall within the Government regulations and the applicant must hold the relevant licences. Proposed survival experiments are subject to special scrutiny.

An annual progress report is requested of every grant-holder, and a reprint of all publications stemming from the funded project must be sent to the Research Funds Administrator. All patent rights arising from inventions made by a grant-holder must be assigned to the Foundation, which will pay the necessary registration fees. Site inspections of research projects are made when required, subject to mutual arrangement. If the holder of a grant wishes to move to another institution this is usually acceptable to the Foundation provided the facilities are judged to be adequate and provided the Foundation gives prior approval.

Equipment requested must be for research purposes in the hospital or laboratory; apparatus is not provided for routine or service use. It becomes the property of the host institution, which has to assume responsibility for housing and maintenance. If the grant-holder moves to another institution it is expected that the equipment will also be transferred. Requests for equipment should conform to the requirements of British Standards 5724 Part 1, and purchase is handled by the Administrator and Buyer of the Cardiac Care Committee since, for most items, the Foundation is zero-rated for VAT.

All grant-holders must be employed by the institution in which they work; in no case is a research worker employed by the Foundation. Quarterly accounts, payable in arrears, have to be submitted for settlement to the Research Funds Administrator by the finance officer of the institution concerned.

Requests for payment of salaries of personnel to be employed on the project must detail, in separate amounts, basic salary, National Insurance, superannuation, increases generated by the expected inflation rate and London weighting if applicable. When the recipient of a grant is undertaking clinical duties the Foundation is prepared to pay UMTs up to a maximum of four A units per week. Bench fees and interviewing expenses will not be reimbursed.

The Foundation is able to make some provision for travel expenses for grant-holders to visit a centre to learn techniques essential to their research, and also to attend the Foundation's symposia. But support is not normally given for attendance at large conferences unless the applicant has had a paper accepted for presentation. The Foundation expects that senior members of departments will be able to obtain funding from other sources.

The regulations also include a section on 'Advice to Applicants' in the presentation of an application. It emphasizes that the detailed research protocol which is needed must include the title, an abstract, the background of the project, the original hypothesis, details of the proposed investigation, the reasons for the financial support requested and the expected value of the results.

The advice also informs the applicant that research personnel supported by the Foundation are expected to devote at least 80% of their time to that research and that the application must be for all personnel to be employed on the project as required, together with details of requests for salaries for all named medically qualified doctors and senior scientific workers.

There is also an exhortation to be realistic rather than submit an inflated application in the expectation that it will be cut down, and a reminder of the need for proof of ethical clearance and for a full specification of equipment requested.

THE BRITISH HEART FOUNDATION PRIZE AND GOLD MEDAL

In 1982 the Council approved a suggestion put forward by Professor Shillingford that, from time to time, the Foundation should award a prize of £5,000 and a gold medal for outstanding cardiovascular research carried out by a worker supported by the Foundation.

The British Heart Foundation Prize and Gold Medal were awarded to Professor George Radda, working in the Clinical Magnetic Resonance Laboratory at Oxford University, in 1983. The citation reads: 'For his work on nuclear magnetic resonance for non-invasive study of muscle metabolism.'

In 1985 two Prizes and Medals were awarded. They went to Professor Robert Anderson and Professor Denis Noble.

The citation for Professor Robert Anderson, Joseph Levy Foundation Professor of Paediatric Cardiac Morphology at the Cardiothoracic Institute, reads: 'For his outstanding contribution to the study of conducting tissues and congenitally malformed hearts.'

The citation for Professor Denis Noble, holder of the Burdon-Sanderson Chair of Cardiovascular Physiology at the University of Oxford, reads: 'For his outstanding contribution to the biophysics of cardiac muscle.'

ENDOWED CHAIRS ESTABLISHED BY THE FOUNDATION

London, 1965. The Simon Marks Chair of Cardiology. Cardiothoracic Institute, Brompton Hospital and National Heart Hospital. Professor Peter Harris, followed by Professor Poole Wilson.

Birmingham, 1971. Chair of Cardiovascular Medicine. Professor Sir Melville Arnott, followed by Professor W. Littler.

Glasgow, 1973. The Walton Chair of Medical Cardiology. Professor Lawrie, followed by Professor S.M. Cobbe.

Leeds, 1973. The Chair of Cardiovascular Studies. Professor Linden, followed by Professor S. Ball.

Oxford, 1973. The Field Marshal Earl Alexander Professorship of Cardiovascular Medicine. Professor Peter Sleight.

Newcastle upon Tyne, 1974. The British Heart Foundation Chair of Cardiology. Professor Desmond Julian, followed by Professor Ronnie Campbell.

Glasgow, 1974. The British Heart Foundation Chair of Cardiac Surgery, supported by the Isadore and David Walton Charitable Trust. Professor Philip Caves, followed by Professor David Wheatley.

London, 1975. The Vandervell Chair of Paediatric Cardiology. Institute of Child Health. Professor Macartney.

London, 1976. The Sir John McMichael Chair in Cardiovascular Medicine. Royal Postgraduate Hospital Hammersmith. Professor J. Shillingford, followed by Professor A. Maseri.

Edinburgh, 1978. The Duke of Edinburgh Chair of Cardiology. Professor Michael Oliver.

Cardiff, 1980. The Sir Thomas Lewis Chair of Cardiology. Professor Andrew Henderson.

London, 1983. The British Heart Foundation Chair of Cardiac Surgery. Royal Postgraduate Hospital Hammersmith. Professor K. Taylor.

London, 1986. The Prudential Professor of Clinical Cardiology. St George's Hospital. Professor J. Camm.

London, 1986. The British Heart Foundation Chair of Cardiothoracic Surgery. Cardiothoracic Institute, Brompton Hospital. Professor Magdi Yacoub.

THE BRITISH HEART FOUNDATION PERSONAL CHAIRS

London, 1983. The Joseph Levy Foundation Professor of Paediatric Cardiac Morphology. Cardiothoracic Institute, Brompton Hospital. Professor Robert Anderson.

London, 1981. The Professorship of Cardiovascular Pathology. St George's Hospital. Professor Michael Davies.

Oxford, 1984. The Chair of Molecular Cardiology. Clinical Magnetic Resonance Laboratory. Professor George Radda.

Oxford, 1984. The Burdon-Sanderson Chair of Cardiovascular Physiology. Professor Denis Noble.

London, 1985. The Chair of Cardiovascular Immunology. St George's Hospital. Professor Spry.

London, 1986. The Sir Ronald Bodley Scott Senior Lectureship in Cardiovascular Medicine. St Bartholomew's Hospital. Dr A.W. Nathan.

RESEARCH GROUPS

Papworth, 1980. The BHF Cardiac Transplantation Group. Mr Terence English.

Oxford, 1982. Magnetic Resonance Research Group. Professor George Radda.

London, 1982. Northwick Park Hospital. The Cardiovascular Epidemiology Research Group. Dr Tom Meade.

London, 1984. Guy's Hospital. The Research Group in Fetal Echocardiography. Professor Tynan and Dr Lindsey Allan.

London, 1985. Charing Cross Hospital. Sunley Research Centre. The BHF Molecular Biology Research Group. Dr S. Humphries. This

The Medical Department

group was originally set up in 1984 at St Mary's Hospital under the direction of Professor Williamson.

London, 1985. The Royal Free Hospital. The BHF Regional Heart Study Group. Professor G. Shaper.

London, 1985. The Royal Free Hospital. The BHF Group to Study the Central Nervous Control of Cardiovascular Function. Professor K.M. Spyer.

Birmingham, 1986. Department of Cardiovascular Medicine. The BHF Group to Study Contractile Proteins in Normal and Abnormal Cardiac Function. Dr P. Cummins.

London, 1987. The Royal Free Hospital. Clinical Trials Research Group. Dr. S.J. Pocock.

London, 1988. Guy's Hospital. Clinical Trials Research Group. Dr. E.G. Sowton.

London, 1988. Cardiothoracic Institute. The BHF Group to Study Cardiac Membrane Ion Channels in Reconstituted Systems. Dr A.J. Williams.

Nottingham, 1988. Department of Medicine. The BHF Cardiovascular Statistics Group in Nottingham. Professors Hampton and Smith.

London, 1988. University College. The BHF Group to Study the Mechanisms of Local Control of Blood Flow: Physiological and Pathophysiological Implications. Professor G. Burnstock.

FELLOWSHIPS COMMITTEE

The award of Fellowships as a means of supporting and encouraging workers interested in cardiovascular research has been recognized from the earliest days of the Foundation. The Science Committee, at its first meeting on 6 March 1961, discussed at length the policy to be adopted for the distribution of funds which it was hoped would become available from the appeal, and resolved that this should include the granting of 'Individual Research Fellowships for study in the UK and abroad; in the first instance Fellowships will be granted for limited periods, usually two to three years.'

The original intention of the Foundation was a single appeal for £3,500,000, later raised to £5,000,000, from which to promote research, but it was an uphill task at first, and money came in slowly. Consequently the Foundation's main contribution to current needs had to be to assist existing research projects and to fund, so far as it could, new applications made to it.

It was nearly ten years later, in 1970, before the objective was changed to an ongoing appeal, with the support of research sustained by the income from invested capital. From its first distribution of 34 awards costing £181,000 in October 1963 it was able to disburse £175,000 per annum by 1969.

British/American Exchange Fellowships

The award of Fellowships began during this early period in the Foundation's history with the introduction of British/American Exchange Fellowships. The first report of a discussion about this project with the American Heart Association is in the minutes of the Science Committee of 27 May 1965. Professor Shillingford reported that he had met Mr Joseph Howatch, an Administrative Associate of the AHA, as a result of which the Americans agreed to support financially three Britons in America and the British one American working in Britain. The Council of the American Heart Association, however, reduced the ratio to 2 : 1, with the Americans putting up $10,000 and the British $5,000. With a total of $15,000 two Exchange Fellows could be appointed from each side every year. They were strictly for research and not for gaining clinical experience.

An announcement was made in *The Times* newspaper inviting applications for consideration in October 1966. The selection committee consisted of Sir John McMichael, Professor Ian Hill and Professor A.S.V. Burgen, Professor of Pharmacology at Cambridge University at that time, and the first two Fellows (Dr Michael Lee, Oxford, and Dr B. Rifkind, Glasgow) left for the National Heart Institute, Bethesda, for the academic year 1967–68. The following year the Exchange Fellows were Dr A.S. Abraham, Birmingham, and Dr L.H. Smaje of University College, London. At that time the basic stipend was $7,500, to which a dependancy allowance was added. In 1969 the American Heart Association suggested sending three Fellows but the Foundation was not able to increase its commitment: Dr R. Hainsworth, Leeds, and Dr C. Rosendorff, St Thomas's Hospital were sent. In 1970–71 the two British Fellows were Dr David Jewitt, Hammersmith, and Dr Elliot Shinebourne, National Heart Hospital.

In September 1970 representatives of the Foundation met representatives of the American Heart Association. Dr Graham Hayward, Sir Ronald Bodley Scott, Professor Shillingford and Dr Margaret Haigh represented the Foundation and Drs Elliot Rapaport, Roland Schneckloth and Howard Weisberg the AHA. As a result of this meeting the stipend was increased to $9,000 and it was agreed that Fellows could apply for an extension of support for all, or part, of a second year, according to the needs of their research programme. Dr Jewitt was awarded a second year and Dr Shinebourne an extra six months.

For 1971–72 Dr Malcolm Murray, London Hospital, went to the Johns Hopkins Medical School and Mr Philip Caves, Brompton Hospital, to Stamford Medical Centre. It is recorded that three American doctors came to Britain the same year but, unfortunately, they are not named. At this time the AHA suggested equal funding by them and the Foundation, which was readily agreed.

In 1972–73 the Foundation sent three Exchange Fellows for the first time: Dr D. Banks, Nottingham, to the Peter Bent Brigham Hospital, Dr B.J. Maurer, Hammersmith, to the Alabama Medical Centre, and Dr I. Hutton, Glasgow, to the University of Texas.

Thereafter the pattern of two Exchange Fellows enjoying a year of research in the United States has continued to the present time, with exceptional years in 1979 with five awards and 1987 when four awards were made. The list of those who have held these Fellowships includes many leading figures in cardiology in Britain, with at least two who have subsequently become BHF Professors.

Other international Exchange Fellowships

Following the success of the British/American Exchange Fellowship scheme enquiries were made about the acceptability of similar schemes with the National Heart Associations in a number of countries. Holland, Australia and Sweden were in favour.

The first British/Dutch Exchange Fellowship was awarded by the Research Funds Committee in 1979 to Dr Margaret Petty, Glasgow University, to work in the Institute of Pharmacology, Rotterdam. In 1986 Dr K.J. Beatt, Newcastle University, was awarded a Fellowship, also to work in Rotterdam, and in 1988 Dr A.G. Fraser, University College of Wales, Cardiff, also to work in Rotterdam.

In 1981 Dr Miller-Craig, Glasgow, was awarded a British/

Australian Fellowship to work in Sydney, and in 1986 Dr A.S. Smith, Birmingham University, was also awarded an Exchange Fellowship to work in Sydney. In 1982 a British/Swedish Fellowship was awarded to Dr. J.E. Took, Leeds General Infirmary, to work in the Department of Medicine at the Carolinska Institute, Stockholm.

Junior and Senior Research Fellowships

With the creation of the Research Funds Committee in 1970, in place of the Science Committee, one of its first considerations concerned the Regulations of the Foundation's Research Fellowships.

At its first meeting on 16 March 1970 it defined the Junior and Senior Fellowships in the following terms:

(a) *Junior Fellowship.* These will be held for a maximum of two years, during which the Fellow will be expected to devote at least 80% of his time to research. They will not be renewable. Salary, including National Insurance and Superannuation, will be paid at the level of a Middle Registrar or equivalent University scale. An expense allowance will be paid but will vary individually.
(b) *Senior Fellowships.* Held normally for three to five years, these will be paid at the level of a Senior Registrar. Selection will be by interview. These Fellowships will be comparable to those of other grant-giving bodies such as the Medical Research Council, British Empire Cancer Campaign, Wellcome Trust and Beit Memorial. The pay policy of the Medical Research Council will be followed.

The awards of these Fellowships are listed in the minutes of the Research Funds Committee amongst the awards of project grants, and it is, consequently, impossible to identify with certainty the complete list of applications, or of the Fellowships awarded. From the records, however, it would appear that the first application for a Senior Research Fellowship was made in December 1971 and the first award made in October 1972. It went to Dr F. Michal, Royal College of Surgeons, to work on 'The Pharmacological Inhibition of Platelet Thrombosis'.

The first recorded application for a Junior Research Fellowship was made in March 1971 and it was approved. It went to Mr F.D. Skidmore, working in the Department of Anatomy, Cambridge University, and was awarded to study 'The Early Development of Pulmonary Arteries in Man'. The following year three more awards are recorded.

In 1972 the Scientific Advisory Committee recommended to the Research Funds Committee the setting up of Junior Research Fellowships in defined subjects at named research centres for a trial period of five years. The Research Funds Committee agreed to this scheme, in spite of the fact that it entailed some degree of direction of research, which was contrary to its philosophy, but there is no record of how successful it proved to be. The recommendations of the Advisory Committee were epidemiology at Edinburgh, physiology at Leeds, paediatric cardiology at the Hospital for Sick Children, biochemistry at the institute of Cardiology and cardiovascular disease at the Royal Postgraduate Hospital, Hammersmith.

As the work of the Research Funds Committee increased, and its main concerns were professorial chairs and project grants, the consideration of applications for fellowships tended increasingly to become the responsibility of an emerging subcommittee, which in time became the Fellowships Committee.

The minutes of this committee begin in September 1983, which coincides with the arrival of Valerie Mason as Administrator, but there are reports and recommendations of the 'Fellowships Committee' in the minutes of the Finance and General Purposes Committee as early as November 1981, when the Committee recommended two Senior Research Fellowships, four Junior Research Fellowships, three British/American Exchange Fellowships and the first British/Australian Exchange Fellowship. Again on 12 October 1982 the minutes of the Finance and General Purposes Committee report the recommendations by the Fellowships Committee of nine awards totalling £83,000.

The awards of Fellowships were made on the basis of an annual quota, which was increased in 1984; Senior Research Fellowships were increased from one to two per annum; Junior Research Fellowships in professorial units from six to nine per annum; Junior Research Fellowships outside professorial units from three to six per annum; and Overseas Visiting Fellowships from two to three per annum. The cost of these increases was estimated at £100,000 per annum.

European Travelling Scholarships

In 1973, at the suggestion of Sir Keith Ross, who was a member of the Research Funds Committee, it was agreed to introduce European

Travelling Scholarships worth £300–£400 to enable young research workers to visit centres of their choice on the Continent. The following year three scholarships were awarded to Dr P.W. McFarlane, Glasgow, Dr Eric Silove, Hospital for Sick Children, and Mr Philip Caves of Edinburgh Royal Infirmary. These scholarships have continued over the years but applications have been infrequent, with the result that the regulations have been broadened recently; 1979 was an exceptional year when four were awarded.

Overseas Visiting Fellowships

Around 1981 (the precise date is not recorded) the Finance and General Purposes Committee accepted a recommendation of the Fellowships Committee to introduce Overseas Visiting Fellowships to fund research graduates keen to work in Britain. At first they were restricted to workers engaged in research which was not being undertaken in Britain, but recently these limitations have been relaxed (see p. 162).

Ph.D. students

As far back as 1979 the Finance and General Purposes Committee raised with the Research Funds Committee the possibility of funding Ph.D. students, and the first awards were recommended in 1981 by the newly formed Fellowships Committee. In 1987, at the request of the professorial chairholders, the Committee agreed to consider requests for the funding of unnamed Ph.D. posts in their units, because of the shortage of suitable students. These were easily lost to cardiovascular research by the unavoidable delays caused by the need to apply to the Committee after the name of a student was known. It was also agreed that awards should not be restricted to BHF professorial departments, and that the funding of these studentships would be in line with Medical Research Council regulations.

Intermediate Fellowships

In April 1986 the Committee introduced Intermediate Fellowships of two to three years duration, to fill a need to bridge the gap between Junior and Senior Fellowships. Since 1986, 15 have been awarded. In

The Medical Department

the same period the Council has also awarded 26 new Junior Research Fellowships and 14 extensions, and five Senior Research Fellowships with one extension.

Committee membership

For many years the Fellowships Committee had an *ad hoc* membership which included many senior figures in the worlds of cardiological research and clinical cardiology. Professor Shillingford was its Chairman until he retired in 1986, and he was succeeded, in 1987, by Sir John Badenoch. At this time the *ad hoc* membership was replaced by a formally appointed Committee whose members would serve three years. The members are Professors Spry, Noble and Tynan, and Drs D. Jewitt and D. Gibson, the initial retirements being staggered to maintain continuity.

The Committee works within the framework of a defined budget instead of on a quota basis as hitherto. The budget for 1988–89 was £1,500,000.

Fellowships offered by the Foundation

In August 1988 Fellowships offered by the Foundation were set out as follows:

The British Heart Foundation currently awards the following Fellowships:
1 Junior, Intermediate and Senior Research Fellowships.
2 Ph.D. Studentships.
3 International Reciprocal Fellowships (known as British/American, British/Australian, British/Dutch and British/Swedish Fellowships).
4 European Travelling Fellowships.
5 Overseas Visiting Fellowships.
It is proposed that the BHF continue to offer the fellowships listed in 1–3 inclusive. It is proposed that European Travelling Fellowships (4) be discontinued and replaced by Senior Travelling Fellowships (see below). Overseas Visiting Fellowships (5) will remain but will not be restricted to the applicant bringing special expertise not currently available in the UK, as has been the intention to date (see below).

Senior Travelling Fellowships

Senior Travelling Fellowships are available to established research workers (UK citizens) of proven outstanding talent to undertake research abroad, or to acquire special knowledge which would assist them in their research in the United Kingdom after their return. The duration of the Fellowship would be for a period of up to six months. At the time of application the proposed Fellow should hold a post in a research institution or university with tenure of not less than five years. The proposed Fellow may apply for funds to cover the cost of economy travel and a reasonable subsistence allowance at the place of work. It is expected that the Fellow's salary would continue to be paid by the university or institution in the UK during his or her absence abroad. Application must be made on the appropriate form together with details of the purpose of the visit and what the Fellow expects to gain as the result of the visit. A curriculum vitae of the applicant and a letter of acceptance by the host institution must also be included in the application.

Overseas Visiting Fellowships

Overseas Visiting Fellowships are available to overseas research workers wishing to undertake research in a recognized research centre in the UK for up to two years. The successful Fellow would be an established research worker of proven outstanding talent, able to contribute to the work of the host department. These Fellowships are not given for training. Applications must be made by the Head of Department in the UK on behalf of the Fellow and should include a full research protocol. The role of the visiting Fellow in the research should be clearly stated. A curriculum vitae of the proposed Fellow and two letters of recommendation from the Fellow's country of origin should also be included. The applicant may apply for funds to cover the Fellow's salary and up to £1,000 per annum as a contribution towards research expenses. The applicant must confirm that all other necessary resources for the proposed research will be available. The Foundation will not cover travel costs.

THE EDUCATION COMMITTEE

The Foundation has always included postgraduate medical education in its role and the Science Committee, at its first meeting on 6 March 1961, defined this as being 'to improve the knowledge and practice of cardiology and to raise the standards wherever it is practised'.

In the early days shortage of money prevented the diversion of funds from the main task of financing research, but in 1964 the Council agreed to the provision of up to £1,000 to assist young cardiologists with their expenses if selected to read a paper at the European Congress in Prague; in the event 11 grants of £50 each were made. The following year the Foundation provided £2,000 to assist

The Medical Department

members of the British Cardiac Society who were reading papers at the World Congress in Delhi. In Delhi, in 1966, the decision was taken to hold the Sixth World Congress of Cardiology in London in 1970, with Dr Patrick Mouncey, Secretary of the British Cardiac Society, as Congress Secretary. He was supported by the Foundation with a loan of £1,300 per annum for four years to cover the expenses of organization.

Later involvement of the Foundation in life-style controversies was foreshadowed as early in its existence as 1965, when it was asked for a policy statement on the dangers of animal fat in the diet. The American Heart Association had put out a publication warning of such dangers and some pressure was put on the Foundation to subscribe to this, but the Science Committee ruled that this would be unwise, and restricted itself to condemning fat as a common cause of obesity.

These small beginnings of support of medical education were made on the recommendation of the Science Committee but in 1970 the Postgraduate Education Funds Committee was established and its terms of reference were 'to promote postgraduate training'.

Professor Shillingford was its Chairman for six years and its members were Dr A.M. Johnson, Dr McLean Baird, Professor John Goodwin and Dr Aubrey Leatham, with Dr Margaret Haigh, Medical Administrator, and Brigadier Cardiff, Director General.

In 1976 Dr Elliot Shinebourne became Chairman and he was succeeded in 1980 by Dr Douglas Chamberlain. He was followed by Dr Tom Meade in 1983 and by Dr Kim Fox in 1986. Professor Sleight is to take over the Chairmanship in 1989. With an ever-increasing workload the membership of the Committee was enlarged by the co-option of several distinguished cardiologists and general practitioners. In 1981 it was agreed that the Committee should be strengthened by the inclusion of a BHF professor in its membership. Professor Henderson was the first and he was succeeded by Professor Sleight, who was later joined by Professor Shaper. In 1982 a Regional Director was added; the first was Mrs Gwen Martyn and she was succeeded by Brigadier W. Deller. In 1977 Colonel Malcolm, the Director of Appeals, joined the Committee.

In 1980 Dr Chamberlain proposed a change of name to Education Funds Committee and in 1985, at the suggestion of Dr Fox, it assumed its current title of Education Committee.

As the Postgraduate Education Funds Committee in 1970, it soon became active in its task of promoting education in cardiology in spite of its budget being only £6,000 per annum. By contrast the Education Budget for 1988–89 was £650,000.

Symposia

The Committee's first move was to promote a symposium, which was a meeting of research workers funded by the Foundation to report their work. The title was 'Lipids, Platelets and Thrombosis', and it was held at the Hammersmith Hospital on 4 December 1970. It was followed by the second on 'Cardiac Surgery' at the National Heart Hospital on 1 April 1971; this was followed in November 1971 by a symposium on 'Coronary Heart Disease' held at the Institute for Diseases of the Chest, and in January 1972 by a meeting at the Hammersmith Hospital on 'Instrumentation and Techniques'. March 1972 saw a symposium on 'Congenital Heart Disease' at the Institute of Child Health and June 1972 one on 'Drugs in Cardiovascular Research' at the Cardiothoracic Institute.

The first meeting at the Royal College of Obstetricians and Gynaecologists, which subsequently became the venue of regular quarterly meetings for the next ten years, was in November 1972 and the subject was 'Physiology and Biochemistry'. Since 1982, with the acquisition of the conference room at headquarters, all symposia have been held at 102 Gloucester Place.

Workshops

Workshops were started in 1983 and are also held quarterly in the conference room. Workshops are designed to bring together basic scientists and clinicians with a mutual interest, but the participants are not necessarily funded by the Foundation.

Both the workshops and the symposia have proved very popular, and have been outstandingly successful in promoting the exchange of information and the encouragement of frank debate. The limitation of attendance to invited participants ensures an informality which allows lively critical discussion. They have won a high reputation in the world of cardiovascular research and done much to enhance the standing of the Foundation.

The Medical Department

The Foundation invites a distinguished scientist from Europe or America as participant and leader of discussion to these meetings and pays their expenses.

The full lists of titles of symposia and workshops are to be found on pp. 179 and 181.

European and international meetings

The Committee decided to organize biennial European Congresses in 1973, and the first was held two years later. Since then the pattern has remained unchanged, except for adjustments of dates to accommodate other important meetings. All have been successful scientifically and have paid their way with modest profits.

The Foundation also helped the Sixth World Congress of Cardiology in London, in addition to the financial loan to its organizers, by giving the delegates an evening entertainment with a concert at the Festival Hall at which Sir John Barbirolli conducted the Hallé

Figure 30 *British Heart Foundation display stand at the 6th World Congress of Cardiology in London in 1970.*

Orchestra. The Foundation also mounted a display stand at the conference hall to promote its activities (Figure 30). In 1974 the Foundation gave the Council of the British Cardiac Society £3,000 to distribute, as appropriate, to its members to assist with expenses in attending the Seventh World Congress in Buenos Aires.

In 1982 the Foundation collaborated with the Community Resuscitation Advisory Council (CRAC) and the Postgraduate Medical School and an organization set up by general practitioners called Basics (British Association of Immediate Care Schemes), to stage an International Meeting on Cardiac Arrest and Resuscitation at Brighton under the direction of Dr Douglas Chamberlain. The BHF film on cardiopulmonary resuscitation (CPR) entitled *A Heart Attack – Learn What to Do* was shown to delegates and well received. Subsequently many copies of the film were purchased, mostly by those concerned with teaching CPR.

The following is a list of international meetings hosted by the Foundation:

1st European Congress. Held in June 1975 at the Royal College of Obstetricians and Gynaecologists. Entitled 'Cardiac Arrhythmias' and attended by 200 delegates. It was organized by Professor Shillingford and Dr Krikler.

2nd European Congress. Held in June 1977 at the Royal College of Obstetricians and Gynaecologists. Entitled 'Paediatric Cardiology' and attended by 320 delegates. Dr Shinebourne was the Chairman of the Organizing Committee.

3rd European Congress. Held in June 1979 at Imperial College and run by Conference Services, attended by 400 delegates. Entitled 'Non-invasive Techniques in Cardiology'. Organized by Dr Derek Gibson and Dr Andrew Selwyn.

4th European Congress. Held in July 1981 at Imperial College and run by Conference Services. Entitled 'Recent Developments in Cardiovascular Drugs'. Organized by Dr D. Coltart and Dr D. Jewitt.

5th European Congress. Held in June 1985 at the Cavendish Conference Centre. Entitled 'The Impact of Research on the Practice of Cardiology'. Organized by Dr Fox, Professor Poole-Wilson and Professor Shillingford.

6th European Congress. Held in September 1987 at the Government Conference Centre, Westminster, and run by the Caroline Roney

The Medical Department

Conference Organizers. Entitled 'The Management of Cardiac Arrhythmias'. Organized by Professor Camm and Dr Nathan.

7th European Congress. Held in June 1989 at the Royal College of Physicians. Entitled 'The Management of Acute Myocardial Ischaemia'. Organized by Professor Julian, Professor Sleight and Dr Chamberlain.

International meeting, October 1982, at Brighton. Entitled 'Cardiac Arrest and Resuscitation'. Organized and run by Dr Chamberlain.

Lectures

An early decision by the Committee was to promote lectures as a means of postgraduate education in cardiology. The first attempt was through whole-day regional meetings with several speakers, and these were planned for Southampton, London (West Middlesex Hospital), Glasgow and Edinburgh, but they had to be abandoned through lack of support. The doctors could not give up a mid-week day from their commitments, and the speakers were not willing to give up free time on Sundays.

It is interesting, however, that ten years later, in 1981, when study leave was better organized and the need for refresher courses more widely accepted, regional meetings were successfully reintroduced, and amongst several those at Cardiff and Chichester are recorded as being particularly successful.

Following the early failure of the concept of regional meetings the Committee introduced BHF lectures with a single speaker at postgraduate centres, either in the evening or at lunch-time. The Foundation has compiled a list of 70 speakers and titles which is distributed to postgraduate deans, and states how often each speaker is available. The meetings are then organized locally, with the Foundation paying the speaker an honorarium and expenses. Light refreshments are provided and are sometimes funded by industry. This scheme has been an unqualified success from the start, and the numbers given each year have steadily increased from nine in 1972 to well over 100 in 1987.

An attempt was made to supplement the lecture programme at these centres by the provision of audio-visual tape–slide projection apparatus and some tapes were made, including one on the management of arrhythmias, but the system chosen was overtaken by the introduction of video cassettes and the television screen, and it was discontinued.

Publications

(a) *Heart Research Series (HRS).* Now renamed Heart Information Series. The HRS leaflets are short summaries of current knowledge on subjects of interest to patients suffering from heart disease, and are written in lay terms. They are the earliest attempt at public education by the Foundation, and to date more than 10,000,000 copies have been distributed free of charge.

From 1963 to 1972 the Foundation published a quarterly journal called *Heart* which contained articles on medical subjects, particularly those concerned with research funded by the Foundation, but in 1970 and 1971 six articles appeared which became the first six titles of the series. The first, entitled 'Where do you go from here?', was the forerunner of HRS 1, *Back to Normal*.

In 1967 the Foundation had also started the publication of the *Heart Bulletin*, which was a news-sheet reporting the activities of fund-raising committees nation-wide, and designed to stimulate and encourage their efforts. The issue of January 1971 announced the publication of these six articles as the 'Heart Research Series'. Their distribution was the responsibility of the Appeals Department and remained so, through the intermediary of the Publications Committee set up by the Council in the mid-1970s, until the responsibilities of the Publications Committee were formally handed to the Education Funds Committee in 1980.

In the mean time, however, the series had been increased to 12, with the appearance of HRS 12, *Heart Surgery for Adults*, in 1981, and all had been revised when necessary. By 1984 the number in the series was increased to 15 and the present total is 18 (see p. 183).

The Committee gave much thought to the distribution of these leaflets and a pilot scheme was first tried by distributing them to doctors in the Exeter area in 1982. Following favourable reports by these doctors a larger pilot scheme was undertaken by distributing them to 100 doctors in the Essex area in 1982, and a display box was designed to contain 20 copies of each pamphlet in the set. Following this it was decided to offer sets to all general practitioners and to hospitals and clinics, where they immediately proved popular.

In 1986 the Committee commissioned an enquiry by professionals to determine the reader response to the series and the success of distribution. There was general satisfaction with the content, but distribution to those who could benefit was inadequate. As a consequence the Foundation has provided a leaflet for distribution in chemists' shops and other suitable sites to publicize their availability.

(b) *Fact File.* In 1984 the Foundation started to send a monthly update to all General Practitioners on a single A4 sheet of paper, giving them current thinking on the management of common cardiovascular problems. The information is the distilled wisdom of the British Cardiac Society and the Foundation, both of which bodies agree the wording before distribution. The Education Funds Committee set up a Fact File Subcommittee to handle this important matter, with two representatives of the British Cardiac Society and one from the Royal College of General Practitioners co-opted to it. Dr Fox was its first Chairman and he was succeeded in 1986 by Professor Julian.

The Fact File sheets drew such an overwhelmingly favourable response from general practitioners that a folder was offered in 1986 to take the whole series, and back numbers were made available for any which had been lost, either individually or as a new pack. Within a few weeks of mailing 8,000 folders and 4,000 packs had been requested and distributed.

(c) *Congenital Heart Disease.* In 1983 the Committee approved a series of 14 leaflets prepared by Dr Olive Scott for circulation to doctors and parents. Each leaflet describes and illustrates the anatomical lesion of one of the common congenital deformities, and summarizes the symptoms, treatment and prognosis. The series also includes sheets on 'General Information', the 'Intensive Care Ward' and 'Catheterization'. They are currently still much in demand.

(d) *Other publications.* A full list of publications available from the Foundation is to be found on p. 183. Amongst these several are unique. A calculator compiled from statistics published by the Department of Health is designed specially for businesses, giving figures for days lost per year, potential deaths from heart disease and average costs from heart disease to an organization for male and female employees with work-forces ranging from 50 to 10,000.

A publication written by the nursing staff of King's College Hospital Intensive Care Unit for those facing cardiac surgery, called *A New Start for You and Your Heart*, was funded by the Foundation. It is simple, comprehensive and reassuring, being illustrated with a light touch. It has proved very popular with patients and the staff of surgical departments.

In 1976 the Foundation published a successful hardback cookery-book entitled *Cooking for Your Heart's Content*. In due course this became out of print and out of date, and was replaced in 1986 by a 36-page booklet called *Food Should Be Fun*. Besides containing a number of recipes it includes suggestions for all meals, advice about shopping and making good use of convenience foods, as well as ways to modify diets to meet the needs of a reducing diet, fat restrictions and the use of fibre, together with hints on modification of cooking methods. It is to be revised to bring it into line with the most up-to-date thinking on fat content.

There is also a special publication describing the Marfan syndrome based, with acknowledgement for permission, on the booklet of the American National Marfan Foundation, and a leaflet called *The Gift of Life* prepared by the UK Transplant Coordinators' Association, similarly acknowledged, giving general information on organ donation.

(e) *Publications for children.* The Education Funds Committee inherited a leaflet for children from the Appeals Department when it took over the responsibility for public education, but in 1983 Mrs Martyn, the Regional Organizer on the Committee, said she thought it was too juvenile for teenagers and that there was a need for something more sophisticated. This resulted in the production of a poster which was circulated in a magazine called *Junior Education*, which has a circulation of 35,000 copies. This described the blood and circulation and gave life-style suggestions with clear text and good illustrations. This was followed by a poster specifically targeting the dangers of smoking, which went to 8,000 secondary schools.

From this the concept was developed of producing a series of posters, combined with newsletters so designed that when folded they could be read as a letter and when opened out displayed as a poster. In response to opinions given by schoolteachers, the poster in the first newsletter was a diagram of the heart, showing how it works and how it can go wrong, and in the second the poster concentrated on the ills of smoking. Others are to follow, illustrating healthy living, based on the BHF Guidelines and the sporting image. So far, 2,300 secondary schools (30% of the total) have requested 500,000 copies of the first newsletter, and requests are still coming in.

Much of the credit for the success of the poster campaign is due to the editorial, design and production firm of Burnett Associates, who created the imaginative designs of the coloured educational material. They also redesigned many of the other major publications of the BHF. In these ways they made a significant contribution to the factors which won for the Foundation the Annual Charity Reports Award in 1985.

The Committee has also recently produced a video for schools audiences, which is being offered at cost price, with a request for the addition of a donation when possible. It has also agreed to cooperate with the Health Education Authority to send a free pack to primary schoolteachers to assist them in health education of the younger group of children.

(f) *Look After Your Heart Campaign.* This was under the auspices of the Health Education Authority, which sought and obtained financial assistance from the Foundation in return for including the BHF calculator in the brochure for industry. The campaign involved the production and distribution of 2,500,000 copies of a book called *Look After Your Heart.* The Foundation also produced a leaflet with the same title, but which rapidly assumed its subtitle, *It'll Never Happen To Me,* under which it has proved very popular. As part of the same campaign a poster was devised for use in doctors' surgeries and has been well received.

(g) *Cardiopulmonary resuscitation (CPR).* The Foundation has pioneered public information on this topic for many years and produced a poster under the title 'Heart/Lung Resuscitation' in 1969, a picture of which is to be found in the *Heart Bulletin* of the summer of 1971 (Figure 31). Ten years later a film on the same subject followed, entitled *A Heart Attack – Learn What To Do,* and a new poster was made by the Cardiac Resuscitation Advisory Council (CRAC) with

172   *Chapter 5*

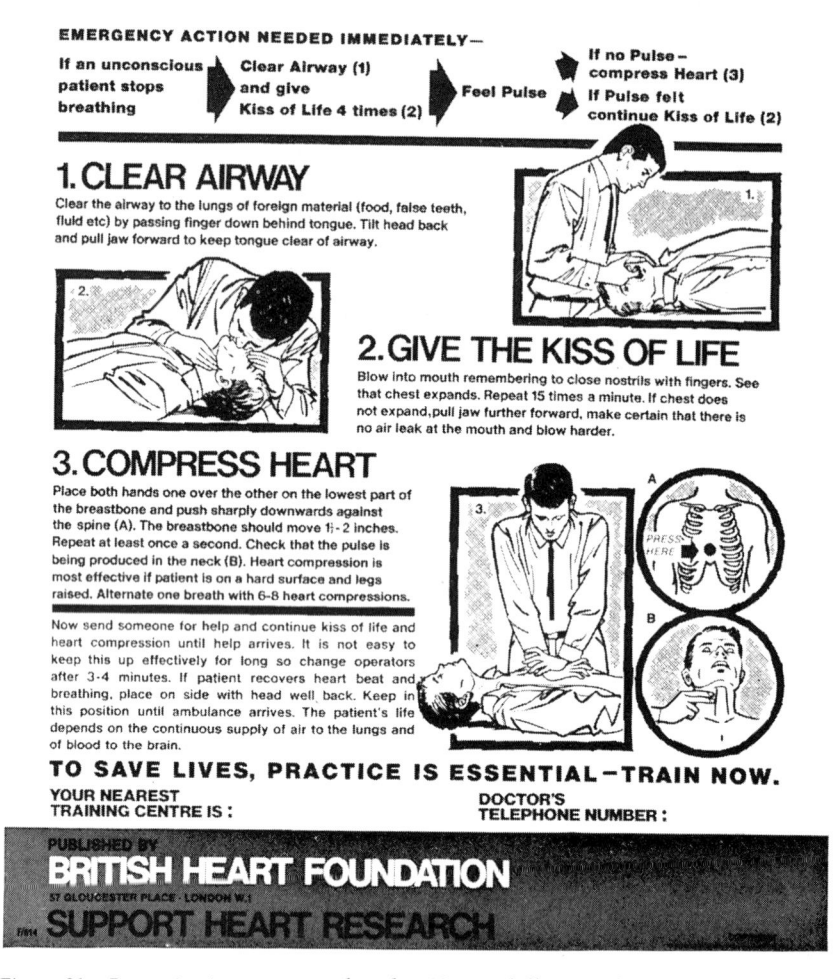

EMERGENCY ACTION NEEDED IMMEDIATELY—

If an unconscious patient stops breathing ▶ Clear Airway (1) and give Kiss of Life 4 times (2) ▶ Feel Pulse ▶ If no Pulse – compress Heart (3) If Pulse felt continue Kiss of Life (2)

1. CLEAR AIRWAY

Clear the airway to the lungs of foreign material (food, false teeth, fluid etc) by passing finger down behind tongue. Tilt head back and pull jaw forward to keep tongue clear of airway.

2. GIVE THE KISS OF LIFE

Blow into mouth remembering to close nostrils with fingers. See that chest expands. Repeat 15 times a minute. If chest does not expand, pull jaw further forward, make certain that there is no air leak at the mouth and blow harder.

3. COMPRESS HEART

Place both hands one over the other on the lowest part of the breastbone and push sharply downwards against the spine (A). The breastbone should move 1½ - 2 inches. Repeat at least once a second. Check that the pulse is being produced in the neck (B). Heart compression is most effective if patient is on a hard surface and legs raised. Alternate one breath with 6-8 heart compressions.

Now send someone for help and continue kiss of life and heart compression until help arrives. It is not easy to keep this up effectively for long so change operators after 3-4 minutes. If patient recovers heart beat and breathing, place on side with head well back. Keep in this position until ambulance arrives. The patient's life depends on the continuous supply of air to the lungs and of blood to the brain.

TO SAVE LIVES, PRACTICE IS ESSENTIAL – TRAIN NOW.

YOUR NEAREST TRAINING CENTRE IS :   DOCTOR'S TELEPHONE NUMBER :

PUBLISHED BY
BRITISH HEART FOUNDATION
57 GLOUCESTER PLACE · LONDON W.1
SUPPORT HEART RESEARCH

Figure 31 *Resuscitation poster produced in 1969 and illustrated in the* Bulletin *of the summer of 1971.*

financial assistance from the Foundation, together with an instructional flip-chart. In 1982 Dr Chamberlain organized the very successful meeting in Brighton on 'Cardiac Arrest and Resuscitation', at which the film was shown, and the Foundation funded an experimental research project, also in Brighton, to test the feasibility and value of public CPR training, where it was reported that 20,000 people had been taught the technique in two years.

In 1986 the Foundation gave substantial financial support to the 'Save A Life Campaign', in which the BBC showed six programmes on CPR. The Royal Society of Medicine were their advisers and Dr Chamberlain represented the Foundation on their organizing committee. It was claimed by the BBC that 100,000 people had been trained and 18 lives saved as a result of the campaign.

(h) *National No Smoking Day.* The Committee has supported this since 1984 when they contributed £15,000 to the expenses. This reversed a decision made 13 years before, in 1971, when a request from the Royal College of Physicians for their fund for Action on Smoking and Health (ASH) was turned down because it was outside the remit of the Foundation to support another charity. In 1988, when Cary Spink, the Education Funds Committee Administrator, was Chairman of the No Smoking Campaign, the Committee gave support of £22,000 on National No Smoking Day.

(i) *Films and videos.* The Education Committee has assumed responsibility for the distribution of the Foundation's audio-visual aids. It took over from the Administration Department the control and distribution of the film dealing with the history of heart research entitled *The Matter of the Heart* and the CPR film *Heart Attack – Learn What To Do.* It also agreed to purchase copies of the film made by Dr J.-P. Rocquebrun, a French cardiologist, entitled *How to Reduce the Risks of a Heart Attack,* and added an English soundtrack. It has proved very popular with fund-raisers and is much appreciated by their audiences. The two videos on the Committee's distribution list are *Coronary Artery Bypass Surgery – For Patients* and the *Healthy Hearts* video for schools. The surgical video is designed for patients facing surgery and is usually shown by the staff of hospital departments. The school video forms part of a talk by teachers.

The oldest film *One in Every Two of US* (Figure 32) is now too old for more than occasional projection and is in short supply. It remains in the keeping of the Administration. A new video showing the objectives, work and achievements of the Foundation is in preparation; amongst its uses it will be valuable if television projection for charity advertising becomes legal.

(j) *Coronary Prevention Group.* In 1985 Dr Michael Oliver agreed to represent the Foundation on the Council of the Group and recently

Figure 32 *His Royal Highness Prince Philip, Duke of Edinburgh, Patron of the Foundation, seen with Professor Sir John McMichael, Chairman of Council (left), and Lord Cobbold, President of the Foundation (right), attending the première of the film,* One in Every Two of Us, *at the Shell Centre on 11 November 1971.*

the Committee has agreed to support a jointly funded data base of statistics on coronary heart disease operated from the Coronary Prevention Group headquarters.

(k) *Library books.* In 1985 the Committee set aside £15,000 per annum for the purchase of books requested by postgraduate centres. At first the amount which could be spent for any one centre had to be restricted, but, with the increase in money available, the maximum for a centre has now been raised to £4,000 per annum; this has so far satisfied all requirements. The awards are made every six months.

(l) *Organ donors.* The Foundation has been at pains to assist in overcoming the chronic shortage of organs for transplantation. Although its primary interest is in heart and heart/lung transplants it has endeavoured to encourage the supply of organs for all transplants.

Besides the publication of the booklet called *The Gift of Life*, the Foundation issues its own donor cards, and in 1985, as part of the Foundation's 'Heart Week', under the slogan 'Research Saves Lives', the Committee arranged the distribution, through Sunday newspapers, of 1,200,000 copies of an insert containing three detachable cards, one of which was a donor card. The others were a CPR instruction card and a returnable card asking for more information about the Foundation. The response was very satisfactory and the cards seeking information are still coming in three years later.

During the same 'Heart Week' the Committee also distributed 100,000 key-rings containing a small donor card tag which was well publicized by the police, the ambulance service and the media, and particularly by local radio stations.

Loans

With the increased availability of money the Committee has been able to look more sympathetically at the requests for assistance in the running of meetings. Every request is scrutinized most carefully but, as a general rule, large meetings can be funded, if worthy, with an interest-free loan of £5,000 to get them set up, and small meetings related to cardiovascular disease can receive an out-right gift of up to £2,500. All applications have to be accompanied by a detailed budget estimate as well as a résumé of the content of the proposed programme and the expected attendance figures.

Travelling expenses

In 1980 the Committee agreed to set aside £15,000 for travelling expenses to overseas meetings and in 1981 the amount was raised to £30,000. The awards of up to £300 per journey were at the discretion of the Medical Administrator. The funds were especially intended for younger cardiologists and particularly for those attending small meetings, for which alternative funding was difficult or impossible to get. Those in receipt of these awards were charged with the duty of submitting a short report of the meeting on their return.

Public education

The Foundation was created to fund cardiovascular research and it has resisted many pressures to deviate from this objective. Although it has perceived its mission as including postgraduate education to ensure that full advantage is taken by doctors of the knowledge gained from research, it has maintained that public health education is primarily the responsibility of the Government through various agencies, of which the most important are the Health Education Authority and the National Health Service. The Foundation's subtitle is 'The Heart Research Charity'.

Its only major concession to public education in the early days was to publish articles in the *Heart Bulletin* on medical topics related to cardiovascular disease. Besides being informative these articles added interest for readers in a news-sheet which was essentially designed to increase awareness of the existence and activities of the Foundation. As has been described, these formed the basis of several of the Heart Research Series leaflets, all of which have been outstandingly successful.

One concession to public education in the early days is recorded, however, in the minutes of the Research Funds Committee of September 1971, when Dr Haigh, the Medical Administrator, reported that the Foundation had printed cards for distribution to the public giving the addresses of emergency pacemaker centres in Britain. No reason is given for this; perhaps it was because the Foundation had been funding research on the development of pacemakers. The publication of such cards has been continued and they have been recently updated.

In 1977 the Director General's report to Council concerning public education states that the policy remains 'to avoid proselytising amongst the general public until there is much more agreement generally about the origins and causes of cardiovascular disease', but the policy review for 1977–78 goes on to recommend that 'some provision should now be made for general education in addition to post-graduate education'.

In the Director General's report in 1978, however, the policy is reaffirmed in the following terms: 'at the present time our policy is to avoid attempting to educate the public until there is much more agreement generally about the origins and causes of cardiovascular disease. For the time being, public education is limited to the issue, on request, of our HRS pamphlets.' Clearly the provision for 'general education' was to cover the costs of producing and distributing these leaflets.

At this time public interest in life-style as a cause of heart disease was being fuelled by media debate, and adverse criticism of charities, including the BHF, for refusing to give dogmatic advice had appeared in the national and medical press and on radio and television.

In 1979 the Director General's report to Council stated that in reply to requests for advice on prevention of heart disease from the public only smoking had been generally agreed to be harmful and went on: 'For the time being we do not wish to suggest any changes in life style. For general bodily health we recommend moderate exercise and avoidance of obesity.'

The following year the Director General stated to Council: 'It has become clear that the medical research charities, together with many other bodies, are under increasing pressure to advise the public on how to improve their health and avoid disease.'

In 1981 the Director General reported that the Foundation had taken two steps to meet the demands of the day. It had made the highly successful film called *A Heart Attack – Learn What To Do*, and it had formed a media panel of medical experts which the Foundation could call upon to answer questions, and which had given answers to the most commonly asked questions, which could be used by Regional Organizers and fund-raisers as official BHF policy.

At the same time the Director General made a cautious statement to Council:

Post-graduate education seems to be on the right lines and we should make haste slowly over the question of public education. We are already spending money on public education under many different headings. We should continue with our policy of making the facts known as they are discovered, and, to this end, we have formed a panel of experts to answer the media. We should not be tempted to speculate publicly about unproven risk factors. Nothing is more likely to confuse the minds of the public than to see the experts arguing amongst themselves.

All this was, of course, of prime importance to the Education Funds Committee, which produced a statement in December 1981 on the 'prevention' of coronary heart attacks. It reads as follows:

The following memorandum was compiled by the Education Committee of the British Heart Foundation after a review of the world's literature on the aetiology of coronary heart disease with the advice of the President of the British Cardiac Society and two independent Consultant Cardiologists. It emphasises the importance of not telling the public anything which may later be refuted.

'Everybody is at a basic risk of developing a coronary heart attack and there is no way of absolutely preventing such an event happening.

'There are factors however which are known to increase this basic risk. These are endogenous (those we are born with) and exogenous (external) factors. The endogenous factors include a family history especially where the first-degree relatives have a history of coronary disease under the age of 55, a family tendency to diabetes, or being born with a high blood fat (e.g.

cholesterol). The major exogenous factor is smoking. Obesity tends to shorten the life span and high blood pressure may lead to strokes and coronary heart disease but its treatment will not for certain reduce the risk of a coronary attack. There is still considerable controversy over the role of food, exercise and stress in altering the exogenous risk factor; although they may play a part, it is possibly only a small one.

'It is therefore probably misleading to talk about "prevention" of a heart attack but more accurate to substantiate the words "increase or decrease the risk".'

In substance the content of this directive remains in force today with, perhaps, some added emphasis on exercise and stress. In 1982 and 1984 Dr Meade, then Chairman of the Education Funds Committee, obtained consensus agreement to guidelines on life-style risk factors which are official BHF policy and are set out in HRS 14.

By 1984 the Director General was able to report to Council that the Foundation's 'role as a research charity, rather than an educational charity is now more generally realised' and in 1985 that the policy was of 'continuing to inform the public of scientifically proven risk factors and advances in treatments through the publication of HRS leaflets'. To this was added the policy of 'improving the facilities for "cardiac care"' and 'keeping under continuous review the question of educating the public in the avoidance of heart disease and ensuring that the facts are publicised as they become known and are agreed by the medical profession as a whole'.

When Dr Fox was Chairman of the Education Committee, as it had now been renamed, he prepared a paper advocating increased participation by the Foundation in public education, which was accepted by the Finance and General Purposes Committee and the Council early in 1987, with the result that the committee was formally charged with the responsibility of carrying out this policy.

In fact this change had been proposed by Dr Chamberlain in 1980 when he was the Committee Chairman, and a subcommittee was formed to explore the possibilities, but it took several years to implement.

It was 1987 when the Director General reported at the Annual General Meeting: 'The activities of the Education Committee have increased substantially in the last year and the Council have given approval to the concept of public education being a function of the Foundation.'

The Medical Department

In December 1985 the Committee supported the suggestion by the Director General that 30% of the education budget should be allocated to public education, and in September 1986 they approved the spending of half their budget on public education and half on medical education.

The Education Funds Administrator

The Committee has been ably served over 17 years by many men and women in various capacities, and serviced successfully by Dr Haigh and Dr Butler in their capacity as Medical Administrators.

Its years of greatest expansion, however, have been since 1982 when Miss Cary Spink was appointed. The energy and innovative ideas which she brought to the job were exactly what were wanted and the Committee was well established in its new role as public, as well as medical, educator when she left in 1988 to become the Director of the Asthma Research Council. She was succeeded by Miss Kate Soutter.

APPENDIX A: TITLES OF SYMPOSIA

1970	December	Lipids, Platelets and Thrombosis
1971	April	Cardiovascular Surgery
	November	Coronary Heart Disease
1972	January	Instrumentation and Techniques
	March	Congenital Heart Disease
	June	Drugs in Cardiovascular Research
	November	Physiology and Biochemistry
1973	January	Clinical Symposium
	March	Pathology
	October	Cardiac Cellular Metabolism
	December	Adrenergic Beta-blocking
1974	February	Non-invasive Techniques in Cardiovascular Research
	May	Electrophysiology of the Heart
	September	The Arterial Wall
	November	Ischaemic Heart Disease
1975	February	Muscle and Myocardial Function
	May	Epidemiology
	October	Cardiac Disease in Childhood
	December	Lipids, Enzyme Chemistry and Hormones

1976	March	Non-invasive Techniques
	May	Thrombosis, Platelets and the Vascular Wall
	September	Cardiac Surgery and Organ Transplantation
	December	Clinical Symposium
1977	March	Clinical Applications in Cardiovascular Research
	May	Electrophysiology
	September	Cardiac Metabolism
	December	Cardiovascular Pharmacology
1978	March	Cardiac Surgery
	May	Thrombosis and Arterial Disease
	September	Myocardial Infarction
	December	Paediatric Cardiology
1979	March	Epidemiology
	June	Biochemistry
	September	Hypertension
	December	Arrhythmias
1980	March	Pharmacology
	June	Physiology
	September	Non-invasive Techniques
	December	Cardiovascular Surgery
1981	March	Clinical Meeting
	June	Cardiac Metabolism
	September	Blood/Arterial Wall Interface
	December	Electrophysiology
1982	March	Non-invasive Techniques
	September	Pharmacology
	December	Pathology
1983	March	Paediatric Cardiology
	June	Cardiac Surgery
	September	Biochemistry
	December	Hypertension
1984	March	Clinical Applications
	June	Myocardial Infarction
	September	Radio-isotopes, NMR, X-Ray Techniques and Doppler Ultrasound
	December	Thrombosis
1985	March	Cardiac Metabolism
	July	Electrophysiology and Electrocardiography
	September	Cardiac Pathology
	December	Non-invasive Techniques

1986	March	Heart Failure
	June	Paediatric Cardiology
	September	Surgery
1987	March	Biochemistry
	June	Myocardial Infarction
	October	Immunology
	December	Role of Ions and Force Production in the Heart
1988	February	Peptides
	June	Hypertension
	December	Electrophysiology

APPENDIX B: TITLES OF WORKSHOPS

1983	February	Manifestations of Ischaemic Heart Disease
	May	Electrophysiology
	October	Heart Rejection
	November	Collagen
1984	February	Genetic Engineering
	May	Hypertension
	November	Immunology
1985	February	Cholesterol
	April	Imaging of the Cardiovascular System
	October	Peptides and the Cardiovascular System
1986	March	Receptors in the Heart
	April	Marfan Syndrome
	July	Computers in Cardiology
	October	Haemodynamics
	November	Arterial Thrombosis
1987	February	Mechanism of Vasomotion
	April	Lipids and Coronary Artery Disease
	October	The Potential of Magnetic Resonance
	November	Of Mice and Men
1988	January	Asians and Coronary Heart Disease
	April	Pulmonary Circulation
	May	UK Multi-centre Study of Cardiopulmonary Resuscitation
	September	Pathology of Pulmonary Vascular Disease
	November	Heart Failure
	December	Platelets and Thrombosis

APPENDIX C: FACT FILE SUBJECTS

1985
1. The Pain of Acute Myocardial Infarction can be Shocking
2. A Slow Heart Rate following a Myocardial Infarction
3. Reducing the Risk of a Heart Attack
4. Acute Left Ventricular Failure
5. Myocardial Infarction – Home or Hospital?
6. Chest Pain – Is it Angina?
7. Detection and Assessment of Hypertension
8. Treatment of Hypertension
9. What to do about Systolic Hypertension
10. Rehabilitation After Acute Myocardial Infarction
11. Palpitation
12. Faints, Blackouts and Dizzy Spells

1986
1. Resuscitation
2. When to use Digoxin
3. Hypercholesterolaemia
4. Transient Cerebral Ischaemic Episodes
5. Heart Disease in Pregnancy
6. Heart Disease and the Contraceptive Pill
7. Marfan Syndrome – Diagnosis and Treatment
8. Use of Aspirin in Heart Disease
9. Atrial Fibrillation
10. Referral in Valve Disease
11. When to refer Patients with Angina
12. Prophylaxis for Endocarditis

1987
1. Pulmonary Embolism
2. Coronary Angioplasty
3. Drugs after Myocardial Infarction
4. Exercise and the Heart
5. Myocarditis
6. Hypertension in the Elderly
7. Indications for and Control of Anticoagulants
8. Peripheral Arterial Disease
9. Diet and Heart Disease
10. Alcohol and Heart Disease
11. Screening for Inherited Heart Disease in General Practice
12. Choice of Drugs in the Treatment of Angina

1988
1. Helping Smokers to Stop
2. Early Management of Coronary Heart Attacks

The Medical Department

3 Aortic Stenosis
4 Heart Disease in Diabetes
5 Treatment of Hypertension (revision)
6 Ventricular Ectopic Beats
7 Use of Aspirin in Heart Disease (revision)
8 Pain of Acute Myocardial Infarction (revision)
9 Thrombolysis for Acute Myocardial Infarction

APPENDIX D: PUBLICATIONS LIST

1 Annual Report
2 Introduction to the BHF
3 General Leaflet
4 Children's Leaflet
5 *Matter of the Heart* – Film and Video
6 *Heart Attack – Learn What To Do* – Film and Video
7 Deed of Covenant Leaflet
8 Legacy Leaflet
9 Christmas Catalogue
10 'Please, No Smoking' Notice
11 *Your Heart* – Newsletter
12 Regional Offices, Map and Addresses
13 Children's Poster
14 Medical Reports. Research, Education Programme and Cardiac Care Awards
15 Grant Regulations
16 Cardiopulmonary Resuscitation Poster
17 All-Organ Donor Card
18 Cardiopulmonary Resuscitation Card
19 Emergency Pacemaker Centres Card
20 Anti-Smoking Poster for Teenagers
21 *Food Should Be Fun*
22 A New Start for You and Your Heart
23 Newsletter for Teenagers
24 Guide to a Healthy Heart
25 The Marfan Syndrome
26 Gift of Life Leaflet
27 Heart Research Series:
   1 Back to Normal
   2 Success in Heart Research
   3 Recovery from a Stroke
   4 What is Angina?
   5 Congenital Heart Disease
   6 Medicines for the Heart
   7 Diet and Your Heart

8   Is it Blood Pressure?
9   Pacemakers
10 Smoking and Your Heart
11 The Heart – Technical Terms Explained
12 Heart Surgery for Adults
13 Valvular Heart Disease
14 Reducing the Risk of a Heart Attack
15 Palpitations
16 Hyperlipidaemia
17 Cardiac Investigation and Coronary Angioplasty
18 Peripheral Arterial Disease

THE CARDIAC CARE COMMITTEE

The Cardiac Care Committee was formed by the Council at the same meeting in February 1970 as the one in which the Research Funds Committee and the Postgraduate Education Funds Committee were set up.

The structure was defined as consisting of 'a Chairman and two members, of whom the Chairman and one other will be medical, and the third the Director General', and its purpose was defined as 'to give aid in cardiac care especially where needs are too urgent to be met by National Health Service resources'.

The existence of the Committee and its objectives were announced to a meeting of the British Cardiac Society within a few months of its formation.

Dr Walter Somerville was its Chairman for fifteen years (1970–85), and its success was, in great part, due to his hard work, and to his knowledge of the cardiovascular scene throughout Britain. Over the years he travelled extensively and repeatedly up and down the country visiting cardiac departments, which enabled him to identify areas of special privation where needs were greatest. Since he knew most of the cardiologists personally he was also able to encourage those whom he knew to have little flair for collecting money to make application to the Foundation for help, and to discourage those who were good at finding local support.

His travels also enabled him to judge the suitability of requests made to the Foundation and, where necessary, to discuss alternatives better suited to the local situation. Moreover, with the two guiding principles of maximum efficiency and economy always before him, he was often able to suggest alternative models at less cost. His visits also sometimes traced a spate of requests in a particular region of the country for an unnecessarily expensive piece of apparatus to a recent tour by an especially persuasive salesman. His objective was always to obtain the 'best buy' to meet a particular need. Dr Somerville's knowledge, energy and strategy were exactly what the Committee needed to ensure success.

For the first five years of its existence the second medical member of the Committee was the then current Medical Administrator, who also acted as its Secretary. This was Dr Margaret Haigh from 1970 to 1972 and Dr Butler from 1972 until 1975, when Dr John Blackburn joined the Committee as the second medical member, with Dr Butler continuing as its Secretary until his resignation in 1983. In the latter part of his time, when the administrative load became very heavy, Dr Butler was ably assisted for several years by Shirley Jacobs and for a shorter time by Julie Stone.

Dr Blackburn was Consultant to the Department of Clinical Measurement at Westminster Hospital and remained a member of the Committee until forced to resign because of ill health in 1984. Dr Somerville paid generous tribute to his ability and to his services to the Committee saying: 'he had encyclopaedic knowledge of the sort of medical equipment that we had particularly in mind when considering requests ... he had great skills in understanding equipment and electrical circuits, and he would take it upon himself to investigate the various properties of different types of, say, defibrillators, and would, at my request, advise most effectively'.

History

The decision to set up the Cardiac Care Committee in 1970 to 'provide life-saving equipment' grew naturally out of the declaration of the objectives of the Foundation, approved at the first meeting of the Founding Committee in September 1959, which included the responsibility to 'improve patients' welfare'.

It was also foreshadowed by the resolution of the Council in May 1964 to support seven requests to supply cardioverters (as defibrillators were then called) for cardiac resuscitation in general hospitals. Besides endorsing this as good publicity for the Foundation's Appeal, this council meeting also affirmed categorically that 'resuscitation is a valid aspect of cardiovascular research to support'.

Disbursement

Within a month of its creation in 1970 it was reported to the Council that the Cardiac Care Committee had met and recommended the acceptance of four requests totalling £5,382; three months later requests for a similar amount of money were also agreed. In 1972 the cost of the awards increased from £11,000 to nearly £18,000, but in 1973 there were no applications and the Council minutes record that the Committee did not need to meet for a year.

In 1974 Dr Butler reported to Council that there 'was not the anticipated flood of requests for grants' although it is recorded that nine were made totalling £13,000. The following year saw 12 requests approved at a cost of £10,000 and in 1976 14 requests totalling £22,000.

It was at this stage that the need for regular quarterly meetings at fixed dates was agreed, but, unfortunately, there are no surviving minutes of these meetings before November 1983. Presumably the earlier records were lost during the move of headquarters from 57 to 102 Gloucester Place. Reliance has therefore to be placed upon extracts from the Director General's Annual Report, and the minutes of the meetings of Council and the Finance and General Purposes Committee, together with personal communications from those who have worked for the Committee.

It appears that in the very early days, once the Committee had approved a request, the hospital concerned purchased the equipment and sent the invoice to the Foundation for payment.

Local fund-raising

Not long after Colonel Malcolm became Director of Appeals in 1976 he joined the Committee, and soon after this made the suggestion that the purchase of life-saving equipment for a local hospital would prove popular with fund-raisers, and benefit fund-raising for research as well. He was proved right and an added incentive was the agreement by the Cardiac Care Committee to make a contribution to supplement the amount collected locally.

This new arrangement gave Regional Organizers a good platform at presentations of equipment to publicize the needs of the Foundation for funds for research, by taking advantage of coverage by local

The Medical Department

media. The Cardiac Care Committee ruled, in order to take maximum advantage of this publicity, that applications for assistance from the Foundation must be made, in the first instance, to the local Regional Organizer, and that the approval of the application by the Committee must be obtained before local fund-raising began; it was also stipulated that the maximum contribution from the Foundation for any one piece of apparatus would be £10,000.

At various times awards financed by local funding have been known as 'local', 'conditional' or 'special' awards, as opposed to those which are funded wholly by the Foundation.

Value added tax (VAT)

This tax was introduced by the Government on 1 April 1973. All goods were taxed at a fixed percentage of cost (currently 15%) but charities were exempt (zero-rated) on such goods as equipment. As a result the purchase of all apparatus through the Foundation saved a lot of money, and it was, therefore, well worth while, even if all the money had been collected locally. This is a legally proper procedure.

Cost of Awards

The annual cost of awards quoted in available sources before 1983 does not differentiate between the amounts contributed by the Foun-

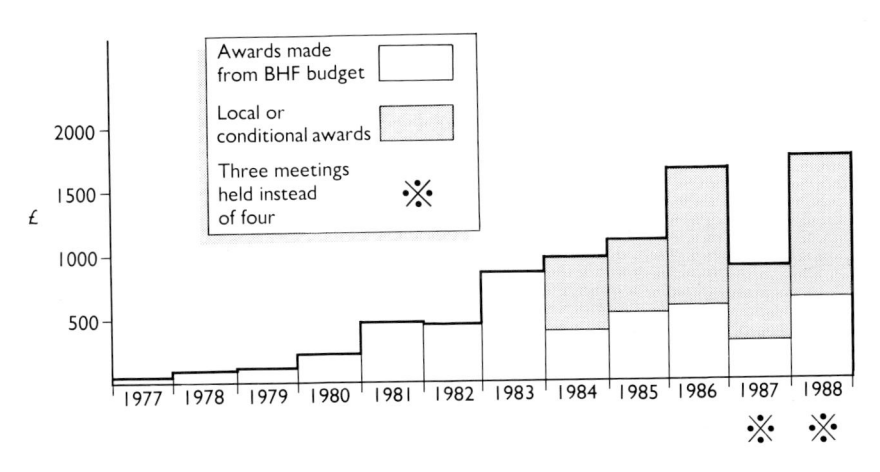

Figure 33 *The value of awards by the Cardiac Care Committee from the BHF budget, and 'local' or 'conditional' awards between 1977 and 1988.*

dation and those subscribed locally. Nor do the records of the number of awards made separate the two categories. The figures are therefore of limited value. But from 1983 onwards the records list the two sources separately as well as giving the total expenditure (Figure 33).

The figures reveal a rapid increase in the amount of money raised locally in recent years. This created a problem for the Committee because it had always made all awards, including 'local' awards, out of a set budget determined by the Council as a fixed percentage of available resources. This started as 5% in 1974, being raised to 8% in 1976 and to 10% in 1978, where it has since remained. With the awards funded locally being deductible from the overall budget, these deductions would have absorbed, by 1986, the whole allocation to the Committee, and left it unable to make any awards, either as contributions to 'local' awards, or as outright grants from the Foundation. To correct this it was agreed, at this time, that the whole allocation to the Committee should be available to it for disbursement, without any deductions arising from locally funded awards.

Buyer

As the costs of the equipment on which the Committee was called upon to adjudicate increased, and the choices widened, it became clear that the services of an experienced Buyer were urgently needed. These were very satisfactorily met by the appointment, in 1981, of Bob Stiller, on a part-time basis. He was just retiring from the post of Buyer and Equipment Officer at the Royal Free Hospital after a lifetime's experience in Government service in this field. Knowing the various manufacturers, and, in many cases, key personnel, he was able to secure the best terms, and, with the help of Dr Blackburn, also the 'best buys'. Besides the Cardiac Care Committee's awards he also arranged the purchase of research equipment for grant-holders and professorial units, with the result that within two years of his appointment the Director General was able to report to Council a saving of £200,000 on equipment costing £1,500,000.

Defibrillators

The value of defibrillators as life-saving equipment for ventricular fibrillation and some other arrhythmias had been widely known for a

The Medical Department

long time, and the Foundation had been sympathetic to requests for money with which to acquire them for many years. In the mid-1980s, however, there was much pressure put on the Foundation to play a major part in supplying ambulance services as well as hospitals in need.

Collecting money for defibrillators was popular with local fundraisers, and enthusiastically supported by Regional Directors because of the good publicity it gave the BHF. Presentation ceremonies of equipment which could save lives so dramatically were good 'seed corn'.

The Cardiac Care Committee, however, had to be realistic and act responsibly before sanctioning such expensive awards in large numbers, and insisted that ambulance crews must first receive adequate training in their use. With this reservation, however, the Committee gave full cooperation and has financed the purchase of a large number throughout the country either as 'conditional' or as total awards.

The supply of defibrillators was the single largest cause of the immense increase in money collected locally in recent years, and also began to absorb a disproportionately large percentage of the Committee's budget. In 1986, therefore, it was decided by the Committee that 20% should be set aside per annum for the supply of defibrillators to ambulances, and that this sum would be allocated to Regional Directors on a per capita basis. They would then have to split their allocations according to the applications, which would be made direct to them. For the financial year 1987–88 the quota for defibrillators was raised to £250,000.

A list of defibrillators approved by the Committee was sent to the Regional Directors for their guidance, and this included the new 'semi-advisory' models which are fitted with fact-finding accessories to identify malignant and dangerous changes of rhythm needing immediate shock therapy. They also have a recording apparatus attached (like the black box in aircraft) which stores the data, and records the action taken at the scene of the emergency, for subsequent study. Assistance in making the right decision in this way is of obvious benefit to paramedical staff, and also reduces the length of time needed for training.

Another difficult problem arose from requests by general practitioners also to be supplied with defibrillators. Their usefulness in the hands of doctors obviously varies with the ready availability of the doctor, the state of supply of defibrillators to the local ambulance service and the proximity of the nearest equipped hospital. It was ultimately agreed that applications could be considered if the doctor concerned had received adequate training and was a member of the 'immediate care accident scheme'.

Personnel

When Dr Somerville retired as Chairman of the Committee in 1985 he was succeeded by Sir Stanley Peart. He resigned in 1987 to become Chairman of the working party investigating the desirability of involvement of the Foundation in clinical trials, and was succeeded as Chairman by Dr Richard Emanuel.

When Dr Blackburn retired in 1984 he was succeeded by Dr Graham Leach (St George's) as Technical Adviser to the Committee; he has done much good work in assessing the relative efficiency, suitability and ease of handling of different pieces of apparatus, and with the preparation of lists embodying summaries and conclusions. Recently he has been heavily committed in the assessment of 'interpretative' ECG machines and the preparation of a paper on the subject for the Committee. To date the Committee has expressed the opinion that, although it recognizes that they have a place in general practitioner referral clinics, they are no substitute for a doctor's ability to read an ECG, and that it is not in favour of making them generally available.

When Bob Stiller retired as Buyer and Secretary of the Committee in 1985 he was succeeded by Caroline Houching, and she, in turn, by Sarah Knight in 1987.

In 1986 it was decided to increase the membership of the Committee by the appointment of a consultant cardiologist, in addition to the Medical Director, who was already a member; Dr R.G. Gold, consultant cardiologist at Newcastle, accepted an invitation to join.

A wise decision was also to invite a Regional Director to membership of the Committee and Wing Commander Jock Heatherill of Region 17 attended for the first time in December 1985. After serving his period of office he was succeeded in February 1988 by Colonel Richard Besly from Region 9.

Colonel Malcolm, the Director of Appeals, who had been a

The Medical Department

member of the Committee for many years, introduced Elaine Snell, the Press Officer in his department, to the Committee in 1988, so that she, in conjunction with the Medical Spokesman, Dr Frank Preston, who also sits in on the Committee as an observer, is aware of, and can take advantage of, any award of potential media interest.

Dorothy Denn, who is the source of much of the information available about the Committee, has been the assistant to the Buyer and Secretary since 1981, and has a wide knowledge of the field of technical equipment and its sources of manufacture. She has provided very valuable continuity during the changes here recorded.

SIX

THE REGIONS

THE NEED FOR fund-raising Committees was immediately appreciated by the Appeal Policy Committee. At its first meeting on 20 July 1960 it passed a resolution to recommend 'that local Appeal Committees be set up in each Region'.

The regions referred to are the Regional Boards of the National Health Service and the Chairman, Dr Maurice Campbell, undertook to write to cardiologists in the regions explaining the need and 'asking for confidential suggestions of leading personalities who might be invited to form the nucleus of a Regional Committee'.

Only Dr W.G.A. Swan of Newcastle replied quickly and enthusiastically, although ultimately nine cardiologists wrote pledging their support.

At the meeting of the Committee in January 1961 Dr William Evans said that he felt it was not too early to set up a regional organization and that the cardiologist in each region should be asked to set up a committee. In discussion, however, it was agreed that it would be a mistake to create committees before the public appeal was launched since their activity would have to be restrained, and that in spite of restraint publicity would inevitably result, which was undesirable prior to the public appeal. In consequence it was generally agreed that action should be deferred.

A memorandum to General Street, who had been appointed Appeal Director, dated 22 July 1963, which was one month after the launch of the public appeal, contains a paragraph, amongst a number of points for consideration, which reads as follows; 'Regional Organisation. Some tentative beginnings have been made in Scotland, and they should be continued as a pilot scheme. The basic essential is to get an energetic business man to act as Chairman; it is hoped he might run the appeal from his own offices to save expense to the Foundation.'

As with most projects in the early days, the Foundation owed facilities and implementation to the Chest and Heart Association. In this instance it was greatly assisted by the Scottish Office of the Association through its Secretary, Miss Hume. With her help the Scottish Appeal Committee was formed in 1965 under the Presidency of Sir Alexander King, and the Chairmanship of the cardiologist Dr Rae Gilchrist; Lord Fraser was one of its members. At the Council meeting in March 1966 the Appeal Director was able to announce that the Scottish Appeal Committee had already raised £50,000, of which, half had been given by Lord Fraser. Following Sir Alexander's death in 1973 Mr Isadore Walton became President and he was succeeded by Mr George Young, who was, at the time, managing Director of the East Kilbride Development Corporation.

Frances Neal records that when she joined the Foundation in August 1966, as assistant to the newly appointed Secretary Denis Blake, there were just five regions: the Scottish Region, based in Edinburgh, which was organized by Major Andrew McIntosh; the Northern Region, based in Newcastle upon Tyne, organized by Richard Hill; the Southern Region including London, organized by Doreen Nicholson and Bill Cutts, with Molly Chandler as their assistant; the North West, based in Liverpool, organized by Kit Keenan; and Northern Ireland in Belfast organized by Wing Commander Masters.

Brigadier Cardiff succeeded General Street as Appeal Director in 1964 after the latter had been the Director for some 15 months, and was assisted by Captain Noel Lyster-Binns; together they were active in promoting the establishment of these five regional organizations.

DEVELOPMENT

In 1966 Brigadier Cardiff became Director General of the Foundation, and he was joined by Geoffrey Davison, on the resignation of Lyster-Binns. Davison's brief was to develop as wide a regional network as possible. When he arrived the organizations in Scotland, London and Northern Ireland had been in operation, as pilot schemes, for between 12 and 18 months, those in the North and North West for only a few months. When he left in 1976, 17 regions were well established.

The Foundation was fortunate to have an organizer, at this critical time of development, who had the energy and skill to invade this difficult field so successfully and, at the same time, inspire new recruits to overcome difficulties and occasional disappointments.

The creation and survival of much of the early regional network owes much to his diplomacy, and to the able help he had from Sarah Corbin (née Hillard) and Frances Neal.

Speaking of these early days Geoffrey Davison said:

We had a very set formula which seemed to work well in those days, where we knobbled anyone who was anyone in the area and had an inaugural luncheon at which they were all asked to do their bit. We tried to form management committees, but they were really only just to oversee and give credibility to the Heart Foundation's operations in the area. Many of these Regions were started by Doreen Nicholson at that time.

Mrs Nicholson had been a professional opera singer with the Carl Rosa Opera Company and started with the Foundation to set up a fund-raising organization in London. She did this so successfully that she was given the title of 'Regional Development Officer', advising and assisting in many parts of the country, besides continuing to run the London Region with Bill Cutts and Molly Chandler.

In October 1966 Brigadier Cardiff was able to report to Council that the committees in Liverpool and Birmingham would be ready to launch appeals in 1967, and that thirteen committees, directed from London, were already active in the South East of England. At the same meeting he also announced that a new region was being set up in the Midlands, based on Nottingham.

Shortly after this, committees in Kent came under the direction of Group Captain du Boulay, who was based in Sandwich. He and his wife, Jane, organized many events including a garden party at Walmer Castle, in 1967, hosted by Sir Robert and Dame Pattie Menzies, the Governor General of Australia and his wife. At the time Sir Robert held the appointment of Warden of the Cinque Ports. Another successful event was an Elizabethan pageant, which was much enjoyed and attracted good publicity for the Foundation amongst other charities.

In June 1968 the Director General was able to report to Council the formation of regional organizations in Hampshire, Wiltshire, Dorset and Cornwall, and in 1969 there followed Yorkshire, Buckinghamshire and Thames Valley, with committees in Leeds, Derby and Leicester.

A total of 15 regions had been achieved by this year, and the Regional Organizers attended a conference in London in January 1969 convened by Geoffrey Davison. The following year Brigadier Cardiff reported the existence of 100 local committees.

Geoffrey Davison recalls that he visited each region at least three times a year: 'It was a very lonely occupation for Regional Organiser,' he said, and went on:

I carried information of what was going on at headquarters so they could be kept up to date. This was important because their voluntary committees wanted to know. There was also the *Bulletin*, which I edited; it was a gossip sheet provided to praise voluntary endeavour, and a way of patting people on the back for their efforts. For someone with no knowledge of print it was hard work, and I used to sit, many a night, working out with a ruler how the photographs would fit. Then we made a splendid arrangement with Warners, the printers. I listed the ones for prominence and they assembled the jig-saw.

After the regional framework had been established for a few years it became the custom to invite about six Regional Organizers to London at a time, usually twice a year, for a day's seminar. This was held at the National Heart Hospital and included a medical talk. Geoffrey Davison recalls that Donald Ross, the cardiac surgeon, often undertook this task and was highly successful.

All voluntary workers and Regional Organizers were invited to a fashion show and variety evening at the Festival Hall in 1969, which was generously hosted by Marks and Spencer. Although the occasion provided good publicity for the Foundation, its primary objective was to acknowledge the hard work done by fund-raisers throughout the country.

In recent years Regional Organizers and Directors and County Organizers have been invited to a social gathering at headquarters after the annual public meeting, and to a seminar the following day in the conference room. It has also been the custom to invite them in turn to sit in on meetings of the Research Funds Committee, and to serve as members of the Education and Cardiac Care Committees with the intention of involving senior regional management as closely as possible with the running of the Foundation at headquarters.

The performance and even the survival of voluntary committees frequently depends on one key figure. Inability to continue for any reason may lead to collapse, or at best to a need to reorganize, during which time income inevitably falls. Newly formed committees are unavoidably at maximum risk, and in the early days of the Foundation regional organizations were subject to the same hazards. There were ups and downs, and failures as well as successes.

In the early 1970s it seems that the number of committees fell back from the 100 reported to Council by Brigadier Cardiff: certainly the impetus of expansion of the late 1960s had died down and was followed by a period in which efforts were concentrated on consolidating the gains already made.

REORGANIZATION

Colonel Malcolm recalls that, when he became Director of Appeals in 1976, 'there were only about seventy voluntary committees and committee creation had dried up'. He went on:

When I came there were about eighteen Regions and there seemed to be no particular strategy as to how the Region was laid out. When breaking new ground the right person had to be found first, and the Region developed where he or she lived, which meant they were unbalanced in many ways. You would get a Region with about ten million people in the Midlands, and another in the South West with half a million, and both organised by the same sized staff.

Building on the sound framework which had been created from nothing by the hard work of so many people he had the vision to see the need for restructuring. By reducing the number of regions a better balance of population was achieved with a saving of personnel, office accommodation, cars and equipment, which reduced expenses by over 30%. His aim was to create ten large regions out of the existing 18, by amalgamations when retirements presented the opportunity. At present there are 11 regions and this number is shortly to be reduced to ten.

Speaking of the Regional Organizers he found them 'very dedicated and working way beyond the call of duty'. He thought they were overworked and underpaid, and he was shocked by the accommodation in which some of them worked. He recalls that this included the sixth floor of a warehouse in Glasgow, a rehabilitated coal shed in Wales, a caravan in the West of England and several attics.

His principal concern, however, was that they were too involved personally in fund-raising, instead of organizing others to do it, and felt that, as Regional Directors, their role should be delegating re-

DO	DON'T
1 **Enjoy** the work to the utmost. Only happy committees are successful	1 **Beg.** The cause of heart research is more than just charitable: it is a public service which concerns everybody and you are providing the community with an opportunity to help themselves
2 **Be Independent** and assume complete responsibility for your area. Our full and part-time organizers are widely scattered and their job is to create new committees. Every time you can tell them to 'mind their own business' you will have made a major contribution to the work of the Foundation	2 **Over reach.** Your ultimate aim is to influence **every** household. This cannot be achieved if you take on too large an area (we need another 750 committees to help you out)
3 **Generate Publicity.** Over 80% of BHF's funds come from unsolicited donations and legacies; from people who have heard or read about our work. Heart disease affects nearly every household; yet how many in your area know about the BHF? Do appoint a publicity officer; it is the most important job on any committee	3 **Attempt too much.** The happiest and most effective committees are often those which concentrate on just one major fund-raising event, which is repeated and improved annually
4 **Think Big.** So often it takes more time and trouble to raise £500 than it does to raise £5000. Make sure that your efforts are properly rewarded and **publicised**	4 **Accept Passengers.** Too many committees leave all the work to the chairman or secretary, or even to the regional office. Every member should make some specific or specialized contribution. Willing 'pairs of hands' can be co-opted when needed
5 **Delegate.** Within your area there are dozens of voluntary organizations which want to help. Give them the opportunity	5 **Pass the Buck** to your regional office or county organizer. A prudent committee seeks advice when it starts; but it becomes effective when it runs its own show from A–Z

Figure 34 *'Dos and Don'ts' for fund-raisers as recommended by Colonel Malcolm, the Director of Appeals.*

sponsibility to fund-raising committees. Somewhat cryptically he remarked that as a general rule he found commitees most effective when they were far enough away not to have Regional Organizers breathing down their necks! When replacements were needed, as Regional Directors he looked for those with experience of senior management and the ability to delegate responsibility (Figure 34).

To make this new concept successful, however, he needed people who were good communicators to foster new committees; these were County Organizers. Of them he said:

I invented the role of County Organisers; their job is to create new committees and keep the existing ones happy. They work from home and have no administrative chores. They are essential to the concept of large regions administered by Regional Directors. The number of committees has gone up from 70 to about 500, and the regional income from a quarter of a million to over three million pounds [1987].

Colonel Malcolm recalls going down with a bottle of champagne to congratulate Dorothy Curtis, the Regional Organizer for Hampshire, in 1978, and celebrate the first time a region had raised £50,000 in a year.

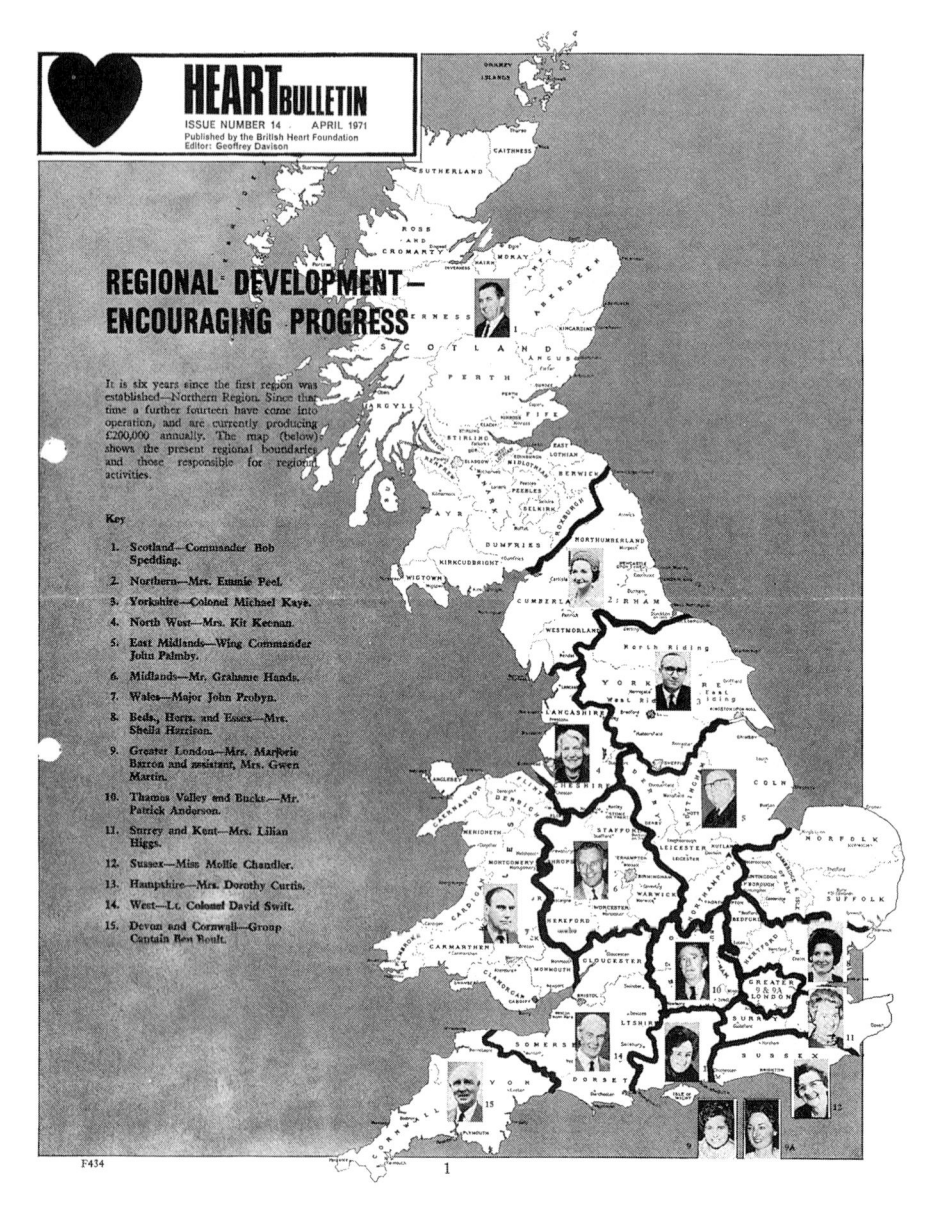

Figure 35 *Map of the regions published in the* Bulletin *in 1971.*

The Regions

By 1981 the Director General was able to report to Council that eight regions had raised more than £100,000 each, and that the total regional income had exceeded £2,000,000 for the first time. In 1984 he was able to report that four regions had each collected more than £250,000. In 1985 this figure went up to £400,000, and in 1987 to more than £600,000.

REGIONAL GEOGRAPHICAL PATTERNS

The original intention of Brigadier Cardiff and Geoffrey Davison was to base a British Heart Foundation Region on each Region of the National Health Service, but it proved impracticable to follow this pattern consistently because regions had to be created round suitable personalities. These were difficult to find, but of supreme importance to the Foundation in setting up the network.

The pattern as seen today is further confused by changes in the numbering of the regions which have taken place over the years, and by amalgamations, realignments and closures which have resulted in many variations in the numbers of active regions at any one time. Overall, Colonel Malcolm's policy of creating larger regions, with no relation to the National Health Service structure, has resulted in a reduction from the maximum numbers of the early years.

None the less it will be of interest to all who were involved in regional staffing and in membership of the numerous committees at different periods in the Foundation's history to have recorded the sequence of events, as well as the records permit.

The situation in 1967 is illustrated in the map published in the *Bulletin* (see p. 61). Another followed in 1971 which included photographs of the Regional Organizers in post at the time (Figure 35). In retrospect it is a pity that the *Bulletin* did not follow this with a series of maps every few years to chart changes. Happily, however, an up-to-date map was published in 1988 (Figure 36).

When David Reynolds joined the Foundation in 1977 he recalls the following pattern:

Region	Area	Regional Officer
1	Northern Region	Norman Bell
2	East Anglia (including Essex and Cambridge)	Major Ray Stokes

200   *Chapter 6*

BRITISH HEART FOUNDATION
The heart research charity
— where to find us:

The British Heart Foundation has 11 regional offices covering the whole of the United Kingdom. Each area has many volunteers organising local fundraising events. To find out what is going on near you – contact your regional office.

REGIONS

A SCOTLAND:
16 Chester St, Edinburgh, EH3 7RA
Tel: (031) 226 3705

B NORTH-EAST AND NORTH ENGLAND:
393 Westgate Road, Newcastle-upon-Tyne, NE4 6PA
Tel: (091) 2731568

C NORTH-WEST ENGLAND, N. IRELAND & I.O.M:
5 Castle St, Liverpool, L2 4SW
Tel: (051) 236 6988

D YORKSHIRE AND NORTH HUMBERSIDE:
4-6 Bridge Street, Tadcaster, North Yorkshire, LS24 9AL
Tel: 0937 835421

E WALES, SHROPSHIRE, HEREFORD & WORCESTERSHIRE:
Brighton House, Temple St,
Llandrindod Wells, Powys, LD1 5DL
Tel: (0597) 2051

F MIDLANDS, STAFFS, LINCS AND SOUTH HUMBERSIDE:
32 Park Row, Nottingham, NG1 6GR
Tel: (0602) 417835

G E. ANGLIA, ESSEX, HERTS, BEDS, BUCKS AND NORTHANTS:
1 Market St, Saffron Walden, Essex, CB10 1HZ
Tel: (0799) 21420

H SOUTH-WEST ENGLAND (INCLUDING OXON):
6 Terrace Walk, Bath, Avon, BA1 1LN
Tel: (0225) 63616

J WEST LONDON:
102 Gloucester Place, London, W1H 4DH
Tel: 01-935 0185

K GREATER LONDON: NORTH, SOUTH AND EAST:
Langthorne Hospital, Langthorne Road, London, E11 4HJ
Tel: 01-539 8828

L SOUTH-EAST ENGLAND:
33 High St, Ticehurst, Wadhurst, East Sussex, TN5 7AS
Tel: (0580) 200443

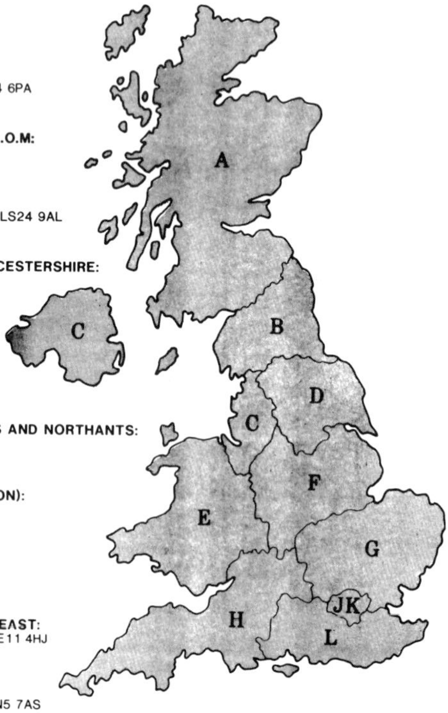

Figure 36   *Map of the eleven large regions of the Foundation in 1988.*

The Regions

3	Scotland	
	East Scotland	Micheal Shale
	West Scotland	Jane Black
4	London	
	Greater London	Gwen Martyn
	West London	Bernie Lane
5	Northern Home Counties (Bedfordshire, Hertfordshire and Buckinghamshire)	Sheila Harrison followed by Miriam Collett
6	West Midlands (based on Solihull)	Graham Hands
7	North West (based in Liverpool; Lancashire, Northern Ireland and Isle of Man)	Kit Keenan
8	Jersey	No RO
9	South East (Kent, Surrey and East Sussex)	Lilian Higgs
10	South West (Oxfordshire and Gloucestershire)	Major Peter Johnstone
11	Staffordshire	Leslie Barker
12	Surrey (closed before 1977)	
13 & 14	Not in existence in 1977	
15	Hampshire, Berkshire and Isle of Wight	Dorothy Curtis
16	Wiltshire and Somersetshire	Colonel David Swift
17	East Midlands (Nottingham)	Wing Commander John Palmby
18	Devonshire and Cornwall	Basil Curtis
19	Yorkshire and Humberside	Colonel Michael Kaye
20	West London (just starting)	Bernie Lane
21	Wales	John Probyn

As a result of extensions and amalgamations the geographical situation at the beginning of 1987 was as follows:

Region	Area	Alteration
1	Northern	Substantially unchanged
2	East Anglia	The old Regions 2 and 5.
3	Scotland	Combination of East and West Scotland
4	Greater London	Unchanged
7	North West	Includes part of the old Region 11, including Greater Manchester
8	Jersey	Unchanged
9	South	Includes the old Region 15
10	West	Includes the old Regions 16 and 18
17	Midlands	Includes the old Region 17 (East Midlands) and part of the old Region 11 (South Staffordshire)
19	Yorkshire	The same with parts of North Humberside and Tyne and Wear added
20	West London	Unaltered
21	Wales	The same with parts of the old Region 11 added. Shropshire and Worcestershire added

REGIONAL HISTORIES

An account of some of the personalities who have made major contributions to the development and success of the regions will be of interest to all who have helped in fund-raising, as will also a record of some of the outstanding events.

The record is unavoidably incomplete, however, because it can only be as good as the memory and cooperation of the participants. Some have been more helpful than others, and this is reflected in the detail available for inclusion.

It is also difficult to see the early endeavours in the light of the present-day concept of a region, its structure and activities, since it was not until 1970 that the Council made the fundamental change of Foundation policy, by replacing the objective of a single defined appeal for £5,000,000 with an ongoing appeal unlimited in time or by financial target. Thus in the early days a region tended to be set up, in the first instance, as a Regional Fund-raising Appeal Committee, and the need to increase the number of local voluntary committees as the

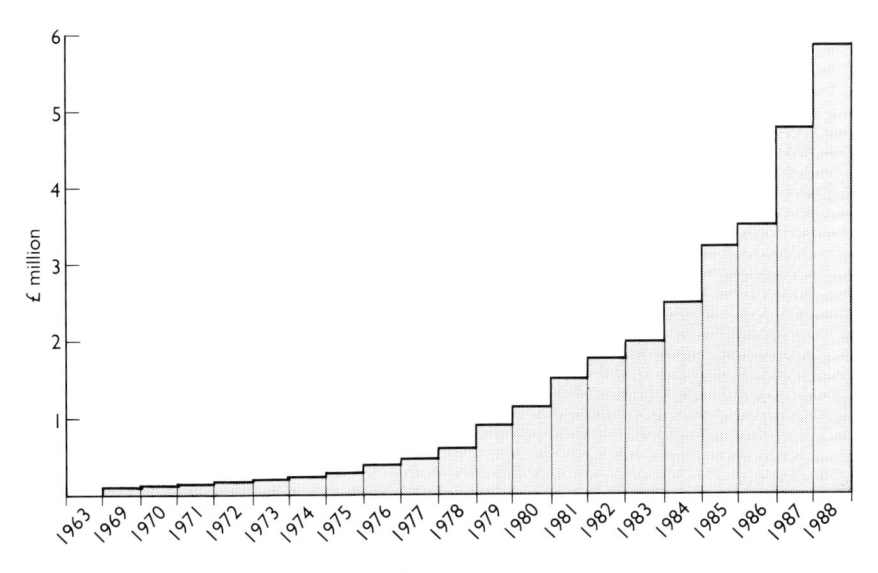

Figure 37 *Chart showing the regional income 1963–88.*

key to increasing regional revenue had not been generally appreciated before Colonel Malcolm's arrival in 1976.

It was fortuitous that this coincided with Brigadier Cardiff's pronouncement that, in his view, the days of prestigious events and expensive participation were over, and that the burden would fall increasingly on the efforts of very many through the regions nationwide. The dramatically successful response by the regions to this challenge is shown in the accompanying chart (Figure 37).

The North

In the map published in the *Bulletin* in 1971 the North is listed as Region 2, with Scotland as Region 1. Shortly after this, however, the Northern Region assumed the premier title and has held it ever since.

The earliest record is of a meeting held on 29 May 1964 at the offices of Mr Neil McQueen in Emerson Chambers, Blackett Street, Newcastle upon Tyne, which set up a Regional Appeal Committee. The Chairman was Dr Adrian Swan, the consultant cardiologist, and the meeting confirmed him as Chairman, with Field Marshal Sir Francis Festing as President, Mr Cecil Geeson as Treasurer, Miss Holmboe as Secretary and Mr Maurice Fraser as Vice-Chairman. The meeting was attended by seventeen persons with one apology for absence.

Captain Noel Lyster-Binns attended the meeting from headquarters in his capacity as the Foundation's Appeal Secretary, and described 'the organisation of the British Heart Foundation and how it works'.

Mr McQueen explained that in accordance with the Articles of Association of the Foundation all members of a Regional Committee had to be members of the Foundation. All agreed to join and to serve on the Committee. After some discussion the name 'British Heart Foundation, Northern Committee' was adopted, and the boundaries defined as covering the counties of Northumberland, Durham, Cumberland, Westmorland and part of North Yorkshire as defined by Region 1 of the National Health Service.

Amongst those present were the Reverend Unwin, representing the Bishop of Newcastle, and Mr P. Stephens of the *Newcastle Chronicle*, who promised good support from the press provided they received good copy frequently from the Branch Secretary, whereupon Captain Lyster-Binns prepared a press hand-out.

The majority of those present at this inaugural meeting were local businessmen, and Dr Swan promised to write to those he felt would be interested living outside the Newcastle area, and to invite some to serve on the Committee.

Dr Swan, who has recently died at the age of 82, remained Chairman of the Committee until 1973 and gave devoted service to the affairs of the Foundation. He was succeeded by Dr Hewan Dewar, who, in turn, handed over to Dr Charles Henderson. He retired in 1985 in favour of Dr Stewart Hunter, who is the current Chairman.

The first Regional Organizer was Richard Hill, who was appointed in 1964 and stayed two years, being succeeded by Mrs Emmy Peel, who had previously been a fund-raiser for Dr Barnardo's Homes. She worked at first from an office in Newcastle but later from her home in County Durham. On her retirement in July 1974 she was succeeded by Norman Bell, who has been Regional Organizer, and later Regional Director, ever since. He retired at the end of 1988, when the region was combined with the Yorkshire Region under the direction of Brigadier Roger Preston. In anticipation of this Bill Rowe was appointed County Organizer for Northumberland, Tyne and Wear and North Durham, and Reg Sigsworth County Organizer for South Durham,

Cleveland and North Yorkshire. They joined Cath Paton, who has been County Organizer for Cumbria since 1983.

When Norman Bell took over he was disturbed that the region, which had been very successful financially at first, had the smallest income of any region (£10,000), whilst the Foundation's income had just passed the £1,000,000 mark. He was not prepared to accept that this was related to a high rate of unemployment, and set about an extensive public relations programme designed to set up new Voluntary Committees, of which the region was 'woefully short' at the time. This was so successful that there are now 22 committees and the regional income for 1987-88 was in excess of £600,000.

Norman Bell stresses the importance he has always placed on the selection of committee officers, and acknowledges his good fortune in those who have served. He believes that the most important role of a committee is to assist the Regional Office in furthering the identity of the charity, which makes all committee members ambassadors for the cause. Whilst not belittling the need for fund-raising events he regards this as secondary and points to the Penrith Committee, which, following this dictum, raised £7,000, of which only £1,000 was from organized events.

There were many pioneers who did stalwart work as fund-raisers. Amongst them the background to the contribution of Mary Robinson, currently the Secretary of the Derwent and Tyne Committee, is remarkable. She was one of the first people in the UK to undergo successful open-heart surgery for valve replacement, and to have it replaced again with a second valve in 1983. She contrasts the long and painful convalescence of her first stay in hospital with her return home in eight days after the second, acknowledging this as an advance secured by research.

Another pioneer who has done much for regional fund-raising is Harold McIntyre, who, when he had to retire from the post of Deputy Managing Director of Swan Hunter, the shipbuilders, because of ill health, organized a successful lottery on behalf of the region. After this he established hospital stalls at the Freeman Hospital, which proved so popular and financially rewarding to the Foundation that similar stalls have now been established in hospitals in Barrow-in-Furness, Middlesbrough, Darlington, Hartlepool and Durham.

Norman Bell acknowledges the help in raising money which resulted from the massive support from the Foundation which made possible the British Heart Foundation Chair of Cardiology in Newcastle. Taking advantage of this he was quick to set up his Regional Office near the Newcastle General Hospital, which, at the time, housed the major Cardiovascular Centre.

The office has a shop front and he has utilized this facility to start a window display, which, in spite of occasional breakage, has been successful, earning a profit from sales of nearly £7,000 per annum.

Of the many large regional fund-raising events the Newcastle Heart Ball, run by the Heart Ball Committee, originally established by Dr C. Henderson, is one of the social events of the North. From humble beginnings, this year the ball grossed £22,000 profit.

Another successful, venture is the 62-mile sponsored bicycle ride following Hadrian's Wall, which was started in 1983 and has become an annual event. In 1987 the ride grossed £17,813 profit.

Scotland

The history of the Foundation in Scotland was punctuated, in the early years, by alternations between two regions, one in Glasgow and another in Edinburgh, and one region for the whole of Scotland. The single region has been sited in Edinburgh except for the earliest days (1965), when it was in Glasgow.

Andrew Mackintosh was the first Regional Organizer. He was succeeded by Margaret McKenzie, the wife of an architect; she, in turn, was followed by Commander Bob Spedding, a retired naval officer. He did much to promote the Foundation's cause, and is remembered as quiet, tall and good-looking, besides being very energetic on the Foundation's behalf. He lived in a fine castellated house in Walter Scott country, and ultimately left to manage an estate in Wales.

Bob Spedding was succeeded by Angela Jennings, who had been a secretary at head office in London before moving to Edinburgh, when she joined Spedding as Assistant Organizer, before taking over in 1970. She remained three years before moving to Jersey on her marriage. She was succeeded in Edinburgh by Michael Shale, who has served the Foundation with distinction as Regional Organizer, and later Regional Director, over a period of 15 years. He took over the whole of Scotland in 1976 when the Glasgow office was closed; in

1979 three subsections were created, as reported in the minutes of the Finance and General Purposes Committee.

The Glasgow Region, which was responsible for the West of Scotland, was organized by Ann Donaldson from 1973 to 1975, and then by Jane Black, a pharmacist, who had been Ann Donaldson's assistant, from 1975 to 1976, when she had to retire because of ill health.

The Foundation shared the Chest and Heart Association's office in Edinburgh until 1969 when it moved to its own premises in Chester Street during Bob Spedding's term of office.

In January 1987 Michael Shale was joined by Major John Prosser as Field Director for Scotland.

Over the years many very successful social fund-raising events have been held under the auspices of both the Glasgow and Edinburgh Regional Offices. As early as 1967 a ball held in Glasgow, raised over

Figure 38 *Scottish Queen of Hearts 1980. Loraine Kelly receiving her prize of two return tickets to Rio de Janeiro from Mr Gordon Mason (right), General Manager of British Caledonian Airways in Scotland, and Mr George Young, President of the Scottish Appeal and Chairman of the judges.*

£1,500, and in 1980 'dozens of Scottish lassies' competed for the title of 'Scottish Queen of Hearts'. To qualify for a place in the final they had to raise £500, entirely on their own initiative. The 19 finalists were judged on 'personality, character, community spirit and funds raised'. Over £25,000 was raised for the Foundation and the winner was Loraine Kelly, a journalist, from East Kilbride (Figure 38).

The North West

The North West Region started from a small executive committee formed to establish a Merseyside branch of the Foundation. It first met in March 1966 at the Liverpool Regional Cardiac Centre in Sefton Hospital under the Chairmanship of Brigadier Sir Douglas Crawford. It had four other members, one of whom was Dr McKendrick, the senior cardiologist.

This became the Merseyside Regional Appeal Committee. Before it met for the second time in May 1966 Mrs Kit Keenan was appointed Regional Organizer with effect from June 1966. She was a Justice of the Peace and an ex-Mayoress of Bootle, besides being the widow of a local Member of Parliament. Consequently she was very well known in the locality. She was very friendly and well liked.

She remained Regional Organizer until succeeded in April 1979 by Alan Ware, who had been an officer in the Royal Marines and knew the area well, having been, at one time, recruiting officer in Liverpool. He has recently been succeeded, on reaching retiring age, by Bertie Brown, who had been County Organizer for Lancashire and Merseyside since 1986.

At its third meeting in June 1966 the Executive Committee had set targets and objectives, and named some personalities to be approached for offers of help. A target of £100,000 was mentioned with a launch date in 1967. In the event the Committee was able to raise only £42,483 in its first three years. It suffered greatly from the enforced resignation of Sir Douglas Crawford through ill health.

An early objective was the creation of 12 committees within a twenty-mile radius of Liverpool; eight were achieved, at Liverpool, Birkenhead, Wallasey, Southport, Chester, Runcorn, Widnes and Crosby. Of these the last was short-lived, and those in Widnes and Runcorn had a struggle to survive. When Alan Ware took over in 1979 there were only eight, including one in the Isle of Man, and these were soon reduced to five by the transfer of Chester, Runcorn and Widnes to Region 11. One of the five survivors, in Blackburn, was dissolved shortly afterwards. Thus the region had fewer committees than any other. Alan Ware recalls his depression at the time, comparing his four with Dorothy Curtis's 32 in Hampshire. He did have, however, two consistently good fund-raising committees; one was in Liverpool, chaired from 1970 until 1983 by Patrick Rathbone of Barclays Bank, and the other in Wallasey, chaired from 1970 until his death in 1988 by Councillor Jack Redhead.

Records of the early years are scanty, but it seems that the regional income averaged £16,000 to £20,000 per annum between 1973 and 1979. This rose to £34,000 at the end of Alan Ware's first year as Regional Organizer.

Kit Keenan, writing of the very early days, expresses warm appreciation of the support she received from universities, polytechnics, the police and Rotary, Lions and Inner Wheel Clubs.

Amongst the many fund-raising activities she recalls are the annual Liverpool Swim at the University Baths and the generosity of Owen Owen, the department store, in allowing the BHF to have the use of a display stand for a week every year in their shops in Chester and Liverpool; at the latter members of the Liverpool Football Club agreed to appear to sign autographs.

The Chester Committee, which was one of the first to be formed in the region (September 1967), had as its Secretary Mrs Wilson, whose husband had one of the earliest valve replacement operations. She is still its Secretary today, and the Committee has raised a total of over £100,000. Amongst its activities were successful fashion shows, including the showing of his autumn collection by Norman Hartnell on one occasion. All the proceeds of these shows were given to the BHF, and the cheque from the Hartnell show was received on behalf of the Foundation by the Duchess of Westminster.

Kit Keenan also has fond recollections of the loyal support she received from other committees, mentioning in particular the Sherratt family in the Lake District and Mrs Ruth Caldwell at Halten, where she has been Chairwoman for many years, after first serving the Runcorn Committee out of which it grew.

As in other regions many of her leading helpers were drawn to the BHF as a result of family involvement with heart disease. One had two sons who underwent successful heart surgery, one of whom, now

22 years old and fit, was not expected to live; he was too weak, Kit Keenan says, to do anything active, but she remembers seeing him, at the age of 7, propped up in bed to do a sponsored 'Yo-Yo' to raise money for the Committee funds.

Kit Keenan also remembers meeting the boat which brought the new 'Pacemaker' rose from Dickson's, the rose-growers in Ireland, which was to be launched the following day on behalf of the BHF at the Southport Flower Show. At this ceremony, and many others, she pays tribute to the wonderful publicity and support she received from Jim Black, who was in charge of the local radio station.

From her account of her activities during her stewardship as Regional Organizer one senses a wide and warm-hearted involvement in countless aspects of the local scene, as a result of which she is widely remembered with great affection.

Upon his appointment Alan Ware immediately set about launching campaigns for the creation of committees in new areas in the region, and managed to form 14 in the next seven years.

In 1986 the size and population of the region was dramatically increased by the acquisition from Region 11, which was closing, of Greater Manchester and Cheshire; this raised the total population of the region to nearly 8,000,000.

This amalgamation brought with it a number of new branches, although several were small and had not been very active in recent times. But an important new branch was started in Leigh shortly afterwards and another in Central Manchester, based on the Manchester Royal Infirmary, which led to the appointment of Keith Malyon as County Organizer for Greater Manchester and Cheshire.

The true situation was somewhat obscured, however, by the advanced training taking place in the ambulance service, largely pioneered by Greater Manchester. Many ambulance stations set up 'Heart-Start' Groups, under the banner of the BHF, to obtain money for the purchase of defibrillators; these were emotive projects and the appeals were largely successful. Unfortunately, however, they mostly disappeared as soon as their target had been reached, and the money they raised has distorted the figures for regional income for 1986–87 and 1987–88 as the income records show:

| 1973–74 | £15,552 | 1981–82 | £84,734 |
| 1974–75 | £14,946 | 1982–83 | £99,640 |

1975–76	£14,221	1983–84	£155,603
1976–77	£17,579	1984–85	£196,149
1977–78	£20,799	1985–86	£242,114
1978–79	£33,910	1986–87	£623,339
1979–80	£51,004	1987–88	£824,826
1981–82	£77,897		

A steady source of increased income during the years when Alan Ware has been in charge is from *in memoriam* donations, which through advertising and liaison with funeral directors throughout the region, as opposed to only in Liverpool, have progressed steadily. Within three years of starting this campaign the income from this source increased from less than £10,000 per annum to over £80,000 per annum.

Efforts to raise funds in Northern Ireland have been made from the earliest times in the history of the Foundation, and a Wing Commander Masters is recorded as being the regional Organizer, based in Belfast, in 1965. He does not seem to have been very successful, however, and Geoffrey Davison recalls a sad journey towards the end of 1967 to close the office down. For a number of years after this the Province was represented only by an entry in the telephone book, giving the name, address and telephone number of the North West Regional headquarters in Liverpool.

But in the late 1970s a County Organizer was appointed and he was succeeded after about a year by Harris Johnstone, who organized a considerable level of publicity in the Province but only one committee in West Tyrone. He left in 1986 and was succeeded by Peter Welsh, who has created a new committee in his home town, Limvady.

Obviously the troubles in Northern Ireland in the last decade and more have made fund-raising very difficult, and it is to be hoped that an improvement will enable more to be done before too long.

Yorkshire and North Humberside

The beginnings of regional activity in the area resulted from a visit by Brigadier Cardiff to the medical staff of Leeds General Infirmary in 1967. This resulted in the formation of a Steering Committee whose Chairman was Sir Malcolm Stoddart-Scott, MP. Other members were

Dr John Towers (Secretary), Professor Linden, Dr Whittaker and Mr Kendall, who was the manager of the Midland Bank in Leeds.

The Steering Committee held a number of meetings, as a result of which Doreen Nicholson, the Regional Development Officer, came to Leeds and set up a small office, to which she recruited Audrey Gale as Secretary. This was a most fortunate choice, and she remained with the Foundation until retirement on 31 March 1987. Writing of her Colonel Kaye said: 'The greatest asset at the Leeds office was Mrs Audrey Gale ... her greatest strength was her empathy with people, not only in person but also on the telephone.' Major B. Chadwick, Colonel Kaye's successor, echoed the same sentiment when he said, 'Audrey was extremely good with people ... all the Committees liked her and she made a lot of friendships which was good for the BHF ... I quickly learned the value of this kind of public relationship.'

It was decided by the Steering Committee and Mrs Nicholson that the best way to launch the Foundation in Yorkshire would be to hold an inaugural luncheon for invited guests, and this was held at the Queen's Hotel in Leeds on 15 October 1968.

The organizers took the sensible step of putting a questionnaire at the side of each place asking guests if they would be willing to help by:

(a) Signing a deed of covenant.
(b) Making a donation.
(c) Starting a committee in their own area.
(d) Holding an event to raise money.

The replies were sorted at the Leeds office. Covenant forms were sent out where requested and arrangements were made for Doreen Nicholson to visit those who had expressed an interest in forming a committee or holding an event.

By December committees had been formed in Beverley (the Hon. Clodagh Farrell and Mrs D. Scott), Pontefract (Mrs D. Enright), Ossett (Mrs Nettleton), Castleford (Mrs Hattan) and Ilkley (Mrs Rust). These were followed by a committee in the North Riding at Wensleydale (Lady Jean Christie and Mrs D. Hunt) in February 1969, and in Knaresborough (Mrs Herbert), Harrogate (Mrs J. Towers and Mr and Mrs Illingworth), Wetherby (Mr and Mrs Roscoe and Mrs D. Nicholson) and Rothwell (Mr A. Roberts and Mrs B. Roberson). Mrs Nicholson, who had remarried, retired from the Leeds office in 1969 when she left the area. Committees were also started in 1969 in Leeds (Mr Stuart Barr) and Wakefield. The Wakefield Committee still has its original Chairman (Mr M. Shaffner), and has produced significant amounts of money year after year.

During this time further meetings of the Steering Committee took place, usually in Sir Malcolm Stoddart-Scott's home, where it was decided to convene a meeting with the purpose of founding a 'British Heart Foundation Council for Yorkshire'.

This took place on 29 November 1968 at the Royal Station Hotel in York. Mrs Nicholson outlined the purposes of local and area committees and Professor Linden spoke on developments in heart research, following which a resolution was passed creating the Council with 31 named members.

Sir Malcolm agreed to become Chairman despite already being Chairman of the Yorkshire Cancer Research Campaign, and also being heavily committed by his parliamentary duties. Dr Towers was appointed Vice-Chairman, Professor Linden Secretary, and Mr Kendall Treasurer.

Colonel Kaye, the recently appointed Regional Organizer, was introduced to the Council by the Chairman. He had been Deputy Lieutenant of the County and a fine cricketer, and so was well known in the area. He was a very hard worker and directed the region with great success for 14 years, retiring in September 1982. It is interesting that he and his two successors, Major Chadwick and Brigadier Preston, have all served in the King's Own Yorkshire Light Infantry Regiment. Bert Chadwick, who was Regional Organizer from 1982 to 1986, recalls that he and Michael Kaye both served in the same company in the expedition to Norway in 1940, and that he first met Roger Preston when they served together in Kenya in 1955 in the days of the Mau Mau troubles.

The next meeting of the Council was held in the board room of the Leeds General Infirmary in June 1969, and it has been an active force in the affairs of the region over the years. Since the retirement of Sir Malcolm its Chairman has been Mr Philip Morris, who has also been the Chairman of the consistently successful Harrogate Committee for 15 years.

As time has passed some of the earlier committees have disappeared, usually because the chairman has gone, but several which were formed in the comparatively early days have survived, amongst which are those in Hull, Sheffield, Brighouse, Mirfield, Whitby, Birkenhead, Doncaster, Filey, Malton and Northallerton.

Colonel Kaye recalls with pleasure that in the year 1987–88, out of 15 Committees raising over £4,000, eight were amongst the earliest ones to be formed. The recently formed York Committee (Mrs Heavens) raised nearly £12,000 in that year.

To attempt to list notable committee events would lead to unacceptable omissions; all have had praiseworthy successes in plenty. But meriting special mention is one of historical interest. Though the Leeds Committee had organized several good fund-raising events its younger members formed a breakaway committee called 'the Valentines', of which no one over 29 years of age could be a committee member. The biggest function held by the Valentines was a 'Soap Box Derby' on the Harewood Hill Climb on an Easter Monday Bank Holiday, with many side shows in addition to the ride down Harewood Hill. The event was widely publicized, including several advertisements on television which cost them over £1,000. 'They weren't worried', remarked Colonel Kaye, 'but I was!' The day was fine and warm and the event a huge success, with so much traffic congestion that Stuart Barr, the Chairman of the Leeds Committee, who was due to present the prizes, was unable to get there. For the next year's event he arranged to come by helicopter but the weather was wet and cold, and the expenses were little more than covered. The Derby was entirely run by young people, led by Michael Inman. Colonel Kaye said of the Valentines: 'They went like a bomb for three or four years and then faded away as they started marrying each other and family life became the priority.'

The Yorkshire Region has always been outstandingly successful in collecting money from *in memoriam* donations, a feature it shares with the Welsh Region, which has been even more successful. Both were, for many years, well ahead of all the others. Colonel Kaye attributes this to regular advertisements in the *Yorkshire Post* alongside the obituary column, to cooperation by undertakers in using the display boxes made to explain the scheme, to publicity by local committees and to letters of sympathy and the meticulous keeping of records by Mrs Audrey Gale.

Before accepting the position of Regional Organizer Colonel Kaye consulted Admiral R. Alexander, who was Regional Organizer for Hampshire at the time, and found him most enthusiastic. He thought the object of the Foundation well worth while and the work interesting. He spoke highly of Ereld Cardiff, with whom he had served at SHAPE (Supreme Headquarters Allied Powers in Europe), and added that if he got into any difficulties or wanted any help he used to ring up 'a splendid young man called Davison who knew all the answers'. Colonel Kaye said: 'I discovered for myself in the years to come how right he was.' One of the ways in which Geoffrey Davison put this help into practice in the early days was to provide the Leeds office with the card index at headquarters of all those who had expressed an interest in the Foundation since its inception and lived in Yorkshire. This list formed the basis of the Yorkshire Regional Index, which has been of great value for publicity and fund-raising over the years.

Before Major Bert Chadwick took over from Colonel Kaye as Regional Director in 1982 he had been part-time County Organizer for West Yorkshire for about a year; on his retirement in 1986 he went back to his old job and has continued in this role to the present time.

He pays generous tribute to Arthur Mills, who has been County Organizer for North Yorkshire and North Humberside since 1981. He regards him as outstandingly successful in persuading supporters to form new voluntary committees, and appreciates his hard work and his infectious sense of humour.

Brigadier Roger Preston, who became Regional Director in November 1986, modestly insists that he has not been in the job long enough to offer a contribution to the history of the region, but its future is in safe hands with him and Philip Morris, the Chairman of the Yorkshire Council. Both are experienced in senior management, and have as County Organizers to assist them, in addition to Bert Chadwick and Arthur Mills, Jack Collins representing South Yorkshire, operating from Bakewell in Derbyshire.

Wales

The first attempt to represent the Foundation in the Principality was made in 1969 by John Green, who was the Regional Organizer for about a year and worked from his home.

When he resigned Major John Probyn and his wife Calista took over, and built the region over a 15-year period, retiring in July 1985. Geoffrey Davison recalls how nearly Major Probyn came to losing the job, because he failed to turn up to the appointment committee because of a road accident *en route* to it. Fortunately Davison was staying in Cardiff over night and Probyn made contact with him. 'We got on very well', said Davison, 'and I thought he had the dedication and interest to do the job and he was appointed.'

John and Calista are Canadians, and John had been a regular soldier in the Canadian Army before joining the Foundation on his retirement from the service. Speaking of him Frances Neal recalls him as 'witty, efficient, brusque and easy to get on with'. James Malcolm's comment was: 'a splendid man'.

In a personal communication John Probyn writes: 'without Calista's help, work and telephone-watch we would not have got very far – the Foundation was very fortunate'. He also writes appreciatively of the work and help of Mrs Brenda Evans, who was part-time secretary and bookkeeper from the earliest days.

When John Probyn retired in 1985 the Foundation was equally fortunate in his successor, Derek Heasman. He had been associated with the Foundation for four years as chairman of an important committee in Glamorgan before taking over. He is an energetic active man, well known and well liked, who has himself undergone bypass surgery and has since ridden four times in the London-to-Brighton Bicycle Ride.

John Probyn, who is a keen fisherman, decided to live at Llandrindod Wells, and built a house there, which is why the Foundation's headquarters are based in the town. The first office was opened in Emporium Buildings in December 1970. It had the merit of being very cheap, with a rent of only £2.10 a week, but it was dingy and needed much cleaning before occupation, to remove the film of coal dust, resulting from previous use as a local coalman's office. As soon as finances allowed the office was moved to Aden Chambers, where it remained until 1986, when it was transferred to Brighton House.

Both Probyn and Heasman pay warm tribute to the help and encouragement the Foundation received from the earliest days from Dr Arthur J. Thomas, the foremost cardiologist at the time, at the Royal Infirmary, Llandough, and Sully Hospital, and later at the University Hospital at the Heath. Heasman writes: 'He and his wife virtually got the Foundation off the ground in Wales by holding a cheese and wine party.' He is still actively concerned with the Cefn Sidan Committee in Dyfed. Dr William Evans, one of the original members of the Founding Committee of the Foundation, appointed by the British Cardiac Society in 1959, who lived in Tregarron in Dyfed, was also of great help and gave a number of talks in support of efforts to increase public awareness of the Foundation's objectives; he continued to assist until ill health made this impossible, only a few years before his death in 1988 at the age of 94.

John Probyn has a wealth of reminiscences about his time as Regional Organizer, and of none of which he is more proud than the day he overcame the understandable suspicion aroused by a military man proclaiming a British Foundation in Wales. It came about the day he was adopted by the Plaid Cymru in North West Wales as a kind of Heart Foundation mascot, and became 'ap Robyn y Galon', which is 'Probyn the Heart'. From then on, he says, he never looked back.

His first real breakthrough in fund-raising was through the Rotary Clubs, to most of which he wrote offering a free talk at their luncheon meetings. Wryly he remarked: 'at that time [1971] free speakers were in short supply.'

Amongst his talks he remembers one in a new town near Pontypool called Cwmbran, after which he was approached by a 'jolly gentleman in a black coat and pepper-and-salt trousers', which he recognized as the 'service dress' of his profession, the undertaker, who invited him to seek him out at his place of business, the crematorium. This meeting resulted in the placing of regular small advertisements in the obituary column of the *Western Mail* and the *South Wales Echo* soliciting *in memoriam* donations from friends and relatives of the deceased in lieu of flowers.

In those days such advertisements were relatively unknown and he had to convince both editors before they accepted that this was not unseemly or disrespectful. To his astonishment donations poured in, and this source of income soon amounted to half the regional total.

Another fortunate outcome of one of Probyn's Rotary Club talks was after he addressed the Swansea Rotary, which is powerful and backed financially by leaders in the business world of Swansea. He readily admits being daunted by the size and elegance of the occasion at the Dragon Hotel and said: 'the time came when I was called upon to perform; and how bad I was. After sitting down and wiping the sweat from my brow I crept away back to Llandrindod – most downcast.'

However, some days later, he received a telephone call from a Rotarian who had been present, and turned out to be a selector of the

Glamorgan Cricket Club, who informed him that the Club, which was looking for a charity to sponsor for their annual fund-raising drive, had picked the Foundation. John Probyn continued: 'I asked why, and he said: "you were so bad" – referring to my Rotary talk – "that you couldn't possibly have been a professional – and we thought you needed help."'

The story may well have been embellished by Probyn, or completely untrue, but it is a fact that the Glamorgan Cricket Club raised large sums over several years for the Foundation. Tony Lewis was the County captain at the time, and with his association with national radio he was able to make the presentations of the donations with the accompaniment of valuable media coverage.

The Welsh Rugby Union was another powerful and influential sponsor which was equally generous with support, and brought large sums to the Foundation. It was closely associated with the cricket club in membership and interests, so that, together, they were the most influential partnership in Wales.

Since Derek Heasman became Regional Director in 1985 the Health Promotional Authority for Wales has undertaken a major educational publicity campaign concerning heart disease called 'Heart Beat Wales', under the direction of Professor John Catford, who is Executive Director of the Authority. Its objective, although circumscribed, is essentially the same as the Foundation's public education policy; both aim to reduce the incidence of premature death or disablement so that all can live their full life span in good health and without fear of heart disease. Both organizations need financial support and since it would obviously be counter-productive to have two appeals competing with each other the Foundation has negotiated a joint fund-raising agreement with Heart Beat Wales called the Welsh Heart Appeal, which is to run for two years in the first instance.

Following Alan Ware's retirement as Regional Director of the North West, advantage has been taken of the proximity of his home in the Wirral to North Wales, to obtain his services as County Organizer. Although committees have been formed right across the Principality from Anglesey to Cardiff geographical features make it difficult to give the North as close attention as would be ideal, and the appointment of such an experienced man as County Organizer will undoubtedly be of great help.

The Regions

The West

As Region 10 the West was one of the first large regions to be set up. It started in its present form in 1982 with Major Peter Johnstone as Regional Director; upon his retirement in 1985 he was succeeded, after a short interval, by Mr Peter Pelly, who was a businessman in Bath. Speaking of Peter Johnstone, James Malcolm said: 'He was really the pathfinder of the large Region.'

The new grouping includes Oxfordshire, Wiltshire, Dorsetshire, Devonshire, Cornwall and Somersetshire, together with Gloucestershire and the newly formed County of Avon, which had made up the original Region 10.

A fund-raising structure for the Foundation in the South West of England was amongst the first areas in the country to be developed.

The earliest was probably in Cornwall with Lieutenant Colonel Belcher as part-time Regional Organizer, starting late in 1966 or early in 1967. His most successful venture was a county football draw in which participants bought a ticket every week throughout the season. Half the money collected was spent on prizes, a quarter on expenses and a quarter for the BHF. It was an excellent fund-raiser, making over £4,000 per annum, which was a big sum for those days. It was run for many years by John Williams from his home in Cury near Land's End, and, after his death, by his widow, Eleanor. It was called the Cornish Region Supporters Association and is still in operation.

The leading representative of the Foundation in the South West of England for many years was Lieutenant Colonel David Swift. He was recruited by Brigadier Cardiff and joined on 8 February 1968, the day after his retirement from the army; he served the Foundation nearly 13 years, retiring on 31 December 1980.

His first appointment was as Regional Organizer for Wiltshire and Dorsetshire, which he ran from an office in the village of Fovant, in the home of Mr Hawksworth, who acted as his part-time secretary with Mrs Adams as part-time typist. There was little money available and Colonel Swift was very conscious of the need to be as economical as possible.

He set about trying to form committees but readily admits it was a hard task. His first success was in Salisbury, where Mrs Nancy Bare became the organizing secretary. She had run a boys' preparatory school in the City for many years, and a large number of her former pupils were by then successful local businessmen, who gave her generous support. The committee has continued to prosper and Colonel Swift has enjoyed being a member of it for the last eight years since his retirement as Regional Organizer. Other committees followed including successful starts in Bridport, Weymouth and Portland and Swindon.

After he had been Regional Organizer for about 18 months Colonel Swift was asked to add Devonshire, and, after 18 months again, Somersetshire and Gloucestershire including Bristol. Thus he became responsible for five counties. The burden of travelling was very great, and put considerable limitations on the number of committees for which he could be responsible, since, in those days, the duties of the Regional Organizer were held to include regular participation in the meetings of committees, and in helping to arrange events undertaken by them.

He was pleased when Group Captain Ben Boult, who had undertaken responsibility for Cornwall upon the retirement of Lieutenant Colonel Belcher, extended his area as Regional Organizer to include Devonshire. Ben Boult pays generous tribute to Swift saying of him: 'He was wonderfully helpful ∴ he was very popular and introduced me to all the Committee Chairmen and members at special meetings which he organised for the occasion ... through him I met many helpful people around whom it was not too difficult to organise more Committees.' When he handed over to Major Basil Curtis in 1978 he had established ten new committees.

Basil Curtis had worked at headquarters in London in the Special Events Department and had, on occasion, assisted Ray Stokes in East Anglia before going to Cornwall; he stayed as County Organizer for Devon and Cornwall after the reorganization which created the new large region in 1982. He was experienced in public relations having been involved in this work in the army during the war, and subsequently as a BBC tennis commentator at Wimbledon after his retirement as a leading player.

He exploited all opportunities to publicize the work of the Foundation on radio and television, and in contacts with the regional press, making full use of presentation ceremonies of equipment to hospitals and the ambulance service.

He also employed all the customary forms of sponsorship to

encourage fund-raising by voluntary committees, and enjoyed the novel idea suggested to him by a schoolgirl of a sponsored 'silence', which was a reverse of her normal behaviour, and made her the most popular girl in the school for as long as it lasted, according to her headmistress.

Curtis recalls that when he took over in 1977 there were five committees in Devonshire, at Plymouth, Exeter, Sidmouth (East Devon), Barnstaple/Braunton (North Devon) and Dartmouth, and six in Cornwall, at Truro, St Austell, Bude, Week St Mary (North Cornwall), Wadebridge and Falmouth. By the mid-1980s the number had increased to 28 with further additions in preparation. He writes that in 1977 the income from the two counties was £34,000 and that when they were absorbed into the large West Region in 1982 this had tripled to over £100,000.

Colonel Swift was responsible for the creation of many committees in the large area over which he presided for so many years. Many of these came under the aegis of Peter Johnstone when he took Gloucestershire and Avon on his appointment in December 1972. Johnstone was an experienced fund-raiser, and joined the Foundation after meeting Brigadier Cardiff by chance in Scotland when both were there on fund-raising exercises. Johnstone was working, at the time, for Clyde Fair International. He was drawn to the South West because of family friendships with Colonel and Mrs Swift.

Johnstone's first office was in Dursley in Gloucestershire, in the office of a local solicitor, but he moved after about a year to Colerne, outside Bath, where premises in a chemist's shop and post office became available. His headquarters remained in Colerne from 1974 to 1982 when he moved to the present office in Bath, which was generously made available by an insurance company at a charity rate.

After being Regional Organizer for about five years Peter Johnstone recalls having about 12 active committees by 1978, which was 'about the limit of the number one could handle'.

Several of these committees had been started by David Swift and their transference to Peter Johnstone was facilitated by the ease with which the two worked together. Many were very influential, such as the Bristol Committee based on the Bristol Royal Infirmary and under the Chairmanship of Professor Bruce Perry, one of the original members of the Executive Committee of the Foundation. After a short period under Michael Moore, James Wishart, the surgeon, became

Chairman and remained in office for many years. In Bath the committee was run initially by Professor Ansell, and later by Jim Mearns, both of the School of Pharmacy, before being taken on by Dr John Cosh, the rheumatologist.

Amongst the many committees, all of which made valuable contributions, Ben Boult recalls, in the very early days, the work of Mrs Drysdale in Falmouth, after losing her husband from heart disease, and of Mrs Paulowski, known affectionately as 'Auntie Vi', who was 'the life and soul' of the North Devon Committee, never taking 'no' for an answer, and being a brilliantly successful fund-raiser. Swift and Johnstone recall the long service as Chairman of Roger Hand at Poole, Neil Wood at Yeovil, Bill Ellis at Dorchester, Nick Turnbull at Chippenham and Bernard Jago at Taunton, besides Nancy Bare in Salisbury.

They also recall long records of fund-raising in Cheltenham, Marlborough, Swanage and Torquay, and in Bridgewater, where the Sedgemoor Committee holds an annual sponsored walk.

Speaking of the ways in which funds can be raised Peter Johnstone points out that sponsorship, coffee mornings, with or without the sale of goods, social events and *in memoriam* donations cover the majority, although he remains firmly convinced that 'tin shaking' is well worth while, pointing out that it requires minimum organization and realizes almost 100% profit.

He stresses the importance of publicity and believes that there is room for much improvement at local level, taking advantage of the recent extensions of regional radio and television, perhaps even appointing press officers to each of the large regions. 'We so often miss the opportunity of publicity,' he remarked, adding: "the BHF should be a household name but it is not yet.'

He also emphasized the value of presentation ceremonies of equipment and to award-winners of project grants, stressing the power of the ambulance service as ambulance men are 'so often the first contact with heart patients'. In support of this he recalls the publicity resulting from the saving of the life of the husband of a committee member in Stroud by an ambulance man, using a defibrillator presented only the previous day at a ceremony led by Brigadier Cardiff, the Director General.

Whilst commending the perception by James Malcolm of the urgent need to change the role of Regional Directors, and reorganize the managerial concept, he is concerned that the new business approach can lead to the loss of the personal touch. Believing, as do most professional fund-raisers, he says, that 'people give to people, not causes', he regrets the unavoidable loss, in some degree, of the close personal approach, which was easier when the organization was smaller.

Johnstone believes the formation of a new committee is a combination of luck and hard work, heralded almost always by good local publicity, and by the ability to seize an opportunity. One such occasion was his meeting with Maureen Marks at a prize-giving ceremony at which her husband had won a 'slim' competition, when Johnstone was looking for someone to run a sponsored swim. She turned out to be a swimming instructress, and has run the Bristol swim with great success for 15 years.

David Swift also stresses the need to accept whatever help is offered, even though its quality is unknown. After accepting the offer, on one occasion, of an enthusiast to become treasurer of a committee, he was taken aback, when asking for the annual accounts to be presented, to be given a large shopping bag full of receipts. As he said: 'If people volunteer it is difficult to say no. You cannot say, "can you add?" You have to say "yes" and then find out.'

When Peter Johnstone took over as Regional Director in 1982 there were about 40 voluntary committees; when he retired in 1985 the number had risen to 65, and in 1988 it was 80, with a ceiling target of about 100.

When the new large region was set up in 1982 the appointment of County Organizers was a factor vital to success, and the Foundation was very fortunate in availability and selection.

Basil Curtis agreed to continue as County Organizer for Devon and Cornwall, on retiring as Regional Organizer for these two counties. Colonel Leo Macey became the County Organizer for Wiltshire and Dorset; he had recently retired from the army Pay Corps and was able to assist James Malcolm with some of the problems relating to the new administrative structure, in addition to fostering the old inheritance of David Swift.

Rear Admiral Sir Hugh Janion became County Organizer for Somerset and Avon, and remained so until his retirement at the end of 1988. His area included the important City of Bristol for which he was particularly well suited, having been Captain of HMS *Bristol* and recently in command of the royal yacht. Gloucestershire and Oxfordshire were equally fortunate in having the services of Mr Adrian Holloway, a retired solicitor and magistrate in the City of Gloucester.

At the end of 1982, after the existence of the new large region for one year, Colonel Malcolm remembers congratulating Peter Johnstone on being the first Regional Director to raise £100,000 in a year. In 1988 the income from the region was nearly £750,000.

The South

The first fund-raiser in the South of England, so far as records can be traced, was Group Captain Guy du Boulay. He started in 1965 working from his home in Sandwich. His principal committee in those early days was in Deal, and was run by Mrs Perez, who had herself been treated for heart disease.

The most noteworthy event was the summer garden party at Walmer Castle (see Figure 10), which was held over a period of four years starting in 1967. It came about because Sir Robert Menzies, the Prime Minister of Australia, who was Warden of the Cinque Ports at the time, was also the President of the flourishing Australian Heart Association. This gave him an interest in the welfare of the fledgeling British junior partner. Not only did these events raise considerable amounts of money but they also attracted excellent and widespread publicity in the national as well as the local press, at a time when the existence and objectives of the Foundation were little known.

Other functions from which the Foundation benefited, were the Roman Holiday Carnival in 1968 and the Elizabethan Pageant; both were held in Sandwich. Unhappily by the time the pageant was held Guy du Boulay was already seriously ill, and much of the work for it, and for the Foundation, was being undertaken by his wife, Mrs Jane du Boulay. She had an additional interest in the Foundation since the Treasurer, and first Chairman of the Finance and General Purposes Committee, was her brother-in-law, Sir Rudolf de Trafford. A few years after her husband's death in 1974 Mrs du Boulay became the Mayor of Sandwich, during which time a second pageant was staged from which the Foundation again benefited.

As illness made it increasingly difficult for Group Captain du Boulay to continue to work for the Foundation he and his wife were assisted by Lilian Higgs. She joined the Foundation at the end of 1967, having previously worked as a fund-raiser for Doctor Barnardo's Homes for six years.

Her first assignment was to launch the Foundation in South and South West London. For this purpose she set up an office in Croydon, which she shared with Molly Chandler, who was undertaking a similar task in Sussex.

In 1969, however, it was decided to put the whole of London under one Regional Organizer, so Lilian Higgs concentrated her efforts on Surrey and parts of Kent. By 1970 Guy du Boulay was not well enough to do much for the Foundation and by 1972 he had been forced to retire completely.

In this year Lilian Higgs moved her office to Ticehurst, where it has remained ever since. When she moved from Croydon, Molly Chandler also moved. She went to live in Arundel, in a cottage on the Duke of Norfolk's estate, to continue to develop regional activities in Sussex. Unhappily she also had to retire because of ill health, and her work was divided, in 1974, when Lilian Higgs took over East Sussex and Dorothy Curtis West Sussex.

When Lilian Higgs retired on 30 April 1984, after more than 16 years' service to the Foundation, she was succeeded by Lieutenant Colonel Richard Besly. The Southern Region assumed its current coverage the following year by the addition of Hampshire to the counties of Surrey, Kent and Sussex upon the retirement of Dorothy Curtis.

At her retirement luncheon Lilian Higgs said: 'In 1967, when I joined the Appeal staff of the BHF it was equivalent to the 'corner shop', but now in 1984, with much hard work on the part of many, it has advanced to the 'supermarket', and I am very proud to have been a small cog in the works.'

She recalls how difficult it was to get things started for the Foundation at first because it was virtually unknown, in contrast to Dr Barnardo's Homes, which were a household name. She appreciated at once that publicity was the prime requirement for success in the collection of money, and set about achieving this by sponsored events, and by making contacts with people who had newsworthy stories to tell of treatment for heart disease. Many of the chairmen and chairwomen of her most successful committees were former patients. Swims were her most popular sponsored events, and she organized no fewer than 24 in her region in one year at the height of her work; sponsored walks were also a good source of income and in the earliest days a charity shop in Croydon, run by Miss Burnett, was profitable for some time.

Amongst the committees set up by Lillian Higgs were those in Bexhill, Brighton, Crawley (Mr Page), Dartford (Mrs Bruning), Dover, Eastbourne, Haslemere, Mepham–Gravesend (Mrs Coote), Oxshott (Mrs Guthrie), Reigate (Mrs Dewar), Sevenoaks (Mrs Inlis), Staines and Weybridge–North Surrey. Gwen Martyn, for many years the Regional Organizer for London, is now a member of the committee in Bexhill, where she has lived since retirement. Mrs Dewar, Mrs Coote, Mr Page and Mrs Bruning all came to assist the Foundation after family concerns with cardiac problems.

In the early days Lilian Higgs was visited by a number of newly appointed organizers to learn from her experience before starting in the field; amongst these were Sheila Harrison, Marjorie Barron and Alan Ware.

Lilian started with no money being raised in the areas to which she was assigned, and, as a result of immense personal endeavour, left with a regional income, in 1984, of nearly £250,000.

Hampshire. As Region 15, Hampshire was one of the earliest to be formed. It was launched in February 1968 after preliminary meetings of a Wessex Council, with Admiral Robin Alexander as Regional Organizer and Dorothy Curtis as his secretary and personal assistant. The Admiral retired about 15 months later because of heavy commitments as a County Councillor, and Dorothy Curtis took over. She remained Regional Organizer until 1985, when Hampshire became part of the large Southern Region, and she is now the County Organizer for the area. Admiral Alexander recalls that the region raised the commendable sum of £4,000 in its first year.

By 1974, with the retirement of Molly Chandler, the region had been enlarged to include West Sussex, and again, about a year later, it was further enlarged to include Berkshire on the retirement of Major Tony Chiesman.

Originally the region had four committees, in Bournemouth, Winchester, Southampton and Basingstoke, which were instigated by Doreen Nicholson as Regional Development Officer. All have survived and flourished, and were followed by many more, notably in

Portsmouth, Petersfield, the Isle of Wight, Reading, Slough, Windsor and Maidenhead.

With the change of county boundaries in 1974 Bournemouth became part of Dorset, but because of its long association with Dorothy Curtis it remained under the administration of the Hampshire office in Fareham. The committee had been set up at an inaugural meeting in 1969 organized by the Mayor and addressed by Dr Ian McMillan, the cardiac surgeon at the Southampton General Hospital. It is now in the area overseen by David Morse, the County Organizer for Dorset.

Dorothy Curtis has always believed in the importance of local community involvement to secure continuing long-term support. 'Right from the beginning', she said, 'we needed to collect as many people as possible who could put on events when I could not get there, so that we could duplicate or triplicate each event. Eventually we found we could have four or five sponsored swims on the same Saturday in different areas.'

At the same time she was conscious that well-intentioned supporters sometimes needed help, particularly at first, in the administration of events, and took much time and trouble assisting them, so increasing their confidence and their willingness to repeat their efforts.

She was particularly keen to involve children in sponsored swims and walks, appreciating that they were ideal ambassadors for the Foundation, when they called asking for sponsorship, and again to collect the money, quite apart from the event itself. The schoolteachers, whose cooperation she much valued, were greatly impressed by her insistence that the children realized and accepted the responsibilities of the promises they made.

To encourage competition she had heart-shaped shields made by a local jeweller, which were awarded annually at presentation ceremonies at school assemblies, to the school whose children had obtained the greatest number of sponsors (not money). The name of the school was inscribed on small shields which were mounted all round it, and if the same school won for three consecutive years they were given a replica to keep. At the same ceremony children who had obtained sponsorship received badges, differing with varying levels of achievement. She initiated a similar scheme with cups for sponsored walks.

Another successful fund-raising scheme involving children was the 'Mend a Heart' project, which was originally devised by Geoffrey Davison. The children were given a heart-shaped card with 20 holes in it and a strip of stamps which they stuck on the holes each time they did a job to earn sixpence. A full card was rewarded with a badge, and six cards with a special badge and a certificate called a gold award. At first this campaign was run from the office but it became so popular, and such a vast undertaking, that schoolteachers gave willing help with its administration.

As a special reward all gold award winners were given a day out in the summer on a Gosport ferry boat with refreshments provided by local traders. It was very popular and provided excellent publicity. The scheme ran, with increasing success, for ten years. Dorothy Curtis remarks of the first outing in 1969: 'it was the first time the surprised Rear Admiral Alexander found himself in a position of authority on a ferry boat'.

Speaking of the sponsored swims, which started in Portsmouth in 1968, she remembered one lady who has swum for the Foundation for more than ten years and is still doing so at the age of over 70, swimming 50 lengths and raising over £1,000 each time.

Dorothy Curtis was also the originator of the sponsored slim, running a Regional Slim under the slogan. 'Put Your Heart into Slimming', which raised over £4,000 in its first year. Its success led to the subsequent National Slim, which has raised around £1,000,000 for the Foundation since its inception.

Over the years many variations were devised on the theme of sponsored fund-raising. One highlighted the dangers of smoking long before this was nationally recognized. The region was flooded with sponsor forms and a poster with a skull and crossbones, the latter being crossed cigarettes. Sponsorship was for the number of days the smoker had given up.

Another fund-raiser was sponsored knitting, in which she persuaded the Lady Mayoress of Portsmouth and several members of the Portsmouth Football Team to sit knitting with her in the window of a department store.

She emphasized the immense importance of presentation ceremonies of equipment and of research grants awarded in the region, not only for the publicity they attract, but to help the voluntary workers understand better the benefits conferred as a result of their hard work.

Speaking of Dorothy, Geoffrey Davison said: 'She was a real live wire, an absolute natural, and in my time by far the top fund raiser for a very long time. Everything she touched turned to gold.'

London

A regional fund-raising organization for London started in 1965, and although precise information is missing it seems almost certain that the headquarters, from an early date, was in Bromley at the home of Doreen Nicholson. She was assisted for some years by Molly Chandler before she moved first to Croydon to develop Surrey and then to Arundel to develop Sussex; Mrs Nicholson had previously worked for the *Daily Mirror* newspaper, besides having been a professional opera singer.

When Mrs Nicholson moved to Yorkshire to assist the formation of the Yorkshire Region in her capacity as Regional Development Officer the continuation of her efforts in London fell into the capable hands of Marjorie Barron. She was a Justice of the Peace and a Local Councillor, in consequence of which she knew the area well, and had access to many influential people in the community and in Local Government.

Gwen Martyn, who was to play such an important part in the development of the London Region over a period of $16\frac{1}{2}$ years, joined Marjorie Barron in July 1970 as Assistant Organizer, and took over from her as Regional Organizer in January 1973, following Marjorie Barron's retirement because of ill health.

London – western boroughs (Region 20). Efforts had been made in the mean time to set up a second office to cover West London. This was first undertaken by Bill Cutts, an ex-naval officer, working in the Ealing district, but this does not seem to have lasted long, and was followed by the opening of an office in North London, in Finchley Road, by Patrick Anderson. At the time he was a member of headquarters staff with responsibility for running Heart Cards, the trading company which pioneered the sale of Christmas cards for the Foundation. When he left headquarters to develop the North London area his work for Heart Cards was taken over by Mrs Roderick, assisted by Nicky Saunders until, in 1970, Mrs Roderick was followed by Mrs Den Hartog, and she by Stephen Johnson who kept it alive through lean years up to the present time.

After a few years Patrick Anderson moved his home to Henley and the North London office was closed. From Henley, however, he developed a successful region known as Thames Valley and Berkshire, which was continued by Major Tony Chiesman until it was subsequently absorbed into the Hampshire Region under the direction of Dorothy Curtis.

A second regional office for London did not return until 1978 when Bernie Lane made a start, working from head office, where she was in charge of the Special Events Department. As the work increased, however, she found that it was not possible to give enough time to both jobs, and the post of Regional Organizer for West London was advertised. This led to the appointment of Ann Chiesman, who started on 1 July 1980 and has run the regional office from her home in Fulham ever since.

The administrative arrangement is different from other regions in that headquarters undertakes the accounting and bookkeeping, thus saving the Foundation considerable office expenses.

For the first two and a half years all income went direct to headquarters, and since 1983 *in memoriam* and general donations still do. In some respects, therefore, Ann Chiesman's role is the combination of a Regional and a County Organizer.

The sums paid to headquarters by her do not, in consequence, represent all the income for the Foundation generated in the region. None the less they are impressive, and show an eightfold increase in five years. In 1983 the total was £17,500; by 1987 it had risen to £84,000, of which the contribution from her five committees was £54,000 and from 'one-off' special events £28,000. In 1988 the total had risen to £148,000, with committees raising £79,000 and events £69,000.

The first of her five committees is the Westminster Committee, whose Chairman is Joan Scott. This committee was started by Bernie Lane before Ann Chiesman's appointment and is very successful financially. Amongst the events it organizes are the annual 'Pace-Maker Plod' on Hampstead Heath, which is a sponsored walk, and the annual sponsored swim in the Porchester baths. Together these two events regularly earn more than £10,000.

The second committee is the Harrow, Brent and Ealing Committee run by Peter Reichwald and his wife Sonya, who has undergone successful cardiac surgery. Amongst events organized by this committee is the annual sponsored swim at the Harrow Leisure Centre which has been held since 1981 and regularly raises more than £10,000.

Another is the Fulham Committee, which organizes the 'From Scratch' classical concerts at the Albert Hall. These bring together several hundred musicians who perform Handel's *Messiah* at Christmas-time without rehearsal (hence 'From Scratch') and Verdi's *Requiem* or some other work in the spring. Sponsorship of these concerts is very successful.

The fourth – the Ball Committee – has organized several prestigious occasions. The first was at the Hurlingham Club in 1981, the second at the Hilton hotel, and the third and fourth at the Intercontinental. The last, in 1987, made a profit of over £20,000. The Ball Committee is under the direction of Mr Ian Burnett, who is also its Treasurer.

The fifth committee of the West London Region is the New Malden Committee, which has been formed more recently, and is becoming increasingly successful under the energetic Chairmanship of Mrs Dorothy Maurice.

Among the special events, Ann Chiesman recalls with pleasure the sponsored bicycle ride by two Gordonstoun schoolboys to Pisa, in Italy, and back, which started and ended at Westminster Bridge, raising over £11,000 in sponsorship money.

She also recalls with some embarrassment, shared by other Regional Organizers and specially mentioned by Colonel Swift, her involvement in the selling of tights on behalf of the Foundation. It came about as a result of the kindness of a manufacturer donating the output of one of his hosiery factories in gratitude for the successful outcome of treatment of a cardiac problem in his family. They were specially packaged with the name of the Foundation on the wrapper. The venture was a financial success but Regional Organizers, for the most part, expressed incredulity to find themselves peddling ladies' underwear.

London – northern, southern and eastern boroughs (Region 4). When Gwen Martyn joined Marjorie Barron the Regional Office was still in Bromley, but shortly after taking over in 1973 she moved it to Stratford in East London, and subsequently to the Langthorne Hospital in Leytonstone where it has remained ever since. When she retired on 31 December 1986 she was succeeded by Mary Ames.

Over her many years with the Foundation Gwen Martyn organized countless fund-raising events, and was the inspiration and driving force behind many more set up by members of her committees, with whom she was a very popular figure; this is a fact always emphasized when her work for the BHF is under discussion.

One of the first large events she undertook in 1971 was to visit all 21 Top Rank Bingo Clubs and make collections, which brought in over £2,000. Another spectacularly successful event she organized was the annual Crystal Palace Sponsored Swim. The first, in 1971, realized £2,500 and the last she organized in 1986 brought in over £28,000. The swims were always opened by the Mayor of Bromley and were well supported by radio and television celebrities. The swimmers mostly came from South East London and the southern counties, being drawn from schools, swimming clubs, hospital staff, police and fire brigade personnel, and church and community groups. Also many individuals took part who had recovered from heart problems, and their families and friends.

In 1979 a sponsored swim organized by Chief Inspector Ken Smith of the Metropolitan Police, in which all the participants were policemen, raised over £4,500. The cheque was presented to the Director General, Brigadier Thursby Pelham, by the Commissioner, Sir David McNee, at a ceremony at Scotland Yard. The Brigadier, in return for the wonderful support from the police over so many years, presented Sir David with a warrant nearly 150 years old signed by King George IV and Sir Robert Peel, the latter being a kinsman of the Brigadier. The warrant is now in the Police Museum.

Financially the most successful event organized by Gwen Martyn was the sponsored jog in the City of London round the moat of the Tower of London. This is held in the lunch hour and attracts excellent publicity. From a modest start in 1979 the jog raised over £62,000 on a summer day ten years later.

Another event in the City was when Mr Richard Shaw, who had undergone heart surgery, paraded his winning Grand National race horse, Hullo Dandy, through the streets accompanied by the well-known rider and trainer Sir Gordon Richards. This raised around £2,000 in a few hours.

The London Fire Brigade were also very supportive, raising big

The Regions

sums of money through a variety of events including bike rides, boxing matches, and long-distance stilt walks.

Gwen Martyn developed an extensive committee network over the years, amongst which were those in Bromley (Mr M. Freedman and Mr and Miss Piper), Croydon (Mr C. Mills), Greenwich (Mrs D. Long), Bexley (Mr B. Sullivan), Enfield (Mrs S. Whetstone), Waltham Forest (Mr and Miss Page), Redbridge (Mr and Mrs Elson) and Southwark (Miss W. Chandler, for which she was awarded the OBE).

Of the many patients who assisted the fund-raising efforts Gwen Martyn recalls that none was more tireless on behalf of the Foundation than Keith Castle, the outstandingly successful recipient of a heart transplant in the early days of the operation. He was prepared to travel long distances to appear at events, often at personal inconvenience, and Gwen Martyn, together with other Regional Organizers, remembers his enthusiastic support with much gratitude.

East Anglia

The area of East Anglia started as Region 2 in January 1973 with the appointment of Major Ray Stokes as Regional Organizer. It consisted then of the counties of Norfolk, Suffolk and Cambridgeshire. Essex, which had previously been looked after by Sheila Harrison, was annexed to Region 2 in November 1975, and the Northern Home Counties of Bedfordshire, Buckinghamshire, Hertfordshire and Northamptonshire, hitherto Region 5, became part of the East Anglian Region in April 1983.

Region 5 (Bedfordshire, Buckinghamshire and Hertfordshire) was originally under the direction of Sheila Harrison, who worked from an office in Bushey in Hertfordshire. She is described as always cheerful and enthusiastic, and very popular with her committee members. Amongst the many whose interest in the Foundation was due to her was Eric Morecambe, who made such an immense contribution to BHF fund-raising over the years. It came about because she knew Eric and his wife, Joan, who were her near neighbours. Following Eric's death Joan is continuing with support in many ways. In February 1986, at a special 25th Anniversary Appeal organized by some of the members of the old Region 5, she launched a national sponsored 'Slide and 24-hour Skate Aid' at the campus of Welwyn Garden City, called a 'Great To Be Alive' Day, to raise funds for a Doppler electrocardiogram for the Cardiac Surgical Centre at Harefield Hospital. This was arranged largely by Miriam Collett, who took over Region 5, with the subsequent addition of Northamptonshire, on the retirement of Sheila Harrison on 1 July 1977; she had a special interest in fund-raising for Harefield Hospital because her husband had been successfully treated there. She remained as Regional Organizer until Region 5 was absorbed into East Anglia (Region 2), after which she continued to give valuable help as a County Organizer until her retirement. Her region first reached the target of an income of £100,000 in 1979, and when she handed over there were 19 committees and she ran 23 annual swims. She pays generous tribute to her committees, to local radio and television, and to the backing she received from innumerable other sources, including the local press, the scout and guide movements and the Rotary, Lions and Round Table Clubs. Her enthusiasm is undiminished by retirement and she writes: 'How about a Charity Day for the BHF in the Channel Tunnel before it opens?'

The first office of the East Anglian Region was set up by Major Stokes at his home in Downham Market in Norfolk in April 1973, with his wife, Joan, as his secretary. But as the region enlarged it became necessary to find a more centrally situated headquarters to ease the burden of travelling, which was very extensive and expensive since a Regional Organizer, in those days, was expected to be an active member of all his committees. Consequently, in November 1987, the office was moved to Saffron Walden, where it has remained.

In the earliest days of the region important committees were formed, amongst which were those in Cambridge, Norwich and Ipswich. Miss Kathleen McBrearty, a medical secretary at Addenbrooks Hospital, has been with the Cambridge Committee since 1974 and is still its Secretary. Mrs Pauline Barker joined the Norwich Committee as its Secretary in 1975 and subsequently took over as Chairman. In Ipswich Mr Herbert Stollery became Chairman in 1975, had major heart surgery in 1977, and is still a very active Chairman of the committee in 1988.

Major Stokes continued as Regional Organizer until his untimely death from a heart attack in May 1982. Brigadier Bill Deller joined the Foundation as Regional Organizer (later Regional Director) six months later in November 1982, and the region was very fortunate to have the services of Mrs Iona Pettit at this difficult time of transition. She had joined the Foundation as secretary to Ray Stokes in April

1978, and had spent five years building up the region with him before she suddenly found herself in sole charge. The Foundation owes much to her able conduct of the affairs of the region at that time, and to her continuing services as Regional Administrator up to the present day.

At first, as is almost inevitable, regional expenditure exceeded income. In its first eight months it spent £351 and earned £50. The first large amount of money recorded as received is an *in memoriam* donation of £154.70p in August 1973. After this there was a steady improvement and the monthly income quickly rose to between £300 and £600. Five years later the monthly income averaged £3,500, and an annual income of over £100,000 was reached, for the first time, in 1981–82. As at the start, *in memoriam* donations have continued to represent a large percentage of the total.

As with other regions a wide variety of sponsored events has contributed to the success of fund-raising. Sponsored swims were started in Thetford and St Ives in 1975, and in Peterborough in 1976, and have raised large sums over the years. Other sponsored events are the first Snetterton Race Day in 1980, the Sandringham Jog in 1979, when members of the Royal Family joined in, and the Charity Race Day at Newmarket in 1985, which was an outstanding success.

Included in Iona Pettit's recollections of happenings in the line of duty for the BHF is the memory of being stuck in a snow drift till 5 a.m. on returning from a dance in 1978 in the company of Ray Stokes – and her husband! Her worst memory, she recalls, was when she arrived to run a sponsored swim by more than 200 children to find that the helpers from the local committee had forgotten about the event. Undaunted she organized the parents to help and the children to swim, with the result that the evening was a success socially and financially.

Amongst the regional archives is a photograph of Ray Stokes with Eric Boon, the boxer, and Keith Castle, the successful heart transplant patient. The interest in the picture is that Keith Castle received the heart of a young boxer (named in the picture) who was being trained by Eric Boon when he died tragically in a motor-cycle accident.

The Midlands

The large area presently covered by the Midlands Region comprises the original East Midlands Region, based in Nottingham, with parts of the West Midlands Region, which was based in Birmingham at Solihull, and parts of the old Region 11, based in Newcastle under Lyme in Staffordshire.

The East Midlands area covered Nottinghamshire, Leicestershire, Lincolnshire, South Humberside and Derbyshire. With the closure of the West Midlands office on the retirement of the Regional Organizer, Graham Hands, on 16 January 1981, Warwickshire was added and the region assumed the title of Midlands. With the closure of Region 11, on the retirement of Leslie Barker on 1 April 1986, it also took over responsibility for Staffordshire.

East Midlands. The East Midlands Region started in 1967, and its first organizer was Mrs S. Ford. She was followed by Mrs Newson Smith, and she, in turn, by Wing Commander John Palmby in 1968. He remained in office until his untimely death in 1978, and was a mainspring of energy, which ensured the uninterrupted progress which was made during the seventies. He was a big man physically, with a capacity to make friends to match. His engaging personality and his friendly jovial manner evoked a warm response in all his contacts, and secured the willing help of leading figures in the region, including the Duke of Rutland, who became the Patron of the Nottingham Committee, and the Duke of Devonshire, who became Patron of the Derbyshire Committee. He also received much help from Colonel and Mrs Hilton; Colonel Hilton was then High Sheriff of Derbyshire and subsequently Lord Lieutenant of the County.

Through these and other influential people it was possible to arrange prestigious events at stately homes, amongst which were Chatsworth House, Belvoir Castle, and Melbourne Hall, where the then Duchess of Gloucester attended a Foundation Ball as guest of honour.

During this exciting period of expansion John Palmby was fortunate to have Dorothy Hunt as Assistant Regional Organizer. She joined the East Midlands office in 1970 and made an immense contribution to the successes of the early days. When Wing Commander Jock Heatherill succeeded John Palmby in September 1978 Dorothy Hunt continued as his deputy, and she assumed the title of Regional Administrator when Jock Heatherill's title was changed to Regional Director. After 18 years' service she is still as busy and enthusiastic as ever.

The Regions

Jock Heatherill brought very valuable expertise in statistical planning and analysis to the headquarters of this very large region at a time when financial expansion was accelerating at a hitherto unprecedented rate.

The office, which had started in very modest accommodation, and with no sophisticated equipment, has gradually progressed to more spacious premises, and has acquired urgently needed electronic office equipment. This has been achieved without increasing the number of headquarters staff. Jill Porter, who joined in 1978, and Mildred Heath, who came later, both work in the office part-time, and manage to cover all the secretarial needs of the Administrator and Director.

Besides the prestigious balls, dinners and dinner-dances which have always been a feature of the East Midlands Region, there were also, as in other regions, a multitude of sponsored fund-raising events; amongst these a sponsored horse ride at Chatsworth was unique. Dorothy Hunt recalls that she took part 'on a great muscular steed and got round the course, to my great relief, without "taking off", by the simple expedient of keeping him amongst the other horses taking part'.

Income from sponsored events stems, as always, from the hard work of many voluntary committees. They all do so much that individual mention can be invidious, but it is right to recall the 20 years of continuous service to the Chesterfield Committee by Mrs Ryan, from its inauguration in 1968 until her retirement in 1988.

Another success story in the region is the start of a BHF shop in Leicester in 1982 by Mrs Ann Cook. This has now been followed by a second one in Leicester and another in Nottingham; all three are highly successful and are run entirely by voluntary help. Another, equally successful, and started at about the same time, is run by the Selston Committee.

As in other parts of the country the income from *in memoriam* donations has risen steadily, with wider knowledge of the scheme, and increasing acceptance by the public of this as a fitting memorial to a friend or relative.

On the assumption of the title and duties of Regional Director by Jock Heatherill, with responsibility for the coordination of fund-raising efforts, four County Organizers have been appointed to support and promote Voluntary Committees. Dennis Owens is the County Organizer for the West Midlands and Warwickshire, Patrick

Holden for Nottinghamshire and Leicestershire, Jeff Leadbeater for Staffordshire and Derbyshire, and Colin North for Lincolnshire and South Humberside.

West Midlands. In October 1966 Brigadier Cardiff, the Director General, reported to Council that a Birmingham Regional Committee was to be formed early in 1967, with Mr Burrows, a chartered accountant, as Chairman. The committee would consist of Sir Robert Aitkin, Vice Chancellor of Birmingham University, Sir Eric Clayson, owner of the *Birmingham Post and Mail*, Professor Melville Arnott and Professor de Burgh.

In 1968 Graham Hands, a Justice of the Peace, was appointed Regional Organizer, and remained so until the absorption of the region into the Midlands in January 1981.

Most of the original regional committees which were set up in the early days have been disbanded but the Birmingham Regional Committee has survived. Mr Burrows was followed as Chairman by Mr Eccles Williams, who served from 1974 to 1977, and he was followed by Mr Charles Davidson, a Director of Lucas Ltd, from 1978 to 1982. The current Chairman is Mr C.J.W. Smith, who is a Director of the Touche Ross Company.

Region 11. The area which was known as Region 11 comprised Staffordshire, Cheshire and Greater Manchester. It began in 1974 and was incorporated into the neighbouring regions of Wales, the North West and the Midlands in 1986.

Leslie Barker was the Regional Organizer during the whole of its independent existence, and she ran all the fund-raising events from her home in Newcastle under Lyme, starting 'in a small box room, with no filing cabinets; just box files stacked on a bed'.

She had formed a local Heart Research Fund in 1968 in memory of her husband, whom she had lost from a heart attack at an early age. Her aim was to equip the coronary care units of the local and neighbouring hospitals with monitors and other life-saving equipment. The first donations came from Mr Barker's colleagues in the legal profession, as a personal memorial, but fund-raising soon gathered momentum under her energetic leadership, and she found herself, after a few years, with substantial sums at her disposal. This gave her much concern because, as she said: 'my fund was rapidly outgrowing me and I was a lay person making decisions about equipment costing several thousand pounds'.

After much consideration she came to London to meet Brigadier Cardiff and Geoffrey Davison at BHF headquarters. She was impressed by both of them, and by the organization and objectives of the Foundation, so, after seeing the problems for herself through visits to the National Heart Hospital and the Hospital for Sick Children, Great Ormond Street, with Brigadier Cardiff, she decided to join her Fund to the Foundation's fund-raising efforts for research. She joined the Foundation on 1 July 1974.

She continued to be highly successful in raising money through weekly advertisements in the local newspapers and a wide variety of sponsored events and by personal donations, many of which were from friends and relatives of victims of heart disease.

Before her retirement in March 1986, after more than 12 years as the Regional Organizer, Region 11 joined the select band of those which had raised more than £100,000 in a year.

Her only regret at joining the Foundation is that she had to retire at the age of 65, commenting: 'had I persevered with my own Charity I would still be working. It took me a long time to get used to be able to have a bath without the telephone ringing, or someone knocking at the door with a donation,' but she added: 'I am proud to have been part of a Charity which has done so much, not only in saving lives, but also in improving the quality of the lives of so many sufferers. I shall always remember with deep affection the loyalty and support which Brigadier Cardiff gave to all his staff.'

The office of Region 11 was closed on 1 April 1986.

Jersey

The organization in Jersey is different from other regions in that there is no Regional Organizer or Director, nor is there a Regional Administrator or County Organizers.

All fund-raising is organized by the Jersey Committee, which is an informal unpaid body of Jersey men and women who work voluntarily for the Foundation. Many have been attracted to the work as the result of heart disease in family or friends, and some have been sufferers themselves.

The committee started in 1972 and has been continuously active ever since, raising big sums of money, all of which are sent to headquarters in London.

There has always been close cooperation with headquarters, and main events held by the committee have been attended on a number of occasions firstly by Geoffrey Davison and later by James Malcolm.

The committee has received a number of grants with which to purchase equipment for the island's coronary care unit, amongst which have been an image intensifier, two monitors, a treadmill exerciser and ambulatory electrocardiograph apparatus.

The first President of the committee was the cardiologist, Dr Alastair McInnes, who was succeeded in 1983 by Dr Bill Ginks, also a cardiologist.

The committee was started by Daphne Wagstaffe and Christine Bailhache, who were respectively the first and second Chairwomen. Daphne Wagstaffe was in office for three years and Christine Bailhache was followed in turn by Sandra Biddle, Julia Tranfield and Cheryl Stanley, until in 1978 Colin Hill took over. He remained in office until he was recently succeeded by Graham Boxall, a Jersey advocate. Colin Hill is a local schoolmaster and was the mainstay of the Committee over a number of years, as was also Geoffrey Grime, an accountant, who was Treasurer from the start in 1972 until 1987, when he retired in favour of Ian Ling, a stockbroker. Geoffrey Grime has made an immense contribution to the success of the committee, and has been very active in supporting its fund-raising activities.

Virtually all those who have been in the Chair have also served the committee as its Secretary. The current Secretary is John Scarborough, who is also an accountant.

Amongst others who have done sterling work for the committee are Sally Thompson, who was its Secretary, Lynn Troy, who was Secretary and then Chairwoman, and Maria Gleeson, the wife of one of the island's consultant physicians, who is currently Vice-Chairman.

The general pattern has been for the committee to hold two major fund-raising events every year. One has often been a ball, which has usually been held in the summer. Other events have included fashion shows, flag days and high-value raffles for expensive prizes such as motor cars.

The annual income from the Jersey Committee has shown a progressive increase, starting in the first three months of its existence to March 1972 with £330, and rising to £30,000 in the year in 1988, with an overall total in the 16 years of its existence of over £200,000.

FRAUD AND DECEPTION

All charities are potential targets for the unscrupulous collection of money and the Foundation has not escaped the attention of rogues, although it has been relatively fortunate. From time to time organizations have appeared in different parts of the country, under a variety of beguiling titles, purporting to collect for the Foundation. They have rarely amounted to more than a nuisance, but on at least three occasions it has been necessary to involve the police and take, or threaten to take, court action.

Vigilance by all in charge in the regions and at head office is the key to success, together with instant investigation of any suspicious circumstance; otherwise much harm to the public image can be done in a very short while.

Also of great importance is the need for expert supervision of fund-raising events, which, through the inexperience of well-intentioned voluntary workers, can result in harmful adverse publicity. The most obvious possible cause of such a mischance is the failure to control the cost of an event in relation to its likely return.

Another, which can cause great resentment, is through securing over-generous sponsorship pledges, with the result that well-wishers find themselves obligated for more money than they can reasonably afford. Enthusiasm, however laudable, has to be tempered by tact and common sense. These, and other points on similar lines, were repeatedly stressed in conversation with regional organizers, and there was a strongly expressed wish that reference should be made to this important aspect of their work.

SEVEN

THE WAY AHEAD: 1987

A NEW ERA commenced in 1986–87 with the arrival of a new Chairman of Council, a new Medical Director and a new Medical Spokesman.

Sir Raymond Hoffenberg, President of the Royal College of Physicians, succeeded Sir Cyril Clarke as Chairman of Council. Sir Cyril came to the Foundation in 1976 to become the Chairman of the Research Funds Committee and relinquished this appointment in 1982 to become Chairman of Council. His wide experience of chairmanship was a great asset to the Foundation in both these committees, where his ability to listen to all shades of opinion and, at the same time, lead debate was matched by his puckish sense of humour, ably used to defuse tension.

Brigadier Peter Tower was appointed Director General to succeed Brigadier Thursby Pelham in July 1986; he had been an officer in the Coldstream Guards, where he had commanded a battalion and had been Chief of Staff of London District. He inherited from his predecessor a very healthy state of affairs with an annual gross income raised from £1,000,000 to £16,000,000 since 1976.

These changes of personnel coincided with the Foundation's Jubilee year and Brigadier Thursby Pelham rightly received warm congratulations on all sides for his stewardship, during which the Foundation had increased immensely in stature and responsibility in the field of cardiovascular research. His achievements were recognized by the award of the decoration of Officer of the Order of the British Empire (OBE).

In 1986 Professor Shillingford was joined as Medical Director Designate by Professor Desmond Julian, at that time President of the British Cardiac Society, and until recently BHF Professor of Cardiology at Newcastle University Medical School. He took over from Professor Shillingford on 1 April 1987. Thus 24 years of unbroken service to the Foundation by Professor Shillingford came to an end.

Speaking of him at a farewell dinner on 29 June 1987 Brigadier Thursby Pelham said:

His knowledge and experience of cardiology have been of inestimable value to the Foundation over the years and have greatly helped to shape the course taken by cardiac research. The depth and breadth of his knowledge of every aspect of cardiology has enabled the Foundation to steer a steady course between the shifting shoals of 'expert' opinion. Many lay members of the Foundation have reason to be grateful for his patience in explaining science in a manner that is readily understandable.

In the autumn of 1987 Dr Frank Preston, lately Senior Medical Officer to British Airways, succeeded Dr David Matthews as Medical Spokesman, an appointment he had held for four years.

Unhappily, in the summer of 1988, after he had been in post for two years, Brigadier Tower suffered a breakdown in health, which led ultimately to his resignation. Fortunately for the Foundation Brigadier Thursby Pelham was able to return as Acting Director General, and he agreed to continue in this capacity until September 1989, pending the appointment of a new Director General.

POLICY

An 'Aim and Policy' document is prepared each autumn by the Finance and General Purposes Committee and passed to the Council for its meeting the following February. When agreed by Council it becomes official BHF policy for the ensuing year.

For 1985–86 this document reads as follows:

1 Aim
To enable man to live out his full life free from the threat of premature death or disablement from heart attack or blood vessel disease by:
(a) Encouraging and financing research into the causes, diagnosis and treatment of cardiovascular disease and its ultimate prevention.
(b) Informing doctors throughout the country of advances in the diagnosis and treatment of heart disease and identification of risk factors.
(c) Continuing to inform the public of scientifically proven risk factors and advances in treatment through the publication of Heart Research leaflets [now called Heart Information Series].
(d) Improving the facilities for 'cardiac care'.

2 Policy
(a) Research remains the prime activity and about 80% of funds available will be used in this area.

(b) The work of identifying promising areas of research will continue as well as identifying the most talented research workers. Such research workers will be supported to the fullest possible extent.
(c) Education and 'cardiac care' continue to be important activities.
(d) Ethical considerations are covered by the Foundation's Grant Regulations. All research projects involving investigations in Man must receive appropriate clearance in writing from the host institution's Ethical Committee prior to submission of the application for a grant. A copy of this clearance must be enclosed with the application. No grant will be awarded in the absence of this.

3 Action recommended

With this aim and policy in mind it is recommended that the Foundation should:
(a) Review the areas of research currently covered with the object of identifying any gaps or unnecessary duplication.
(b) Continue the drive to identify more fields which we should be particularly interested in supporting, not to the exclusion of, but in addition to, all the existing ones; continue to do all that is possible to interest and attract able research workers within these fields and support them to the fullest possible extent.
(c) Encourage the exchange of ideas by arranging symposia and meetings of research workers in various disciplines.
(d) Further the understanding between basic research workers and clinicians by arranging workshops at regular intervals.
(e) Monitor research progress supported by the Foundation, by site visits to Chairholders and individual grant holders, and to publicise the benefits deriving from that research.
(f) Keep general practitioners informed of up-to-date clinical practice in the treatment of various conditions of cardiovascular disease through the British Heart Foundation Information Service 'Fact File'.
(g) Keep under continuous review the question of educating the public in the avoidance of heart disease and ensure that the facts are publicised as they become known and are agreed by the medical profession as a whole.

The 'Aim and Policy' documents for 1986–87 and 1987–88 are identical except for the addition of a sentence under 2 Policy (d), which reads: 'When a project entails the use of animals the applicant must explain why no alternative model can be used,' and of a new paragraph under 3 Action Recommended: '(h) Interpret and publicise the benefits deriving from research.'

ANNIVERSARY REVIEW

In a '25th Anniversary Review' dated June 1986 Brigadier Thursby Pelham undertook a critical survey of the strengths and weaknesses of the Foundation, looking at its structure and the way it operates. He set out to review its work objectively and offered suggestions concerning the direction in which it should move over the next 25 years.

Against the background of the Foundation's uninterrupted success, without which, he observes, 'research into cardiovascular disease would have shrunk very materially in the UK', he poses the following questions: 'Is the Foundation mobilising sufficient talent into the field?'; 'Is it making sure that enough work is being done in the most promising fields?'; and 'Could it get better value for the money it spends?'

In attempting to answer these difficult questions he suggests that: 'there is a strong case for considering how much money the Research Funds Committee [the main spending committee] actually needs to do an optimum job'. He goes on: 'It is always easy to spend money: there is often a shortage of applicants of the right quality. But we do seem to lack a clear view of what level of expenditure might produce the best value in results – even if it turns out that the Foundation could not afford whatever the figure turned out to be.' At the same time he has 'little doubt that some applications which deserve support have been turned down for lack of funds'.

He also raises the question as to whether the current balance between clinical and non-clinical research is right, concluding: 'there appear to be strong grounds for thinking that more clinical research is needed, though clinical applications are comparatively rare'. To improve the situation he suggests setting up more clinical Fellowships in the lecturer and senior lecturer grades.

In attempting to answer the sensitive question as to whether the Foundation should guide research applications into specific areas he concludes that 'there appears to be increasing evidence that some guidance, at any rate, is necessary'. In support of this view he quotes a sentence from the report of the then Medical Director, Professor Shillingford, concerning the setting up of a task force on the blood/arterial wall interface, which reads: 'although it has not been the policy of the BHF to direct research in any way, some encouragement of this vital area may now be desirable'. The Brigadier comments: 'It may well be a matter of semantics, but the message seems clear that guidance is becoming increasingly necessary.'

Writing about the great success for research, and for the Foundation, of the policy of funding professorial chairs at universities he sees much benefit from site visits as a means of assessing financial needs and of monitoring standards of work. From this it follows that it might be of greater value to research to withhold further support to a unit if it was shown to be less successful than others, and, instead, to reinforce the success of outstanding units by deploying the money to them.

Whilst not underrating the difficulties in arriving at such a decision he faces it directly by suggesting that:

In those cases where the Foundation is critical of a particular unit it does seem that the Foundation should consider doing two things – firstly decline to give additional financial support to the unit until it is satisfied with its performance; and secondly, send a carefully stated, but very frank, letter to the Dean of the School, and to the Chairholder, setting out the reasons for its decision.

The Director General also has comments to make on the allocation of funds by the Foundation. His statement reads:

The distribution of moneys to the various spending activities of the Foundation has tended, almost inevitably, to be settled year by year in relation to the allocations of previous years. On the whole this has achieved a reasonable balance, even if made somewhat arbitrarily.

There are good grounds for thinking that a new approach might from now on be more appropriate. This would be for each of the spending bodies to make a reasoned case each year, say in October, for the money they think they could spend productively during the following financial year. They would in effect be bidding for whatever they felt to be a necessary allocation: and would be required to support their applications with proper reasons. This would require a good deal more effort and expenditure of time than the present system.

Such a procedure might well stimulate constructive thought in each spending area, might clarify ideas of how moneys could best be spent, and would almost certainly prove of great value. It would then be for the Finance and General Purposes Committee, on the report of the Director General, to make a final overall allocation based on an evaluation of the different bids for each spending activity.

Writing of fund-raising the Brigadier recognizes the immense successes achieved as the result of much hard work by very many people, but he reminds his readers that the causes of heart disease, which the Foundation was set up to discover, still remain largely unknown, and that, in consequence, there is a continuing need for more and more money.

Gratefully acknowledging that in fund-raising 'the trend is steadily upwards', he goes on: 'the question must be asked "can this trend be accelerated?" We must keep asking this question.' Conscious of the key role of increasing public awareness, and the benefits already conferred by rapidly expanding media coverage, he expresses his disappointment that, to date, exploitation through television has been on such a relatively small scale.

He concludes by stating that his review is 'an attempt to provide a general overview of the work of the Foundation and to indicate some, at least, of the areas which may need to be reappraised'. He goes on: 'It is therefore suggested that it would be helpful to the Foundation, and certainly instructive to the individuals concerned, to ask the new Director General and the Consultant Medical Director to conduct a critical and objective overall review of the structure, method of operation and practices of the Foundation as their first task.' He urges that this should be done expeditiously and completed within a defined timetable.

ANNUAL REPORT 1987

In his report to the Annual General Meeting in July 1987, Brigadier Tower advocated a pause for consolidation of recent achievements. At the same time Dr Jeffrey Fryer, a member of Council and Managing Director of the Pharmaceutical Division of Ciba Geigy, was asked to make a study and prepare a report on the overall organization and methods of operation of the Foundation in order to chart a course for the future. This is exactly in line with Brigadier Thursby Pelham's thinking.

A study of the methods and running of charity shops was also commissioned, to be undertaken by Mr Christopher Britten, following the successful outcome of a pilot scheme of ten shops launched and managed by Mr Keith Barker in the South East of England. The average annual return from each of these shops was £10,000.

The Foundation had made a number of tentative forays into the business of charity shops over the years but none had been permanent. As early as May 1966 a shop was opened in Harrow by the Mayor and subsequently adopted by the Harrow Committee. It is recorded as being successful and in the issue of the *Bulletin* for September 1967 an advertisement appeared asking for children's toys, games, jewellery, books, china and pottery, stamps and cigarette cards, concluding: 'we hope that the BHF shop will eventually become a pilot for a chain of Foundation shops throughout Britain. It can sell almost everything. All gifts are welcome.'

Again, in 1982, a shop was opened in Leicester by the Lord Mayor. It paid off its overheads and made a profit of £4,000 in its first year, after which, running on a five-day week and manned by a group of 25 volunteers, it produced, on average, £750 per month, and is reported as still running profitably six years later, together with a second one in the same city.

The outcome of Mr Britten's enquiry was the decision to build up a network of 100 charity shops across the country in the next three years requiring investment capital of about £3,000,000. The operation would be a trading arm of the BHF under a Shops Director with wide experience in the retail business. Mr Colin Sandford, who had been Commercial Director of Curry's stores and had worked for them for 22 years, was chosen from a short list of applicants experienced in this work.

REORGANIZATION

Following Dr Jeffrey Fryer's report on the organization of the Foundation Brigadier Thursby Pelham announced decisions about future plans in a memorandum dated 29 November 1988, which made the following points:

Organization of head office

Chief Administrator. The administrative responsibilities for the Foundation will in future be undertaken by the holder of the new post of Chief Administrator, who will be directly responsible to the Director General for Personnel Management, Buildings and Material (other than medical). He will be supported by a Personnel Manager and an Administration Manager [formerly called the Administrator]. This will relieve the Secretary of the Foundation of these administrative duties.

Secretary. The main tasks of the Secretary will be those of Company Secretary, with responsibility for legal matters, tax and VAT requirements, Accounts, Investments, Legacies and management information. The Secretary will be supported, as at present, by an Assistant Secretary, a Legacy Officer and an Accountant.

The Way Ahead

Shops. Colin Sandford, Chief Executive of BHF Shops, is responsible to the Director General in the same way as other Heads of Departments. The shops operation will be directed from its Head Office at 9a Victoria Road, Surbiton in the near future.

When these changes have been effected the organization of Head Office will be as follows:

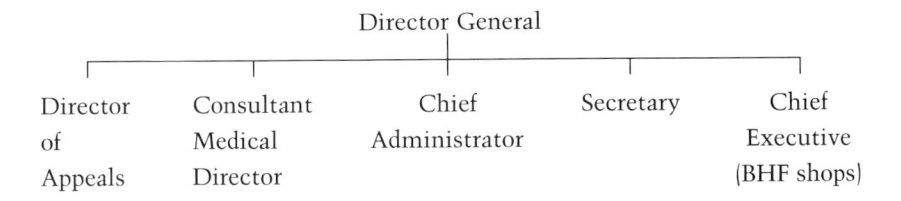

```
                        Director General
    ┌───────────┬───────────┬───────────┬───────────┐
Director    Consultant    Chief      Secretary    Chief
of          Medical       Administrator           Executive
Appeals     Director                              (BHF shops)
```

Despatch department

A Section Head and an Assistant will be appointed as soon as possible to deal with the despatch of leaflets.

Accommodation

There is already a danger of over-crowding and the Finance and General Purposes Committee has authorised a search for new premises with a view to moving towards the end of 1989 or in the first half of 1990. It is hoped to find a large enough building in the same part of London as at present to accommodate all headquarters departments comfortably and efficiently under one roof.

Salaries

A review of present salary scales to ensure that the Foundation is in line with comparable charities will be undertaken in the next few months. In the meantime, a cost-of-living increase will be awarded on 1 April 1989 and upgradings will take place on 1 July 1989.

MEDICAL POLICY DECISIONS

Two important decisions of medical policy were also made in 1986–87. The first was to charge the Education Committee officially with the task of educating the public in matters concerning heart disease, and the second to enter the field of clinical trials as part of the Foundation's research programme. It was decided that the first step in this field would be to support Dr Sowton in a ten-hospital, multi-centre trial based at Guy's Hospital to compare the long-term value of coronary artery bypass surgery with angioplasty in the treatment of coronary heart disease, and also to support Dr Pocock, at the Royal Free Hospital, with a project researching methods of statistical analysis of clinical trials to assess results with scientific accuracy. It was agreed that he would use the findings of Dr Sowton's investigation as the first trial of the methodology.

All these important decisions were made by the newly streamlined Council (see p. 84) on advice given by the Finance and General Purposes Committee.

ACHIEVEMENTS

The first Clause in the Articles of Association of the Foundation gives as its aim: 'to undertake and promote medical and scientific research relating to diseases of the heart and circulation and subjects relative thereto, and to promote postgraduate medical training therein'.

The achievements of the Foundation in its first 25 years of endeavour must, therefore, be considered in the above context.

Research

To perform its primary responsibility as the heart research charity, on which it has consistently spent over 80% of its income, three broad patterns of support can be identified. Firstly it has funded individual applications for project grants; secondly it has attracted graduates into cardiovascular research by setting up research Fellowships; and thirdly it has created centres of excellence in university medical schools through professorial chairs and research groups.

Project grants. The amount of money spent on project grants has steadily increased with the passage of time until today the Research Funds Committee usually recommends awards costing more than £1,000,000 at each of its quarterly meetings. The width of the spectrum covered is impressive (see Figure 27, p. 129), and promising new lines of enquiry are assured of sympathetic consideration.

In the last 25 to 30 years there has been an explosion of knowledge in the field of cardiology world-wide, in the realms of both diagnosis and treatment. The Foundation has played a major role in many of these advances, and has contributed, with other research workers in institutions in Britain and overseas, to progress in many more.

The applications of electronics and bioengineering have greatly increased the methodology in the diagnosis of heart disease with the development of the sophisticated electrocardiograph, radio-isotopes and computerized axial tomography, together with magnetic resonance and echocardiography. Research workers supported by the Foundation have been in the van with these and many others; they have been the pioneers in several.

Advances in the field of treatment as a result of research have been enormous and BHF-supported workers have played a full part. There have been very important advances in drug therapy for many conditions, notably high blood pressure, heart failure and irregularities of rhythm.

The development of the defibrillator has greatly improved the survival rate of emergency resuscitation, as has also the introduction of coronary care. This almost coincided with the beginning of the Foundation, which has played an important part by supporting research leading to the widespread introduction of coronary care units; these have had profound effects on the management of coronary disease.

Perhaps the most important advance in therapy has been the introduction of thrombolysis with streptokinase combined with aspirin in the Isis 2 Trial, in which the Foundation played an important supporting role.

Cardiac surgery has become established during this era as a valuable method of treatment in many forms of heart disease. Stemming from the development of the heart/lung machine, open heart surgery has become a practical reality. Valve replacement is increasingly undertaken and surgeons supported by the Foundation have contributed greatly to the development of new types of valve. Similarly, new operations have been devised to overcome the problems created by severe congenital malformations with dramatic improvement in the survival rate and the quality of life. Paediatric cardiac surgeons supported by the Foundation have been among the pioneers in this field.

The Foundation has also contributed to the progress made in heart and heart/lung transplantation through support of research in the

Papworth Unit run by Terence English, and the Harefield Unit run by Magdi Yacoub. The latter is now the BHF Professor of Cardiac Surgery at the Cardiothoracic Institute at the Brompton Hospital in London.

Coronary heart disease is now very clearly the most important heart disease of adults in terms of its impact on the quality of life and on mortality. Progress in its treatment has been made by bypass surgery and by angioplasty. The Foundation has recently financed, in conjunction with the British Cardiac Society and the Department of Health, an important research programme comparing the two forms of treatment.

Mention of individual contributions by workers supported by the Foundation is to risk the omission of others equally worthy, but the volume and scope of outstanding work done by those supported over the years are such that available space prohibits totality.

Doctor Lindsey Allan has pioneered fetal echocardiography and developed it to the point where it is now a valuable clinical diagnostic investigation of cardiac, and other, malformations in the unborn child. At the same time Professor Anderson has played a leading role in advancing the understanding of the pathology of different forms of congenital heart disease, and Professor Michael Davies has made similar advances in the understanding of the pathological changes which occur in coronary heart disease.

Doctor Tom Meade's observations in his unit at Northwick Park Hospital on the predictive value of abnormalities in blood-clotting factors have identified an entirely new risk factor which had not previously been recognized, but which is now thought to be virtually equally as important as the other major risk factors of smoking, high blood pressure and blood fats.

In the field of epidemiology, studies carried out by Professor Shaper at the Royal Free Hospital in London, with the support of the Foundation, in the British Regional Heart Study have clarified the aetiological factors in coronary heart disease and have attempted to explain the variations in its incidence in different parts of Britain.

Mention must also be made of the identification of the 'sick gene' concerned with familial hypercholesterolaemia to which Doctor Humphries and his research group have contributed so much by their work at the Bernard Sunley Research Laboratory in Charing Cross Hospital Medical School, and also of the work of Professor Radda's group in Oxford on cardiac muscle using magnetic resonance.

Fellowships. Perhaps the most important function of a research-funding body is to identify and support young research workers of talent. The value of Fellowships instituted by the Foundation from its earliest days is confirmed by the fact that most of those now reaching the top of the profession in Britain in both academic and clinical cardiovascular practice are those who have been supported during their training by BHF Fellowships or project grants.

The junior fellowships have been particularly valuable in enabling young graduates to explore the possibilities of a career in cardiovascular research in the face of a scarcity of alternative means of support whilst coming to a decision. This far-sighted policy has led many able men and women into heart research who would otherwise have been lost to it through lack of opportunity.

At the same time the Foundation was quick to appreciate that an extension of the scheme through senior research Fellowships with longer tenure was needed to keep and support more experienced researchers whilst awaiting appointments to career posts. These are always in short supply, particularly in non-clinical fields.

Later the need became apparent for an intermediate research Fellowship to bridge the gap between senior and junior. This continuity, for a two- to three-year period, has been an extremely valuable addition to the infrastructure on which the top echelons depend for continuity of availability of high-calibre talent.

Finally the introduction of overseas exchange fellowships further increased the training potential of those fortunate enough to be supported by the Foundation and, once again, several now in leading positions were recipients of these awards during their training.

Professorial chairs and research groups. In no part of its activities has the Foundation had a greater impact on cardiac research in Britain than in its massive investment in chairs of cardiology and cardiac surgery, and in the setting up of research groups with guaranteed continuity of support.

Without the British Heart Foundation cardiovascular research in Britain would, almost certainly, still be as woefully inadequate as it was in 1961 when its parlous state was the spark which lit the fire. The advances which have followed are a measure of its success.

The creation of 14 endowed chairs (eleven in cardiology and three in cardiac surgery) in university medical schools has meant that these centres have become the major foci of cardiac research, particularly in the clinical field. Where British Heart Foundation chairs exist, these centres are widely regarded as the leading centres of excellence in the practice of cardiology and cardiac surgery. This point emphasizes the very close relationship between research and clinical practice; the research centres are those which are most likely to put into practice the major findings of research and at the same time evaluate them most critically.

In addition to the 14 endowed chairs the Foundation has also created six personal chairs, which have ensured that a number of internationally recognized experts in their fields are adequately supported and are, indeed, encouraged to stay in this country in spite of tempting offers from abroad. The first personal chair was set up in 1980.

The introduction of research groups was made to fill a need to sponsor projects which required a team to be kept together with guaranteed support for long enough to produce a valid conclusion. They have been very fruitful of results and have fully justified the policy and the investment. Their leaders are, without exception, pre-eminent figures in their own disciplines, and their findings have, in consequence, been authoritative. Their topicality has frequently led to widespread media interest and coverage.

Postgraduate medical training

Besides the award of individual Fellowships the Foundation has assisted the greater understanding of cardiology by specialists and general practitioners in many ways through its Education Committee (p. 162), and these efforts have undoubtedly made a major contribution towards increasing the standards of patient care. Of particular value have been the lectures given by BHF-sponsored lecturers at postgraduate centres and the 'Fact File' sheets produced jointly with the British Cardiac Society, which are circulated, on a monthly basis, to all general practitioners who want them. The response to this offer has exceeded 90%. They summarize on one A4 sheet of paper current thinking on the commoner problems encountered in clinical practice.

Postgraduate medical training can justifiably be included among the Foundation's impressive achievements during the last 25 years.

Public education

Whilst remaining careful to refrain from making statements supporting unproven hypotheses the Foundation has, over the years, done much to increase understanding of the causes and manifestations of heart disease. This has mainly been done through its eighteen 'Heart Information Series' booklets, about 10,000,000 of which have been given away free to the public, either directly or through doctors and institutions as intermediaries.

The Education Committee has also produced other booklets, together with films, videos, posters and newsletters, all of which have proved popular, and schoolchildren have been specially targeted. Since 1987 the Education Committee has been formally charged with the duty of educating the public as well as with continuing its work of postgraduate medical education.

In recent years it has been increasingly concerned with direct responses to enquiries from individual members of the public about all manner of matters relating to heart disease, and has responded by correspondence and by answering telephone enquiries. It has also assisted the media and the medical journalists with information needed in programmes and articles.

Fund-raising

The success of fund-raising to finance the objectives of the Foundation must also be included in a record of its achievements. From a start as an unknown charity less than 30 years ago it is a remarkable achievement to have reached an income of nearly £25,000,000 a year, with a General Fund Portfolio and a Chairs Maintenance Portfolio standing at over £20,000,000 each. The money has come entirely from the public and industry, without Government support except for the tax relief granted to all charities. This reflects the greatest possible credit on all fund-raisers and testifies to the wonderful generosity of the public.

OBJECTIVES

Unfortunately in spite of all these major advances important problems remain to be solved so long as heart disease continues to be the single largest cause of death world-wide. The main objective of the Foundation, therefore, will remain unaltered, as the supporter of research.

The Foundation's policy to extend the scope and size of its commitment as far as its finances allow will continue to be its endeavour, though the emphasis of its thrust will constantly shift as new frontiers loom and challenge.

Most importantly, perhaps, in the immediate future is the need to learn much more about the causes and treatment of coronary disease; this needs to be pursued on many fronts including pathology, epidemiology and biochemistry. Only if the causes of coronary disease are better understood will prevention be more successful.

There is currently great interest in the potentiality of changing clotting factors following Dr Meade's work, and it may well be that major advances will occur because of new therapeutic methods in this area. The Foundation will be keen to continue to support work in this field.

Among many other areas in which there is increasing interest are the genetics of various forms of heart disease, the fundamental causes of high blood pressure, the mechanism of disturbances of rhythm and their control, and better understanding and management of the problems of heart and lung transplantation. The Foundation will continue to be in the forefront of research in all these areas and many others besides.

By expanding its endeavour into the realm of clinical trials the Foundation is greatly extending its research horizons, and, at the same time, greatly enlarging its financial commitments. It is, however, right that an organization as important and authoritative as the Foundation should spend time, money and effort to assess the clinical value of the spectacular advances which have been made in recent years.

The Foundation's commitment to the support of research workers by awarding Fellowships at all levels of training is certain to be maintained, and is likely to be extended to meet the ever-increasing potentials of research. The Foundation will also continue to be conscious of its torch-bearing responsibility to the support and furtherance of academic cardiology at a time when it is having difficulty in competing with the rewards of clinical practice. To echo the words of Sir John McMichael at the launch of the Public Appeal in 1963: 'a country which fails to develop its research would be committing national suicide because our cultural leadership depends on it'.

Finally the Foundation is firmly committed to an increasing role in education of both the public and the profession. This is essential in the light of the great increase which has come about in the knowledge of the causes and treatment of heart disease.

All modes of communication will be utilized, taking advantage of every opportunity for coverage by radio and television. The programme of public education will be especially targeted at young people as it is widely felt that the long-term prevention of heart disease is something which must start in childhood or adolescence.

The future of the Foundation is assured because of the wisdom and integrity on which it has been built ever since its inception by its Founding Committee. Only with the dawn of the long sought-after day when heart disease is relegated to past history, like other scourges of bygone days, will it no longer need to be the rallying point of so much dedicated endeavour.

INDEX

Bold page numbers refer to illustrations and main references

Abraham, A.S., Exchange Fellowship, 156
Academic professorial units, establishment, as centres of excellence, 53
Accommodation 1987 report, 249
Adams, Mrs, *Western Region*, 219
Administration
 early years, 27–29
 middle years, 48
Advertising
 expenditure, **93**
 recent years, 91–94
Aims and Policy documents, 243–244
Aims of the BHF, video, 74–75
Aitkin, Sir Robert, *West Midlands Region*, 238
Al-Maktoum Senior Lectureship, 143
Alexander, R., (Admiral), *Hampshire Region*, Regional Organizer, 214, 226
Alexander of Tunis, Viscount, first President, 14, **15**, 29–30, 54
Allan, Lindsey
 Research Group in Fetal Echocardiography, London, 141, 154, 252
 speaker, 89, 90
American Heart Association, 115, 156
 advertising ratio, 94
Ames, Mary, *London Region*, northern, southern and eastern boroughs, 232
Anderson, Patrick
 London Region, western boroughs, 229
 Manager, 56, 105
Anderson, Robert, Joseph Levy Foundation, Chair of Paediatric Cardiac Morphology, **55**, 58, **137**, **152–154**, 252
Angioplasty versus Bypass Surgery, Assessment, Guy's Hospital, 142, 252
Animals, use in research, Chairs and Research Groups Committee, 148–149
Anniversary Review, 244–247
Annual General Meetings
 early years, 36–38
 and Public Meetings, middle years, 56
 recent years, 88–90
Annual Reports, 1987, 247–248
 early years, 38
Ansell, Professor, *Western Region*, Bath Committee, 222
Appeal Consultants, 24
 see also Joan Scott Consultants
Appeal Policy Committee
 Annual Report, 1962, 24
 Chairman, Campbell, Maurice, 17
 early years, 18–19, 23–24
 first, 17
Appeals, *see also* Fund-raising
Appeals Department, 78, 80, 81

258

Index

recent years, 90
Appleby, Betty, Secretary, 82
Arnott, Sir Melville, 111, 112
  Chair of Cardiovascular
    Medicine, Birmingham, 153
  Founding Committee meetings, 9
  Science Committee,
    Chairman, 17, **87**, 115, 117, 120
    Vice-Chairman, 49
  West Midlands Region,
    Committee member, 238
Ascot race days, **43**, 44, 100
ASH, and BHF policies, 124–125
Astor, Hon. Gavin
  President, first Appeal
    Committee, 23
  Times proprietor, Appeal
    Committee launch, 20, 23
Audio-visual tape-slide projection
  apparatus, 167
Australia, advertising ratio, 94
Australian/British Exchange
  Fellowship, 158

Badenoch, Sir John, 136–137
  Fellowship Committee,
    Chairman, 161
Bailhache, Christine, *Jersey Region*,
  Chairwoman, 240
Baird, McClean, Postgraduate
  Education Funds Committee,
  163
Balcon, R., speaker, 89
Ball, Stephen, Leeds, Chair of
  Cardiovascular Studies, 131,
  153
Bankers
  Appeal Committee launch, 20
  Glyn Mills Bank, 12
Banks, D., Exchange Fellowship,
  157
Barbirolli, Sir John, Sixth World
  Congress of Cardiology,
  concert, 165
Bare, Nancy
  Western Region, Salisbury,
    Chairman, 222

  organizing secretary, 219–220
Barker, Keith, charity shops,
  247–248, 249
Barker, Leslie
  Midlands Region,
    Regional Organizer, 238
    retirement, 236
  Staffordshire Region, 201
Barker, Pauline, *East Anglian
  Region*, Norwich Committee,
  secretary, 234
Barnes, Fiona, Press Office, 82, 95
Barr, Stuart, *Yorkshire and North
  Humberside Region*, Leeds
  Committee, 212
Barron, Marjorie
  London Region, 229
  Southern Region, 226
Barry, Miss E, Royston Fellowship,
  144
Basset, Brian
  Appeal Committee, 52
  Investment Committee,
    Chairman, 83
  Treasurer, 51, 83
Bayliss, Jill, 79
Bayliss, Sir Richard, **87**
  Chairs Committee, 135
Beale, David, Finance and General
  Purposes Committee,
  Outside Advisor, 83
Beatt, K.J., Dutch–British Exchange
  Fellowship, 157
Beckensale, Richard, 101
Bedford, Evan
  Council Chairman, 29
  resignation, 49
  Founding Committee member, 3,
    4, **6–9**, 9
  reorganization of BHF, 33
  Science Committee, Hon.
    Member, 17, 117
Beecham Group Ltd., covenant, 24
Beeon, Professor, 128
Belgrave Square Residents
  Association Fair, 101
Bell, Norman, *Northern Region*, 199
  Appeal Committee,

260 Index

Regional Director, 204
Regional Organizer, 204–205
Bernard Sunley Research Centre,
　Charing Cross Hospital, 142
Besly, Lieutenant Colonel Richard
　Cardiac Care Committee,
　　Regional Director, 190
　Southern Region, 225
Biddle, Sandra, *Jersey Region*,
　Chairwoman, 240
Bike rides
　Hadrian's Wall, 99, 206
　London-to-Brighton, 63–64, 99, 102
　'National Ride a Bike Week', 100
　'Round Britain', 102
Billimoria, J.D., Westminster
　Hospital Medical School, 116
Biochemistry, research grants
　1979–85, analysis of
　distribution of funds, **129**
Birmingham
　Chair of Cardiology, 130
　Department of Cardiovascular
　　Medicine, Contractile
　　Proteins in Normal and
　　Abnormal Cardiac Function, 142
　group Chair, 131
　Professorial chairs, 54, 115
Black, Jane, *Scottish Region*,
　Glasgow organizer, 201, 207
Black, Jim, 210
Blackburn, John, Cardiac
　Care Committee, Medical
　Administrator, **185**, 188
Blake, Denis, Foundation Secretary,
　34–35, 64, 107, 193
　and Accountant, 78
　retirement, 103–107
Blood/Arterial Wall Interface Task
　Force, Chairs and Research
　Groups Committee, 144
Blythe, Louise (neé Levinson), 79
Bodley Scott, Sir Ronald
　British/American Exchange
　　Fellowships, 157
　Chair of Cardiovascular
　　Medicine, St. Bartholomew's
　　Hospital, 137
　Chairman, 49–50
　Council Chairman, 86, 130, 134
　Research Funds Committee,
　　Chairman, 50, 119
　Royal College of Physicians,
　　President, 116–117
　Science Committee, Chairman,
　　49, 120
　death, 49–50
Bonham, Carter, R.E., 57, 119
Born, G.V.R., speaker, 89, 145
Boult, Group Captain Ben, *Western
　Region*, Cornwall Regional
　Organizer, 220
Boxall, Graham, *Jersey Region*,
　Chairman, 240
Braimbridge, M., speaker, 90
Bransfield, Mary, 82
Breckenridge, A.M., speaker, 57
British Association of Immediate
　Care Schemes, basics, 166
British Cardiac Society, 1–2, 116
British Heart Foundation
　25th anniversary dinner, 87, 88
　accommodation 1987 report, 249
　advertising and publicity
　　expenditure (1977–86), **69**
　Aims and Policy documents,
　　243–244
　Anniversary Review, 244–247
　annual gross income, 68
　Annual Report, 1987, 247–248
　Cardiac Transplantation Research
　　Group, 141
　Cardiovascular Statistics Group, 142
　Certificate of Incorporation as a
　　Company, early years, 18
　Chairs Fund Portfolio, 69
　Chief Administrator,
　　responsibilities, 248
　Constitution of the Foundation, 13
　Council structure, early years,
　　21–22
　creation, 3–17

Director General, 34
display stand, **165**
early years, 1961–1966, 18–39
Education Committee, 249–250
Founding Committee meetings, 9–17
the future, 255–257
General Fund Portfolio, 69
headquarters, 34
income,
  and expense/income ratios (1977–86), **68**
  from voluntary sources (1977–86), **69**
investment portfolio, 68
memorandum and articles of association, early years, 22
middle years, 1966–1976, 40–67
Molecular Biology Research Group, Charing Cross Hospital, 142
objectives, 10, 255–257
overseas funding, 116
Personal Chairs, Chairs and Research Groups Committee, 154
prize and gold medal, 152–153
projects grants, 250–253
Regional Heart Study Research Group, Royal Free Hospital, 142
relationship with Chest and Heart Association, 33–34
  early days, 21
reorganization, 248–249
research achievements of first 25 years, 250
Secretary, responsibilities, 248
Silver Jubilee dinner, 87, 88
university professional chairs, early years, 38–39
British Medical Journal, public education and prevention, 73
British/American Exchange Fellowships, 115
  Fellowships Committee, 156
  Research Fellowships, 39
Britten, Christopher, charity shops, 247–248, 249
Brompton Hospital, Joseph Levy Foundation, Chair of Paediatric Cardiac Morphology, 55, 58, 137, 152–154
Brown, Bertie, *North West Region*, Regional Organizer, 208
Bruning, Mrs, *Southern Region*, Dartford Committee, 226
Bulletin, 95–98
Burdon–Sanderson Chair of Cardiovascular Physiology, 138
Burgen, A.S.V., Selection Committee, 156
Burnett, Ian, *London Region*, Ball Committee, director, 231
Burnett, Ken, Direct Mail specialist, 107
Burnett, Miss, *Southern Region*, 226
Burnstock, G., Mechanisms of Local Control of Blood Flow, London, 142, 155
Burrows, Mr, *West Midlands Region*, Chairman, 238
Butler, Morris, Cardiac Care Committee, Medical Administrator and Secretary, 185
  Education Funds Committee, Medical Administrator, 179, 186
  Medical Administrator, 49, 59, 64, 78, 81, 120–121, 135
Butterfield, W.J., speaker, 57

Cadbury Marvel, National Sponsored Slim, 47
Caldwell, Ruth, *North West Region*, Halten Committee, Chairman, 209
Cameron, Ian, Investment Committee, 83
Camm, John
  Bodley Scott Chair of Cardiovascular Medicine,

137, 138
Prudential Professor of Clinical Cardiology, London, 154
Sixth European Congress, organizer, 166–167
Campbell, Maurice
BHF Chair of Cardiology, Newcastle upon Tyne, 153
Committee, Hon Member, 117
Council Chairman, 9, 37
first Appeal Policy Committee Chairman, 17
Founding Committee member, 4, **9**
letter to members of British Cardiac Society, 2, 3, **8–9**
Medical Director, 131
Regional Boards of the National Health Service, Chairman, 192
reorganization of BHF, 32
resignation as Chairman of Council, 29, 49
Cardiac Care Committee, 50, 81, 119
constitution, 119
cost of awards, 187–188
defibrillators, 188–190
disbursement, 186
formation, 184
history, 185
local fund-raising, 186–187
members, 119
personnel, 188, 190–191
purchasing organization, 188
Value Added Tax, policy, 187
Cardiac Resuscitation Advisory Council (CRAC), 166, 171, **172**
Cardiac surgery, achievements, 251–253
Cardiff, Ereld
Appeals Committee, Director, **32**, 88, 193
Director General, 34–**35**, 40, 41, 65, 66–67, 193
Finance and General Purposes Committee, Chairman, 66–67, 67, 83, 135
Postgraduate Education Funds Committee, Director General, 163
speaker, 89
Vice-President, 86, **87**, 194
Cardiopulmonary resuscitation (CPR), 171–172
Cardiovascular Epidemiology Research Group, 141, 252
Carruthers, Malcolm, 57
Carter, R.E. Bonham, Research Funds Committee, 57, 119
Catford, John
Health Education for Wales, 75
Welsh Region, Heart Beat Wales, Director, 218
Caves, Philip
BHF Chair of Cardiac Surgery, Glasgow, 153
European Travelling Scholarship, 160
Exchange Fellowship, 131, 157
Centres of excellence
establishment, academic professorial units, 53
middle years, 54
CHA *see* Chest and Heart Association
Chadwick, B., *Yorkshire and North Humberside Region*, 212, 213
Chain, Sir Ernst
Medical Committee, 117
Research Funds Committee, 119
speaker, 57
Chair of Cardiac Surgery
Brompton Hospital, London, 130
Glasgow, 131
Chair of Cardiology
Birmingham, 130
Newcastle, 131
Oxford University, 41
Chair of Cardiothoracic Surgery, Royal Postgraduate Hospital, Hammersmith, 138
Chair of Cardiovascular Immunology, St George's Hospital Medical School, 138

Chair of Cardiovascular Pathology,
    St George's Hospital Medical
    School, 137
Chair of Cardiovascular Studies,
    Leeds, 131
Chair of Molecular Cardiology,
    Oxford, 138
Chair of Paediatric Cardiology
  Great Ormond Street, 128
  Vandervell Trust, 128
Chairs Maintenance Fund, 139
Chairs and Research Groups
    Committee, 81, 125
  animals, use in research, 148–149
  BHF Personal Chairs, 154
  Blood/Arterial Wall Interface
    Task Force, 144
  budget, 149
  clinical trials, 147
  Constitution, 136
  personnel, 134–136
  policy reviews, 146–147
  Professorial Chairs,
    established by Foundation,
      153–155
    personal and endowed, 137–140
  Project Grant Regulations, 1988,
    150–152
  research funds administrator, 150
  research groups, 140–143,
    154–155
  rolling tenure, 145–146
  Royston Fellowship, 144
  sabbatical leave, 147
  Standing Orders, 135–136
Chamberlain, D.
  Education Committee, chairman,
    178
  International meeting, Brighton,
    organizer, 167
  International Meeting on Cardiac
    Arrest and Resuscitation,
    director, 166
  Postgraduate Education Funds
    Committee, chairman, 163
  Seventh European Congress,
    organizer, 167
  speaker, 89, 90

Chandler, Miss W., *London Region*,
    Southwark, 229, 233
Chandler, Molly
  Southern Region, 193, 225
  Sussex organizer, 46
Charities Act, 106
Charity, registration as, early years,
    28
Charity Card Christmas Council,
    106
Charity shops, 247–248, 249
Chest, Heart and Stroke
    Association, 2–3
Chest and Heart Association, 2–3,
    192
  Proposed Cardiac Appeal, 5
  relationship with BHF, 33–34
Chief Administrator,
    responsibilities, 248
Chiesman, Ann, *London Region*,
    Regional Organizer, 230
Chiesman, Major Tony, *Hampshire
    Region*, 226
Child, Ann, Task Force, Director,
    145
Children
  education, 76
  publications, 170
Christie, Lady Jean, *Yorkshire and
    North Humberside Region*,
    212
Christmas catalogue, 60, 106–107
Ciba Foundation, 82–83
Clarke, Sir Cyril
  Council Chairman, 86, 87, 242
  Research Funds Committee, 53
  Chairman, 120, 134
Clayson, Sir Eric, *West Midlands
    Region*, Committee member,
    238
Cleland, W.P., Finance Committee,
    117, 119, 130
Clinical cardiology and diagnosis,
    research grants, 1979–85,
    analysis of distribution of
    funds, **129**
Clinical Magnetic Resonance
    Laboratory, Oxford, 138

Clinical trials, Chairs and Research Groups Committee, 147
CNS control of CV function, Royal Free Hospital group, 142
Cobbe, S.M., Walton Chair of Medical Cardiology, Glasgow, 131, 153
Cobbold, Lord
  Finance and General Purposes Committee Chairman, 28, 29
  President, **51**, 52–53
  reorganization of BHF, 32
  Treasurer, 23, 88
  Vice-President, 86
Collett, Miriam
  East Anglian Region, Bedfordshire, Buckinghamshire, Hertfordshire and Northamptonshire, 234
  Northern Home Counties Region, 201
Collins, Jack, *Yorkshire and North Humberside Region*, County Organizer, 215
Collins, Norman, Council member, 14
Coltart, D.J.
  Finance and General Purposes Committee, 137
  Fourth European Congress, organizer, 166
Combe, Simon, Appeal Committee launch, 20
Commonwealth countries, 116
Concerts *see* Fund-raising events
Congenital heart disease, 169, 252
Consultancy, Joan Scott Public Relations Consultancy, 77, 94, **98–100**
Consultant Advisers, 25–26
  Science Committee, 114
Cook, Ann, *East Midlands Region*, Leicester BHF shop, 236
Cooking for Your Heart's Content, 103, 170
Cooper, C.F., legal adviser, 13, 14, 15, 16, 28, 49

Coote, Colon, Appeal Committee launch, 20
Coote, Mrs, *Southern Region*, 226
Coronary Artery Bypass Surgery — for Patients, video, 173
Coronary attacks, 'prevention', 177–178
Coronary Prevention Group, 173–174
Cosh, John, *Western Region*, Bath Committee, 222
Council
  professional membership, reduction in numbers, 84
  recent years, 84–88
Covenants, 105
  industry, 40–41
Cowdray, Lord, Council member, 14
Coxon, Ann, speaker, 89
Crawford, Sir Douglas, *North West Region*, Chairman, 208
Crossed-out Man poster, **92**
Cummins, Peter, Contractile Proteins in Normal and Abnormal Cardiac Function, Birmingham group, 142
Curtis, Dorothy
  Hampshire, Berkshire, Isle of Wight Region, 47, 201, 209, 225, 230
  secretary and personal assistant, 226, 227, 228, 229
Curtis, Major Basil, *Western Region*, Cornwall Regional Organizer, 201, 220, 223
Cutts, W.E. (Bill)
  fund-raising, London, 31, 229
  Southern Region, 193

Davidson, Charles, *West Midlands Region*, Chairman, 238
Davidson, James, speaker, 57–58
Davies, Michael
  Chair in Cardiovascular Pathology, London, 137, 154, 252
  speaker, 145

Index

Davis, Mrs, Chest and Heart Association secretariat, 29, 117
Davison, Geoffrey
  Assistant to Director General, 35, **45**, 47, 48, 63, 76, 193–195
  editor, *Heart Bulletin*, 60
  Jersey Region, 240
De Burgh, Professor, *West Midlands Region*, Committee member, 238
De L'Isle and Dudley, Viscount, Vice-President, **51**, 86, **87**
De Trafford, Sir Rudolf
  Finance and General Purposes Committee,
    Chairman, 33, 48, 51
  Investment Subcommittee Chairman, 29
  retirement, 86
  Southern Region, 224
  Treasurer, 24, 36, 51, 67, 128
  Vice-Chairman, Appeals Committee, 24
Deception, effect on charities, 241
Defibrillators, Cardiac Care Committee, 188–190
Deller, Bill
  East Anglian Region, Reigate Organizer (*later Regional Director*), 234
  Postgraduate Education Funds Committee, Regional Director, 163
Denn, Dorothy, 191
Deverall, P., speaker, 89
Dewar, Hewan, *Northern Region*, Appeal Committee, Chairman, 204
Dewar, Mrs, *Southern Region*, Reigate Committee, 226
Dickinson, C.J., 135
Dodds, Sir Charles
  Chairman, 116
  Council Vice-Chairman, **27**, 29
  first Science Committee, Chairman, 25, 37, 49
  reorganization of BHF, 32

Donald, K.W.
  Science Committee, 117
  speaker, 57
Donaldson, Ann, Scottish region, Glasgow organizer, 207
Donations Department, 82
  Heart Cards Ltd., 105–106
  recent years, 103–107
Donor cards, 174
Donors, new, 105
Douglas Hume, William, 42
Drogheda, Harold, Appeal Committee launch, 20
Drysdale, Mrs, *Western Region*, Falmouth, 222
Du Boulay, Group Captain Guy, *Southern Region*, 46, 194, 224
Du Boulay, Jane, *Southern Region*, **45**, 224
Dudgeon, Alastair, Research Funds Committee, Chairman, 87, 120, 135
Duke of Edinburgh Chair of Cardiology, Edinburgh, 54, 130
Dunn, Mary, Appeals Department, Director, 82, 100
Dutch–British Exchange Fellowship, 157

East Anglia Region, 233
Edinburgh, Professorial chairs, 54, 130
Education
  GPs, 254
  policy, recent years, 73–76
  public, 175–179
  recent achievements, 255
Education Committee, 249–250
  Education Funds Committee, 81
  establishment of current title, 163
  European and international meetings, 165
  symposia, 164
  workshops, 164
Education Department, 81
Edwards, C.R.W. Chairs and

Research Groups Committee, 135, 137
Elizabeth, HM the Queen Mother, 41, **42**
Elson, Mr and Mrs, *London Region*, Redbridge Committee, 233
Emanuel, Richard, **87**
  Cardiac Care Committee, chairman, 190
  speaker, 89
Emery, Richard
  Donations Department, Managing Director, 82, 105
  Donations Secretary, 80, 103–104
English, Terence
  BHF Cardiac Transplantation Group, Papworth, 141, 154, 242
  speaker, 89
Enright, D., *Yorkshire and North Humberside Region*, Pontefract Committee, 212
Epidemiology, research grants 1979–85, analysis of distribution of funds, **129**
European congresses, 166
European and international meetings, Education Committee, 165
European Travelling Scholarships, Fellowship Committees, 159–160
Evans, Brenda, *Welsh Region*, 215–217
Evans, Horace, Cord, **19**, 20, 67
  Appeal Policy Committee, Vice-Chairman, 19, **23**
  Founding Committee meetings, 9
  reorganization of BHF, 33
Evans, William
  Appeal Policy Committee, Vice-Chairman, 17, 19, 20
  BHF statement of intent and objectives, 14
  CHA negotiations, 12
  first negotiations, **4–5**, **6–8**
  regional policies, 192
  Welsh Region, 216–217

death, 88
Exchange Fellowships, 115–116

Fact File subjects, 169
  list, 182–183
Farrell, Hon. Clodagh, *Yorkshire and North Humberside Region*, Beverley Committee, 212
Fellowships Committee, 155–162
  British/American Exchange Fellowships, 156
  creation, 126
  European Travelling Scholarships, 159–160
  Fellowships offered by Foundation, list, 161
  Intermediate Fellowships, 160–161
  Junior and Senior Research Fellowships, 158
  membership, 161
  other international Exchange Fellowships, 157–158
  Overseas Visiting Fellowships, 159, 160, 162
  PhD Students, 160
  policy and structure of Fellowships, 71
  Senior Travelling Fellowships, 161–162
Festing, Field Marshal Sir Francis, *Northern Region*, Appeal Committee, President, 203
Festival of Flowers, Westminster, 101
Fetal Echocardiography, research group, London, 141
Field Marshal Earl Alexander Professorship of Cardiovascular Medicine, Oxford, 128
Finance Department, 82
Finance and General Purposes Committee
  early years, 33
  recent years, 82

recommendations, 118
reconstitution, 50
Fisher, Noel, 107
Food Should Be Fun, 170
Ford, H. *(later Sir Hugh)*, 117
Ford, S., *East Midlands Region*, Regional Organizer, 236
Forrest, Sir Patrick, University of Edinburgh, Chancellor, 143
Forte, Charles, Lord
  Council member, 14, 17
  covenant, 24
  first Appeal Policy Committee, 17, 20
  Science Committee, 27, 117
  Vice-President, 29, 86
Founding Committee agreement, 16
Fox, Kim
  Education Committee, chairman, 178
  Fact File Subcommittee, chairman, 169
  Fifth European Congress, organizer, 166
  Postgraduate Education Funds Committee, chairman, 163
  speaker, 89
Fraser, A.G., Dutch–British Exchange Fellowship, 157
Fraser, Maurice, *Northern Region*, Appeal Committee, Vice-Chairman, 203
Fraud and deception, 241
Freedman, M., *London Region*, Bromley Committee, 233
Fund-raising events, 41–48
  changes, 66
  'Do's and Don'ts' for fund-raisers, 197
  gala evening concert, Sir John Barbirolli, 44
  Gala Variety Performance, 41
  Golden Boy Show, Sammy Davis Jnr, 42
  Marks and Spencer fashion show, 44
  personnel, 62–65
  special and national events, recent years, 100–103
  Wembley Stadium concert, 42

Gala performance, London Palladium, 1984, 101
Gala Variety Performance, 1972, 41
Gale, Audrey, *Yorkshire and North Humberside Region*, Secretary, 212
Geeson, Cecil, *Northern Region*, Appeal Committee, Treasurer, 203
Genetics, research grants 1979–85, analysis of distribution of funds, **129**
Gibson, D.
  Fellowship Committee, member, 161
  Third European Congress, organizer, 166
Gift of Life, 170
Gilchrist, Rae
  first Science Committee, 3, **6**, 17
  Founding Committee meetings, 9
  Scottish Appeal Committee, Chairman, 193
Ginks, Bill, *Jersey Region*, President, 240
Glasgow
  Chair in Cardiac Surgery, 54, 131
  Walton Chair of Medical Cardiology, 54, 131, 153
Glasse, Miss L.M., 117
Glaxo Laboratories Ltd., covenant, 24
Gleeson, Maria, *Jersey Region*, Vice-Chairwoman, 240
Gold Medal of the BHF, 96
Gold Medallists, 152
Gold, R.G., Cardiac Care Committee, Consultant Cardiologist, 190
Goodman, B.W.
  Finance and General Purposes Committee, 48
  Research Funds Committee, 119
  Science Committee, 117

death, 52
Goodwin, John
　Postgraduate Education Funds
　　Committee, 119, 130, 163
　speaker, 145
Grade, Lew, Lord, Council member,
　　42, 49
Grainge, Marion
　BHF secretary, 80, 107
　Research Funds Committee, 135
Great Ormond Street, Hospitals for
　　Sick Children
　Al-Maktoum Senior Lectureship,
　　143
　Chair of Paediatric Cardiology,
　　128
　professorial chairs, 54
Green, F.H.K.
　Scientific Advisor, 117
　resignation, 49
Green, John, *Welsh Region*,
　　Regional Organizer, 215
Grieve, Miss S., Royston
　　Fellowship, 144
Grime, Geoffrey, *Jersey Region*,
　　Treasurer, 240
Guthrie, Mrs, *Southern Region*,
　　Oxshott Committee, 226
Guy's Hospital, Angioplasty versus
　　Bypass Surgery Assessment,
　　142, 252

Hadrian's Wall ride, 99
Haigh, Margaret
　BHF Secretary, 34, 157
　Cardiac Care Committee, 50, 185
　editor of *Heart*, 59
　Education Funds Committee, 179
　Medical Administrator, 49, 117,
　　120
　Postgraduate Education Funds
　　Committee, Medical
　　Administrator, 163
　Research Funds Committee,
　　Medical Administrator, 176
Hainsworth, R., 156

Hamilton, I.D., Chair of Cardiac
　　Surgery, Edinburgh, 143
Hampshire Region, 226–229
Hampton, J.R., BHF Cardiovascular
　　Statistics Group,
　　Nottingham, 142, 155
Hand, Roger, *Western Region*, Poole
　　Committee, Chairman, 222
Hands, Graham
　Midlands Region, Regional
　　Organizer, 236
　West Midlands Region, Regional
　　Organizer, 201, 238
Harold, Samuel, covenant, 24
Harris, Peter
　Research Funds Committee, 119
　Royston Fellowship, supervisor,
　　144
　Science Committee, 117
　Simon Marks Chair of Cardiology,
　　London, 130, 153
Harrison, Sheila
　East Anglican Region,
　　Bedfordshire, Buckinghamshire
　　and Hertfordshire, Director,
　　233
　retirement, 234
　Southern Region, 226
Harrison, Sheila, *Northern Home
　　Counties Region*, 201
Hartog, Mrs Den, *London Region*,
　　western boroughs, 229
Hattan, Mrs, *Yorkshire and North
　　Humberside Region*, 212
Hawksworth, Mr, *Western Region*,
　　219
Hay, John, Science Committee, 117
Hayward, Graham
　Founding Committee meetings, 9
　Vice-Chairman, 49, 157
　death, 86
Head Office
　recent years, 78–83
　reorganization, 1987, 248–249
Health Education Council, later
　　Health Education Authority,
　　75

Healthy Hearts, 173
Heart, 34
Heart Attack — Learn What to Do, 166, 171, 177
Heart Bulletin, 60, 62, 168
Heart Cards Ltd., 105–106
Heart donor cards, 75
Heart Information Series, 73–74, 168
  Pamphlet No. 14, *Reducing the Risk of a Heart Attack*, 74
Heart Journal, 58–62
Heart Problem, The, 14
Heart Research Series, 168
  Pamphlets, 59
  renamed *Heart Information Series*, 73–74
Heart Surgery of Adults, 168
Heart transplantation, organ donors, 75, 174
Heart Weeks, 99
Heart/Lung Resuscitation, poster, 171, **172**
Heasman, Derek, *Welsh Region*, Regional Organizer, 216, 218
Heatherill, Wing Commander Jock
  Cardiac Care Committee, Regional Director, 190
  East Midlands Region, Regional Organizer, 236–237
Heavens, Mrs, *Yorkshire and North Humberside Region*, York Committee, 214
Henderson, Andrew
  Postgraduate Education Funds Committee, 87, 163
  Sir Thomas Lewis Chair of Cardiology, 138, 153
Henderson, Charles
  Heart Ball Committee, 206
  Northern Region, Appeal Committee, Chairman, 204
Herbert, Mrs, *Yorkshire and North Humberside Region*, Knaresborough Committee, 212
Higgs, Lilian

South West Region, 201
Southern Region, 225, 226
Hill, Colin, *Jersey Region*, Chairman, 240
Hill, Ian
  Exchange Fellowships, 156
  first Science Committee, 17
  Founding Committee meetings, 9
  Memorandum and Articles of Association, 86
Hill, Richard, *Northern Region*, 31, 193
  Appeal Committee, Regional Organizer, 204
Hillard, Sarah
  Bulletin, Editor, 96
  Press Office, 58, 60, 63, 76, 194
Hodgson, Adele
  National Appeals Department, Director, 82
  Special National Events Department, Director, 100
Hoffenberg, Sir Raymond
  Chairman of Council, 86, 242
  Chairs and Research Groups Committee, Chairman, 135
  subgroup, Chairman, 146
  Finance and General Purposes Committee, Vice-Chairman, 83
Hogan, Clem, Legacy Officer, 80, 107
Holden, Patrick, *East Midlands Region*, Notinghamshire and Leicestershire County Organizer, 238
Holloway, Adrian, *Western Region*, Gloucestershire and Oxfordshire, 224
Holmboe, Miss, *Northern Region*, Appeal Committee, Secretary, 203
Holmes Sellors, Sir Thomas
  Finance and General Purposes Committee, 57, 88
  Founding Committee meetings, 9,

17, 49
Holroyd, Sir Ronald, consultant adviser, 26
Houching, Caroline, Cardiac Care Committee, Buyer, 190
How to Reduce the Risks of a Heart Attack, 173
Howatch, Joseph, American Heart Association, Administrative Associate, 156
Hume, Miss N.B.
  Chest and Heart Association, 55
  Scottish Office, Secretary, 193
Humphries, Steven
  BHF Molecular Biology Research Group, London, 141–142, 154–155
  speaker, 145
  studies in familial hypercholesterolaemia, 252
Hunt, Dorothy
  East Midlands Region,
    Assistant Regional Organizer, 236
    Regional Administrator, 236
  Yorkshire and North Humberside Region, Wensleydale Committee, 212
Hunter, Stewart, *Northern Region*, Appeal Committee, Chairman, 204
Hutton, I., Exchange Fellowship, 157
Hypertension, research grants 1979–85, analysis of distribution of funds, **129**

Illingworth, Mr & Mrs, *Yorkshire and North Humberside Region*, Harrogate Committee, 212
Immunology, research grants 1979–85, analysis of distribution of funds, **129**
In memoriam donations and names, 37, 104, 105, 214
Inland Revenue, 28

Inlis, Mrs, *Southern Region*, Sevenoaks Committee, 226
Institute of Cardiology, London, 53
Intermediate Fellowships, Fellowship Committee, 160–161
International meetings, list, 166
Isis 2 Trial, 251
It'll Never Happen to Me, 76, 171

Jacobs, Shirley, Chairs and Research Groups Committee, Minutes Secretary, 122, 135, 185
Jago, Bernard, *Western Region*, Taunton Committee, Chairman, 222
Janion, Rear Admiral Sir Hugh, *Western Region*, Somerset and Avon, County Organizer, 223
Jansen, Alderman, Mayor of Hounslow, 46
Jarrold, Julie, 'Nurse of 1970', **47**, 48
Jeff, Albert, 65
Jennings, Angela, *Scottish Region*, 206
Jersey Region, 239
Jewitt, David
  Exchange Fellowship, 156
  Fellowship Committee, member, 161
  Fourth European Congress, organizer, 166
Jim'll Fix-It team, 101
Joan Scott Public Relations Consultancy, 94, **98–100**
Johnson, A M.
  Postgraduate Education Funds Committee, 119, 163
  Science Committee, 117
Johnston, Stephen
  Appeals Department, 78
  Donations Department, 104, 105
  London Region, western boroughs, 229
Johnstone, Harris, *Northern Ireland*, 211

Index

Johnstone, Major Peter
  South West Region, 201
  Western Region,
    Regional Director, 219, 223
    Regional Organizer, 221
Joseph Levy Foundation, Chair of Paediatric Cardiac Morphology, Brompton Hospital, **55**, 58, **137**, **152–154**, 252
Journal of the British Heart Foundation, 60
Julian, Claire, Press Office, 95
Julian, Desmond, **122–124**
  BHF Chair of Cardiology, Newcastle upon tyne, 130, 153
  Fact File Subcommittee, Chairman, 169
  Medical Director, **87**, 131, 242
  Research Funds Committee, Vice-Chairman, 120
  Seventh European Congress, organizer, 167
  speaker, 90
'Jump Rope for Heart', 103
Junior Education, 170
Junior and Senior Research Fellowships, Fellowships Committee, 158

Kaye, Michael, *Yorkshire and Humberside Region*, 201, 212, 213
Keenan, Kit, *North West Region*, 193
Kelly, Loraine, **207**
Kendall, Mr, *Yorkshire and North Humberside Region*, 212
  Yorkshire Council, Treasurer, 213
King, Sir Alexander, Scottish Appeal Committee, President, 193
Kirkwood, Lord, CHA, Treasurer, 36
Knight, Sarah, Cardiac Care Committee, Buyer, 190
Knollys, Lord, Appeal Committee launch, 20

Kossof, David, radio appeal, 42
Krikler, D.M.
  First European Congress, organizer, 166
  speaker, 89

Landon, Jane, Press Officer, 82, 95
Land's End to John O'Groats journey, 102
Lane, Bernie
  London Region, 230
  Press Officer, 76, 81, 95
  Special Fund-raising Events, organizer, 63
  West London Region, 201
  Westminster Committee, Chairwoman, 100
Lawrie, T.D.V.
  Research Funds Committee, 119
  Walton Chair of Medical Cardiology, Glasgow, 54, 131, 153
Lazell, H.G. (Leslie)
  Appeal Committee, Chairman, **19–20**, 23, 30–31, 86, 91
  launch, 20
  resignation, 49
  Finance and General Purposes Committee, first Deputy Chairman, 33
  relations with Chest and Heart Association, 20, 21
  reorganization of BHF, 32–33
Le Cromp, Jocelyne, 107
Leach, Graham, Cardiac Care Committee, Technical Adviser, 190
Leadbeater, Jeff, *East Midlands Region*, Staffordshire and Derbyshire County Organizer, 238
Leatham, Aubrey
  CHA member, 12, 13
  Postgraduate Education Funds Committee, 119, 163

Index

speaker, 57
Lee, Michael
  Exchange Fellowships, 116, 156
  Research Fellowships, 39
Leeds
  Chair of Cardiovascular Studies, 54, 131
  Mauntner Lectureship, 144
Legacy Department, 80
  legacy income, 90, **93**
  recent years, 107–109
Lewis, Tony, 218
Library books, 174
Lincoln, Christopher, 58
Linden, R.J.
  Chair of Cardiovascular Studies, Leeds, 131, 153
  Research Funds Committee, 119
  Vice Chairman, 53, 120, 133
  Science Committee, 117
  Yorkshire and North Humberside Region, 212, 213
Ling, Ian, *Jersey Region*, Treasurer, 240
Littler, W.A., Chair of Cardiovascular Medicine, Birmingham, 131, 153
Liverpool, Ladies' Half-Marathon, 99
Loans, 175
London Region, 229–233
  Ball Committee, 231
  concerts, 231
  western boroughs, 229–231
London-to-Brighton bike ride, 63–64, 99, 102
Long, D., *London Region*, Greenwich Committee, 233
Longmore, D., Royston Fellowship, supervisor, 144
Look After York Heart campaign, 171
Lukoma, Kaleyi, 78
Lyster-Binns, Noel
  Appeals, Deputy Director, 32, 35, 193
  Foundation Appeal Secretary, 204

Macartney, F., Vandervell Chair of Paediatric Cardiology, 89, 130, 153
McBrearty, Kathleen, *East Anglian Region*, Cambridge Committee, 234
Macey, Leon, *Western Region*, Wiltshire and Dorset, County Organizer, 223
McFarlane, P.W., European Travelling Scholarship, 160
McInnes, Alastair, *Jersey Region*, President, 240
McIntosh, Major R. Andrew, fund-raising, Scotland, 31, 193
McIntyre, Harold, 205
McKay, Alex
  Appeal Committee, Chairman, 49
  Finance and General Purposes Committee, Director of Appeals, 33
  Publicity Subcommittee, Chairman, 29, 37
  retirement, 51–52
McKeller, Judy, 82, 100
McKendrick, Dr, *North West Region*, 208
McKenzie, Margaret, Scottish region, Regional Organizer, 206
Mackintosh, Andrew, Scottish region, Regional Organizer, 206
McMichael, Sir John
  Council, Chairman, 49
  Exchange Committee, 156
  project grants, 116, 117
  Research Funds Committee, Chairman, **27**
  Science Committee, Vice-Chairman, 30, 38, 49
Macmillan, Harold *(later Viscount Stockton)*, 54
McMillan, Ian, *Hampshire Region*, 227
McNally, Sue, 81
McNee, Sir David, Police

Index

Commissioner, 232
McQueen, Neil, 203, 204
Mahler, R., 116
Malcolm, James
   Appeals, Director, 78–79, **79**, **87**, 90–91, 186, 190–191
   fund-raising in the regions, 109–110
   Jersey Region, 240
   Postgraduate Education Funds Committee, 163
Mantripp, A.J.
   C&HA, 5
   Public Appeal, 29
Margaret, Countess of Tunis, 41, **42**
Marks, Lady Miriam, Vice-President, 29
Marks, Lord, Vice-President, 29, 39
Marks, Maureen, *Western Region*, Bristol swim, 223
Marley, Claire, 81, 95, 96
Martyn, Gwen
   Greater London Region, 201
   London Region,
     Assistant Organizer, 229
     northern, southern and eastern boroughs, 231
     Regional Organizer, 229
   Postgraduate Education Funds Committee, Regional Director, 163
   Southern Region, Bexhill Committee member, 226
Maseri, A.
   Sir John McMichael Chair in Cardiovascular Medicine, London, 130, 153
   speaker, 89, 145
Mason, Gordon, **207**
Mason, Valerie, Chairs and Research Groups Committee, research funds administrator, 81, 122, 135, **150**, 159
Masters, Wing Commander C.G., *Northern Ireland Region*, 31, 193
Matter of the Heart, 173

Mauntner Lectureship, Leeds, 144
Maurer, B.J., 157
Maurice, Dorothy, *London Region*, New Malden Committee, Chairman, 231
Meade, Tom
   Cardiovascular Epidemiology Research Group, London, Director, 141, 154, 252
   Education Funds Committee, chairman, 74, 163, 178
   speaker, 145
Mearns, Jim, *Western Region*, Bath Committee, 222
Media coverage
   early years, 29–32
   middle years, 45
   recent years, 76–78, 91–95, 176
Medical Department Committee, structure, 81, 118–120
Mellor, Sir John, Appeal Committee launch, 20
Membership
   early years, 28, 31
   recent years, 85–86
   supporters list, 104
Mend-a-Heart Campaign, 47
Menzies, Sir Robert, 46, 224
   and Dame Pattie, 194
Michal, F., Senior Research Fellowship, 158
Midlands Region, 235–238
Mieville, Sir Eric, Appeal Committee launch, 20
Miller, N.E., 145
Miller-Craig, Dr, Australian/British Fellowship, 157–158
Mills, Arthur, *Yorkshire and North Humberside Region*, County Organizer, 215
Mills, C., *London Region*, Croydon Committee, 233
Mitchell, J.R.A., 135
Mole, Brenda, 82, 107, 122
Moore, Michael, Science Committee, 27, 221
Moore, Sir Harry

Index

Appeal Committee launch, 20, 21
  Council member, 14, 17, **67**
  Finance and General Purposes
    Committee, Chairman, 51,
    83, 86, 87, 88, 117
  relations with Chest and Heart
    Association, 21
  reorganization of BHF, 33
Morecambe, Eric, 42, **101**, 233
  Gala Variety Performance, 41
Morecambe, Joan, *East Anglican Region*, 233
Morgan Jones, A.
  first Science Committee, 17
  Founding Committee meetings, 2, 9
Morris, G.K., 57
Morris, Philip, Yorkshire Council, Chairman, 215
Mouncey, Patrick
  Founding Committee, 4, **9**, 116
  Sixth World Congress of Cardiology, Secretary, 163
Marray, Malcolm, 157

Nathan, A.W., 138
  Sir Ronald Bodley Scott Senior Lectureship in Cardiovascular Medicine, London, 154
  Sixth European Congress, organizer, 138, 166–167
Nathan, Peter, 87
National Appeal Fund, 4
National Appeals Department, 82
National No Smoking Day, 173
'National Ride a Bike Week', 100
National Sponsored Slim, 47, 99, 102
Naylor, W., Royston Fellowship, supervisor, 144
Neal, Frances, 45, 64, 78, 193, 194
Nettleton, Mrs, *Yorkshire and North Humberside Region*, Ossett Committee, 212
New Start for You and Your Heart, 170

Newcastle, Chair of Cardiology, 39, 54, 131
Newmarket race day, 100
Newson Smith, Mrs, *East Midlands Region*, Regional Organizer, 236
Nicholson, Doreen
  Hampshire Region Regional Development Officer, 226
  London Region, 31, 56, **194**, 229
  Southern Region, 193
  Yorkshire and North Humberside Region, 213
  Regional Development Officer, 212
  Wetherby Committee, 212
Noble, Denis
  Burdon–Sanderson Chair of Cardiovascular Physiology, Oxford, 153, 154
  Fellowship Committee, 138, 161
North, Colon, *East Midlands Region*, Lincolnshire and South Humberside County Organizer, 238
North West Region, 208–211
Northern Ireland, 211
Northern Regional Board, 203–206
Nuclear Magnetic Resonance, research group, 141

Oakley, Celia, 57
Oliver, Michael
  Coronary Prevention Group, member, 173
  Duke of Edinburgh Chair of Cardiology, Edinburgh, 57, 153
  Science Committee, 89, 117, 130
One in Every Two of Us, 173
Overseas funding, 116
Overseas Visiting Fellowships, Fellowship Committee, 159, 160, 162
Owens, Dennis, *East Midlands Region*, West Midlands and Warwickshire County

Organizer, 237
Oxford
   Chair of Cardiology, 41
   Clinical Magnetic Resonance Laboratory, 138, 141
   Field Marshal Earl Alexander Professorship of Cardiovascular Medicine, 128, 153

Pace-Maker Plod, 230
Pack promotions, 103
Paediatric cardiology, research grants 1979–85, analysis of distribution of funds, **129**
Page, Miss, *London Region*, Waltham Forest Committee, 233
Page, Mr
   London Region, Waltham Forest Committee, 233
   Southern Region, Bexhill, Brighton, Crawley Committees, 226
Palmby, Wing Commander John, *East Midlands Region*, 201, 236
Papworth Hospital Transplant Unit, 141
Parkinson, Sir John, Founding Committee member, **6–9**
Parsons, Clifford
   CHA member, 12, 13
   consultant adviser, 25
'Passion Potion', 103
Pathology, research grants 1979–85, analysis of distribution of funds, **129**
Paulowski, Mrs, *Western Region*, North Devon Committee, 222
Peake, Sir Harold, Appeal Committee launch, 20
Peart, Sir Stanley
   Cardiac Care Committee, chairman, 190
   Chairs and Research Groups Committee, subgroup, chairman, **87**, 137, 146
Peel, Emmy, *Northern Region*, Appeal Committee, Regional Organizer, 204
Pelly, Peter, *Western Region*, Regional Director, 219
Perez, Mrs, *Southern Region*, **45**, 224
Perrin, Michael *(later Sir Michael)*
   first Appeal Policy Committee, 17, **87**, 117
   Founding Committee meetings, 9, 25
   reorganization of BHF, 33
Perry, Bruce
   CHA member, 12, 13
   first Science Committee, 17
   Western Region, Bristol Committee, Chairman, 221
Personal chairs, Professorial chairs, 55
Personnel
   early years, 29
   middle years, 62–65
   recent years, 81–83, 86–88
Peters, T.J., 135
Pettit, Iona, *East Anglian Region*, Regional Administrator, 235
Petty, Margaret, Dutch–British Exchange Fellowship, 157
Philip, HRH The Duke of Edinburgh, *frontispiece*, 15, 100, **101**
Physiology, electrophysiology and anatomy, research grants 1979–85, analysis of distribution of funds, **129**
Piper, Miss, *London Region*, Bromley Committee, 233
Piper, Mr, *London Region*, Bromley Committee, 233
Platt, Sir Robert, Founding Committee meetings, 9
Pocock, S.J., Clinical Trials Research Group, Royal Free Hospital, 142, 155, 250
Policy reviews, Chairs and Research

Groups Committee, 146–147
Poole-Wilson, Professor
  Fifth European Congress, organizer, 166
  Royston Fellowship, supervisor, 144
Pope, George, *Times*, deputy manager *(later Sir George)*, 21
Popjak, Dr *(later Sir)*, 114, 117
Porter, Jill, *East Midlands Region*, secretary, 236
Porter, K.A., Research Funds Committee, 117, 119
Postgraduate Education Funds Committee, 50, 118–119
  constitution, 119
  members, 119
Postgraduate Hospital, Hammersmith, 130
Potter, John, 102
Powell, Trevor, 138
Press Office, recent years, 94–95
Preston, Frank, Cardiac Care Committee, Medical Spokesman, 191, 243
Preston, Roger
  Yorkshire and North Humberside Region,
    Regional Director, 215
    Yorkshire Council, Regional Organizer, 204, 213
Prideaux, Sir John, **87**
Probyn, Calista, *Welsh Region*, Regional Organizer, 215–217
Probyn, John Green, *Welsh Region*, Regional Organizer, 75, 201, 215–217
Professorial chairs, 1977–78 and 1980–81, 132, 125
  Chairs Maintenance Fund, 139
  education and research, 81
  establishment by Foundation, Chairs and Research Groups Committee, 153–155
  exchange professorships, 71
  funding, 29, 39, 53–55, 71, 115
  optimum staffing, 133
  personal chairs, 55

  policy, 127–134
  recent years, 70–72
Project grants, 250–253
  Regulations, Chairs and Research Groups Committee, 1988, 150–152
  Science Committee, 114–118
Proposed Cardiac Appeal, objectives, 5
Prosser, Major John, Field Director, 207
Prudential Chair of Cardiology, St George's Hospital, 138
Public Meetings, recent years, 88–90
Publications
  list, 183–184
  loans and travelling expenses, 168

Radda, George
  Chair of Molecular Cardiology, Oxford, 154
  Gold Medallist, 96
  Magnetic Resonance Research Group, Oxford, 138, 141, 154, 252
Randle, Sir Philip, 120, 135
Rapaport, Elliot, American Heart Association, 157
Rathbone, Patrick, *North West Region*, Chairman, 209
Redhead, Jack, *North West Region*, Chairman, 209
Reducing the Risk of a Heart Attack, Heart Information Series Pamphlet No. 14, 74
Rees, Graham, 78
Regions
  development, 193–196
  geographical patterns, 199–202
  histories, 202–241
  income 1963–88, **203**
  map 1971, **198**
  map and poster 1967, **61**
  middle years, 55
  recent years, 109–110
  Regional Organizers (1971), 56

Index

reorganization, 196–199
Reichwald, Peter, *London Region, Harrow, Brent and Ealing Committee*, 230
Reichwald, Sonya, *London Region, Harrow, Brent and Ealing Committee*, 230
Reid, Donald, consultant adviser, 25
Reid, J.L., 120
Reorganization
  Annual Report, 1987, 248–249
  Committee structure, middle years, 48–53
  early years, 32–36
  regions, 196–199
Research Fellowships
  British — American Exchange Fellowships, 39
  Science Committee, 39
Research Funds Committee, 81, 118, 125–134, 150, 250
  members, 119
Research grants
  1979–85, analysis of distribution of funds, **129**
  chairs and education, income and expenditure, 1963–88, **133**
  early years, 26–27, 36, 37–38
  expenditure, 1972–88, **128**
  Science Committee, 112–113
Research groups
  achievements, 253–254
  Angioplasty versus Bypass Surgery Assessment, Guy's Hospital, 142
  BHF Cardiac Transplantation Research Group, 141
  BHF Cardiovascular Statistics Group, Nottingham, 142
  BHF Molecular Biology Research Group, Charing Cross Hospital, 142
  BHF Regional Heart Study Research Group, Royal Free Hospital, 142
  Cardiac Membrane Ion Channels in Reconstituted Systems, 142

  Cardiovascular Epidemiology Research Group, 141
  Chairs and Research Groups Committee, 140–143, 154–155
  Clinical Trials Research Group, Royal Free Hospital, 142
  Contractile Proteins in Normal and Abnormal Cardiac Function, 142
  Fetal Echocardiography, 141
  Genetic engineering, St Mary's Hospital, 141–142
  Mauntner Lectureship, Leeds, 144
  Mechanisms of Local Control of Blood Flow, London, 142
  Papworth Hospital Transplant Unit, 141
  Royal Free Hospital, CNS Control of CV function, 142
  use of nuclear magnetic resonance, Oxford, 141
Research policy
  early years, 26
  expenditure, **72**
  recent years, 70–72
Reynolds, David, 78, 100
Richards, Sir Gordon, *London Region, northern, southern and eastern boroughs*, 232
Rifkind, B.M., Research Fellowships, 39, 116, 156
Roberson, B., *Yorkshire and North Humberside Region, Rothwell Committee*, 212
Roberts, A., *Yorkshire and North Humberside Region, Rothwell Committee*, 212
Robinson, Mark, 95
Robinson, Mary, *Northern Region, Appeal Committee, Derwent & Tyne Committee*, 205
Robson, Nigel, 83, 137
Roderick, Mrs, *London Region, western boroughs*, 229
Rogers, Sir Philip, 116
Rolling tenure, Chairs and Research Groups Committee, 145–146

Roscoe, Mr & Mrs, *Yorkshire and North Humberside Region*, Wetherby Committee, 212
Rosendorff, C., 156
Rosenheim, Lord, 125
Ross, Donald, 130, 195
Ross, James Davison, 62
Ross, Rosalind, 44
Ross, Sir Keith, Research Funds Committee, 159
Rowe, Bill, *Northern Region*, Appeal Committee, Northumberland, County Organizer, 204
Royal Free Hospital
  BHF Regional Heart Study Research Group, 142
  Clinical Trials Research Group, 142
Royal Melbourne Hospital, 4
Royal Postgraduate Hospital, Hammersmith, London, Chair in Cardiothoracic Surgery, 54, 138
Royston Fellowship, Chairs and Research Groups Committee, 144
Rusby, Lloyd, 86, **87**
  CHA representative, 11
Rust, Mrs, *Yorkshire and North Humberside Region*, Ilkley Committee, 212
Ryan, Mrs, *East Midlands Region*, Chesterfield Committee, 236

St Bartholomew's Hospital, Bodley Scott Chair of Cardiovascular Medicine, 137
St George's Hospital Medical School, Chair in Cardiovascular Pathology, 137
St Mary's Hospital, BHF Molecular Biology Research Group, 141–142, 154–155
Salaries, 1987 report, 249
Salvaratnam, Lakshmi, 82

Samuel, Harold *(later Lord)*
  Appeal Committee launch, 20
  first Vice-President, 29, 86, 88
Sandilands, Sir Francis, **87**
Sanders, Nicky, *London Region*, western boroughs, 229
'Save a Life Campaign', 172
Saville, Jimmy, 101
Schneckloth, Roland, American Heart Association, 157
Science Committee
  Consultant Advisers, 114
  first, 17, 24–25, 111–114
  last meeting, 118
  project grants, 114–118
  Proposed Standing Orders, 112
  replacement by Research Funds Committee, 50
  research Fellowships, 39, 155
  research grants, 112–113
Scientific Advisory Committee, meetings, 124–125
Scientific Advisory Council, 50
Scott, D., *Yorkshire and North Humberside Region*, Beverley Committee, 212
Scott, Joan Scott Public Relations Consultancy, 77, 94, **98–100**
Scott, Olive, 169
Scottish Regional Board, 206–208
Selwyn, Andrew, Third European Congress, organizer, 166
Senior Travelling Fellowships, Fellowship Committee, 161–162
Shaffner, M., *Yorkshire and North Humberside Region*, Wakefield Committee, 212–213
Shale, Michael
  East Scotland Region, 201
  Scottish region, Regional Director and Organizer, 206
Shaper, G.
  BHF Regional Heart Study Group, London, 142, 155
  Postgraduate Education Funds

Committee, 163
studies in epidemiology, 252
Shaw, Richard, *London Region*, 232
Shepherd, Clare, 79
Shillingford, Jack
  Blood/Arterial Wall Interface Task Force, chairman, 144
  Fellowship Committee, Chairman, 157, 161
  First European Congress, organizer, 166
  Postgraduate Education Funds Committee,
    Chairman, 119, **121–124**, 133–134, 163
    Vice-Chairman, 49, 50, 119
  retirement, 242–243
  Science Committee, 6, 8, 81, 115, 117
  Sir John McMichael Chair in Cardiovascular Medicine, London, 153
  speaker, 57
Shinebourne, Elliot
  Exchange Fellowship, 156
  Postgraduate Education Funds Committee, chairman, 120, 163
  Second European Congress, organizing committee, chairman, 166
  speaker, 58
Sigsworth, Reg, *Northern Region*, Appeal Committee, South Durham, County Organizer, 204
Silove, Eric, European Travelling Scholarship, 160
Simon Marks Chair of Cardiology, CT Institute, University of London, 29, 39, 53, 128, 139
Sir John McMichael Chair, Royal Postgraduate Hospital, London, 54
Sir Melville Arnott Chair, Birmingham, 131
Sir Thomas Lewis Chair of Cardiology, University of Wales College of Medicine, 138
Skidmore, F.D., Junior Research Fellowship, 158
Sleight, Peter
  Field Marshal Earl Alexander Professorship of Cardiovascular Medicine, Oxford, 128, 153
  Postgraduate Education Funds Committee, chairman, 163
  Seventh European Congress, organizer, 167
Smaje, L.H., 156
Smith, A.F.M., BHF Cardiovascular Statistics Group, Nottingham, 142, 155
Smith, A.S., Australian/British Exchange Fellowship, 158
Smith, C.J.W., Chairman, *West Midlands Region*, 238
Smith, Ken, Chief Inspector, *London Region*, sponsored swim, 232
Smith, Percy, 102
Smith, Richard, 102
Smith, Shirley, CHA member, 12, 13
Smith, Tony, 96
Snell, Elaine, 95
  Cardiac Care Committee, Press Officer, 191
Somerville, Walter
  Cardiac Care Committee, Chairman, 119, **184–185**, 190
  Research Funds Committee, Chairman, 50
  speaker, 57, 89
Southall, D., 89
Southern Region, 224–233
Soutter, Kate, Education Funds Committee, Medical Administrator, 179
Sowton, E.G., Clinical Trials Group, Guy's Hospital, 142, 155, 250
Special Events Department, 82, 100–103
Spedding, Commander Bob, Scottish

region, Regional Organizer, 206
Spink, Cary, Education Funds Committee, Administrator, 81, 122, 173, 179
Spinks, A., 113, 117
Sponsored events, middle years, 46–47
Sponsored walks, 99, 100
Spry, C.J.E.
 Chair of Cardiovascular Immunology, St George's Hospital, London, 138, 154
 Fellowship Committee, member, 161
 speaker, 145
Spyer, K.M.
 BHF Group to Study the Central Nervous Control of Cardiovascular Function, 155
 Chairs and Research Groups Committee, 137
Staffordshire, Cheshire and Greater Manchester region, 238–239
Stanley, Cheryl, *Jersey Region*, Chairwoman, 240
Stedeford, Sir Ivan, Appeal Committee launch, 20
Steiner, Robert, consultant adviser, 25, 89
Stephens, P., *Newcastle Chronicle*, 204
Stiller, Bob, Cardiac Care Committee, Buyer, 81, 122, 188, 190
Stock, Peter, 117
Stoddart-Scott, Sir Malcolm
 Yorkshire and North Humberside Region,
 Chairman, 211–212, 213
 Steering Committee, 213, 231
Stokes, Joan, *East Anglian Region*, secretary, 234
Stokes, Major Ray, *East Anglian Region*, 199, 220, 233, 234
Stollery, Herbert, *East Anglian Region*, Ipswich Committee, Chairman, 234

Stone, Julie, 185
Street, General Vivian, Appeal Director, 31–32, 67, 192
Sugden, A.E., senior lectureship, St George's Hospital, 139
Sullivan, B., *London Region*, Bexley Committee, 233
Sunday Times Fun Run, 100
Surgenor, Dr, American Heart Association, proposals for exchange of research Fellows, 39
Surgery, research grants 1979–85, analysis of distribution of funds, **129**
Swan, Adrian, *Northern Region*,
 Appeal Committee, Chairman, 203, 204
 Academic Chair, Newcastle University, 39
Swan, W.G.A., *Newcastle Region*, 192
Swedish/British Exchange Fellowship, 158
Swift, David
 Western Region, Wiltshire and Dorsetshire, Regional Organizer, 219–221, 231
 Wiltshire and Somerset Region, 201
Symposia
 Education Committee, 164
 titles, 179–181

Taggart, Peter, 57
Taylor, Keith, Health Education Council, 75
Taylor, Kenneth, BHF Chair of Cardiac Surgery, London, 138, 153–154
Techniques and instrumentation, research grants 1979–85, analysis of distribution of funds, **129**
Therapy
 achievements, 251–253
 Isis 2 Trial, 251

Index

Thomas, A.J., first Science Committee, 17
Thomas, Arthur, J., *Welsh Region*, 216
Thomas, George Viscount Tonypandy, *foreword*, 86, **87**, 97–98
Thompson, Sally, *Jersey Region*, Secretary, 240
Thomson, Edward, 20, 23
Thrombosis and atherosclerosis, research grants, 1979–85, analysis of distribution of funds, **129**
Thursby Pelham, Brigadier Christopher
  Anniversary Reviw, 242, 244–247
  Director General, **52**, 53, **55–56**, 67, 135
  speaker, 89, 90
Tillotson, Allen, Appeal Committee, Chairman 52, 42
Tobacco Research council, 116
Tones, M., Royston Fellowship, 144
Took, J.E., Swedish/British Exchange Fellowship, 158
Tower Brigadier, Peter, **87**, 90
  Annual Report, 1987, 247–248
  Director General, 242, 243
Towers, John
  Yorkshire and North Humberside Region,
    Secretary, 212
    Yorkshire Council, Vice-Chairman, 213
Tranfield, Julia, *Jersey Region*, Chairwoman, 240
Treatment and pharmacology, research grants 1979–85, analysis of distribution of funds, **129**
Trebell, Ron, 63, 65, 78, 104
Troy, Lynn, *Jersey Region*, Secretary *(later Chairwoman)*, 240
Turnbull, Nick, *Western Region*, Chippenham Committee, Chairman, 222
Tuson, Sheila, 82

Tynan, M.J., Fellowship Committee, 89, 161

Underwood, R., Royston Fellowship, 144
Unilever Ltd., covenant, 24
Unwin, Reverend, 204

Value Added Tax (VAT), Cardiac Care Committee, 187
Vandervell Trust, Chair of Paediatric Cardiology, London, 128

Wagstaffe, Daphne, *Jersey Region*, Chairwoman, 240
Walton Chair of Medical Cardiology, Glasgow, 54, 131
Walton, Isadore, 54, 55, 131
  Scottish Appeal Committee, President, 54, 55, 86, 131, 193
Walton Surgical Research Unit, Glasgow, 143
Ware, Alan
  North West Region, 208–209, 210–211
  Welsh Region, County Organizer, 218
Watney Mann Ltd., covenant, 24
Wayne, E.J.
  consultant adviser, 25
  first Science Committee, 17
  Founding Committee meetings, 9
Webster, Nathaniel, 64, 79
Weisberg, Howard, American Heart Association, 157
Wells, Nick, 95
Welsh Heart Appeal, 75
Welsh, Peter, 211
Welsh Region, 215–218
West Midlands Region, 238–239
Western Region, 219–224
Westminster Committee, 99–100
Whalan, Ann, 107
Wheatley, David, BHF Chair of

Cardiac Surgery, Glasgow, 131, 153
Whittaker, *Yorkshire and North Humberside Region*, member, 212
Williams, A.J., Cardiac Membrane Ion Channels in Reconstituted Systems, 142
Williams, Eccles, *West Midlands Region*, Chairman, 238
Williams, Eleanor, *Western Region*, Cornish Region Supporters Association, 219
Williams, Harley, **5–6, 13**
   Administrative Medical Director, resignation, 49, 120
   Appeals Committee, 17, 20
   General Secretary, 32
   CHA representative, 11
   editor of *Heart*, 58–59, 97
   Proposed Cardiac Appeal, 5
   Science Committee, 115, 117
   Secretary, resignation, 34
Williams, John, *Western Region*, Cornish Region Supporters Association, 219
Williams, W.G., 58
Williamson, B., 89
Wilson, Mrs, *North West Region*, Chester Committee, 209
Wilson, Poole, Simon Marks Chair of Cardiology, London, 153
Winston, Philip, 138
Winston Readership, 138
Wishart, James, *Western Region*, Bristol Committee, Chairman, 222
Wood, Paul
   BHF statement of intent and objectives, 14
   first Science Committee, 17
   Vice-Chairman, 25
   first Secretary, 9
   Founding Committee, 4, **8–9**
   death, **25**
Woodroofe, E.G. *(later Sir Edward)*, consultant adviser, 26, 113, 117
Woolton, Lord, Appeal Committee member, 31
Workshops
   Education Committee, 164
Worsfold, Pauline, 64, 78, 80
Wright, Berwick, Institute of Directors, medical department, 38, 57
Wright, J.H., Founding Committee meetings, 9

Yacoub, Magdi
   BHF Chair of Cardiothoracic Surgery, London, 154
   Professor of Cardiac Surgery, Brompton Hospital, 139, 252
Yorkshire and North Humberside Region, 211–215
Young, Ann, 82
Young, George, Scottish Appeal Committee, President, 87, 193, **207**
Your Heart, first issue, 97